P A S T F O R W A R D

PAST FORWARD

French Cinema and the Post-Colonial Heritage

DAYNA OSCHERWITZ

SOUTHERN ILLINOIS UNIVERSITY PRESS

Carbondale and Edwardsville

13   12   11   10   4   3   2   1

Library of Congress Cataloging-in-Publication Data
Oscherwitz, Dayna, 1970–
 Past forward : French cinema and the post-colonial
heritage / Dayna Oscherwitz.
     p. cm.
 Includes bibliographical references and index.
 ISBN-13: 978-0-8093-2996-0 (alk. paper)
 ISBN-10: 0-8093-2996-4 (alk. paper)
 ISBN-13: 978-0-8093-8588-1 (electronic)
 ISBN-10: 0-8093-8588-0 (electronic)
 1. Motion pictures—France—History—20th century.
 2. Historical films—France—History and criticism.
 3. National characteristics, French, in motion pictures.
 4. Imperialism in motion pictures. 5. Collective memory—France. I. Title.
 PN1993.5.F7O838 2010
 791.430944—dc22   2009052300

For Brian, who always believed, and Evan and Emma, who made me believe

Contents

Acknowledgments

There are far too many who inspired and encouraged me along the way for me to thank them all. However, several deserve special attention. I would like to thank everyone at Southern Illinois University Press, particularly Kathleen Kageff, Karl Kageff, and Barb Martin, for the attentive handling of this project from beginning to end. Bridget Brown deserves special thanks because without her very efficient work, this book might never have been. Mary Lou Kowaleski deserves much praise for dotting the *i*'s and crossing the *t*'s and counteracting all of my other bad habits. I am deeply indebted to Southern Methodist University for supporting this project financially and for providing me a room of my own in which to work and intelligent and engaging colleagues and students with whom to share ideas. Among my colleagues, I thank Bill Beauchamp for reading and re-reading various drafts of the manuscript, Gordon Birrell for his unwavering support, and Marlies Gaëttens for helping me keep everything in balance. I would be remiss in not thanking Rosemary Sanchez for lighting candles and saying prayers and Debbie Garland for her calm reassurance. And lastly, I thank Brian for contributions too numerous to list and Evan and Emma for yielding precious time and never (almost never) complaining.

PAST FORWARD

Introduction

*I*n France, the year 1980 was designated the Year of Heritage (*L'Année du patrimoine*). It was devoted to foregrounding, restoring, and transmitting French cultural and ethnological heritage, reviving interest in French culture, and combating Europeanization and globalization (Blowen, Demossier, and Picard 2001; Citron 1987; Lebovics 2004). Heritage as it manifested in France in 1980 was an accumulation of objects, places, and events that were seen to embody national identity. It celebrated everything from the lives of rural ancestors to the works of celebrated artists to France's maritime achievements.[1] This eclectic ensemble of objects, practices, events, and dates was figured as an essential but lost component of national identity, something that had to be rediscovered, remembered, and restored in order to ensure the survival of the nation.

The heritage wave that was inaugurated in France in 1980 was symptomatic of a wider heritage wave that, according to David Lowenthal, swept the Western world in the latter part of the twentieth century.[2] Heritage is a type of state-sanctioned, official, collective memory used to shape "senses of belonging defined and transmitted through representations of place" (Ashworth, Graham, and Tunbridge 2007, 1). As with other forms of collective memory, it presumes a shared vision of the past that reinforces collective identity (Halbwachs 1997; Hobsbawm 1992; Ashworth, Graham, and Tunbridge 2007). It concretizes group identity by providing the basis from which a group derives its "formative and normative impulses" (Assman 1995, 128). Heritage as generally understood is inherently backward gazing and nostalgic, idealizing the past and condemning the present. Paradoxically, although it is obsessed with memory, heritage is sometimes regarded as the death of memory, since it is largely a form of institutional memory, transmitted through museums, monuments, and archives (Nora 1997). In that regard, it can be seen as the opposite of lived or "everyday" memory, transmitted from person to person or from generation to generation rather than through impersonal surrogates of the state (Assman 1995; Citron 1987; Hobsbawm and Ranger 1992; Le Goff 1988; Nora 1997). Heritage is also understood as distinct from history, because it does not consider the past as entirely past in the way that history is presumed to do. Rather, it is both present centered and obsessed with the past (Connerton 1989; Katriel 1999), which it seeks to domesticate in the service of the present (Lowenthal 1998, xvii).

Cinema has played a central role in the rise and reinvention of French *patrimoine* or heritage.[3] During the François Mitterrand years, for example, the French government actively sought to restore French cinema, which is regarded as one of France's greatest technical and artistic contributions, to its former position of artistic and commercial dominance.[4] The French government argued vigorously that the cinema was an integral part of French cultural identity and asked that it be given special protection during the 1993 GATT negotiations (Powrie 1996). The government also subsidized the production of films that it considered quintessentially French. Jack Lang, Mitterrand's minister of culture, used France's system of *avance sur recettes* to promote films that would raise France's cultural and cinematic profile.[5] Although various types of films were funded during Lang's tenure, the principal beneficiary was the French costume drama or historical film, sometimes referred to as the "heritage film" (Austin 1996, 143–44; Hayward 1993, 46; Van Dijk 2002). Such heritage films as Daniel Vigne's *Le Retour de Martin Guerre* (1982), Bertrand Tavernier's *Un dimanche à la campagne* (1984), Claude Berri's *Jean de Florette* (1986), Bruno Nuytten's *Camille Claudel* (1988), Yves Robert's *La Gloire de mon père* (1990), Alain Corneau's *Tous les matins du monde* (1991), Yves Angelo's *Le Colonel Chabert* (1994), Patrice Chéreau's *La Reine Margot* (1994), Angelo's *Le Hussard sur le toit* (1995), Patrice Leconte's *Ridicule* (1996), Philippe de Broca's *Le Bossu* (1997), Raoul Ruiz's *Le Temps retrouvé* (1999), Gabriel Aghion's *Le Libertin* (2000), Benoît Jacquot's *Sade* (2000), Eric Rohmer's *L'Anglaise et le duc* (2001), Jacques Dormann's *Vercingétorix* (2001), Christophe Barratier's *Les Choristes* (2004), Laurent Tirard's *Molière* (2007), and Olivier Dahan's *La Môme* (2007) have done well at the box office, both domestically and internationally and have, as Lang had hoped, returned French cinema to a place of prominence.[6] Apart from an emphasis on particular historical periods, what unites such films is an apparently conventional, linear narrative structure and a tendency to center around so-called heritage properties, culturally prestigious literary texts, historically significant buildings, or culturally resonant landscapes and interiors. As a result of their narrative structure and their mise-en-scène, heritage films have been read as privileging spectacle over narrative, as generating heritage space—a nostalgic space of memory—rather than narrative space (Higson 1993, 177).

The heritage film's tendency to replay the past is symptomatic of the cinema's broader tendency to re-present history and synthesize memory. Cinema as Matt K. Matsuda suggests, has the re-production of the past at its core. The cinema revolutionized modern conceptions of time and memory through its seeming ability to recapture lost time and replay it for a spectator who assumes this reconstructed past as his or her own (Matsuda 1996, 172–73; Connerton 1989, 78). Film, therefore, has rendered modern historical memory in every sense a screen memory—an edited and constructed version of the historical past *and* the version of events as the cinema has depicted them. If the French nation is, as Benedict Anderson argues, an imagined community, the cinema has played a central role in imagining it, particularly since cinema and the nation evolved together in a symbiotic fashion.

Nations imagine themselves to be much older than they are (Hobsbawm 1992, 1–14). Through the invention of founding myths, epic histories, national traditions, and a collective memory of all of these, nations hide their essential modernity, presenting themselves as the logical consequence of actions and processes rooted in the distant past. National identity is, at its core, a story about common origins, common heritage (Hall 1997, 294). In France, this story emerged after the French Revolution, during a period characterized as a national memory crisis, a period during which "people experienced the insecurity of their culture's involvement with its past, the perturbation of the link to their own inheritance" (Terdiman 1993, 3). The idea of national identity as heritage, an inherited national-*cultural* identity rooted in memory, emerged during this period, even if the word "*patrimoine*" was not yet used to describe it (Vadelorge 2003).[7]

History has long been recognized as playing a central role in the creation and transmission of national identity. It was French historiography that first articulated and perpetuated the idea that the French were a single people with a common identity, and it was history that introduced the idea that they were "exceptional." Historiography from Jules Michelet in the nineteenth century to the historians of the Annales school in the twentieth century produced a narrative of French national development that suggests that France and the French were the bearers of democratic traditions and a culture of progress that could benefit the rest of the world. One of the key components of this historical worldview was a linear, progressive concept of historical time that served to reinforce this notion of French exceptionalism.[8]

Almost from its beginning, cinema was involved in history's production of French heritage. Some of the very first films were historical films. These ranged from Auguste Lumière and Louis Lumière's historical scenes, such as *Mort de Marat* (1897) and *Mort de Robespierre* (1897) to early historical reenactments, such as Albert Capellani's *La Mort du Duc d'Enghien* (1909), Émile Cohl's *La Bataille d'Austerlitz* (1909), and Louis Feuillade's *Roland à Roncéveaux* (1910). The existence of these early films testifies to the degree to which history and historiography were bound up with cinema from its origins. By the early twentieth century, the historical film had become one of the cinema's dominant genres (Abel 1998). These first historical films were often overtly patriotic, functioning to "reinforce a sense of belonging to the nation" (Véray and Krohn, 2005, 334–37).

Early historical films did more, however, than simply transmit to the public a specific version of history. They also projected a certain structure of the past, an implicit, linear, historical progression that framed the images within a given film and implicitly situated the events within the broader, linear narrative of the national past. Mary Anne Doane has argued that the early cinema was bound up in the broader "rationalization" or quantification and commodification of time that characterized the late nineteenth and early twentieth century (2002, 6). Cinema reflected this rationalization in its capacity to capture time, to stop it. By its nature, cinema seemed to fulfill the historian's greatest wish, the wish to render the past eternal, to project the past forward, transmitting and reinforcing a certain vision of history and an accompanying model of historicity. Historical films become synthetic memories of an imagined collective past, positioning the spectator at one and the same time inside and outside of the history they re-presented, making the spectator feel as if he or she lived the past and the present at the same time (Connerton 1989, 78). They synthesize both personal and collective memory, creating for each spectator a sense that he or she has directly experienced the past but also creating an identical "memory" for each individual within a population. The creation of this synthetic collective memory functions to create and sustain the idea that the nation is a community of memory, by ensuring that each individual within a generation feels an identical connection to an identical past. Cinema, therefore, functions to personalize the national and nationalize the personal. It functions as the metaphoric bloodline through which a nation's identity is transmitted from generation to generation.[9]

Heritage: An Expression of Nationalism or Multiculturalism?

Heritage films are presumed, like their earlier historical counterparts, to be essentially nationalist narratives that reinforce conservative conceptions of what it means to be French. Heritage in general has been read as an expression of "tribalism," a reaction against the immigration and cultural *métissage* that have resulted from globalization (Hall 2005; Higson 2003; Littler and Naidoo 2005). In France, heritage has become synonymous with French culture, a culture seen increasingly as disappeared or disappearing (Todorov 2004, 21).[10] Heritage responds to this perceived loss of culture by encoding national identity as a product of memory, the consequence of deep, shared, vertical connections binding individuals to one another and to the territory they occupy. Heritage seems, therefore, to exclude from the space of the nation anyone who lacks a long-standing, ancestral connection to the national territory or anyone whose traditions may differ from the idealized norm. For this reason, heritage in France and elsewhere is seen as an attempt to exclude ethnic minorities from the national space.

Heritage or *patrimoine* as it reemerged in 1980 is sometimes seen as a return to the colonial logic of the nineteenth century. It is true that colonialism informs both nineteenth-century and contemporary notions of nation and national identity in France. However, it is also true that contemporary heritage is not identical to the nineteenth-century version. First, the nineteenth century, as discussed later, conceived of the relationship between past, present, and future as an ascending line, what Eviatar Zerubavel terms a narrative of progress, in which France and the French were seen to be progressing toward an idealized future (2003, 16). Contemporary heritage, on the other hand, is most frequently understood as presenting French history as a narrative of decline that regards the present as fallen and that idealizes the past.

Both of these models of the past are linear in nature, and both imply that the present is the consequence of a series of progressive actions linking the present to the past. Both, therefore, tend to reinforce the idea that time, history, and identity are unified and that they unfold across time in a single geographic space. Contemporary heritage, however, seems in many ways to be a reversal of the nineteenth-century version. Where the nineteenth century imagined history as a line marching toward progress, the contemporary era conceives of it as a line leading to decline. This reversal has been explained in various ways. Michel Wieviorka has attributed it to a loss of optimism in the French nation, particularly with regard to French economic and political power (1996, 161). The oil crises of the late 1970s and the economic slowdown that followed almost certainly played a role in undermining confidence in the technological progress and national power associated with the postwar period. The rise of the European Economic Union and related fears about the loss of France's place on the continent and in the world have also provoked doubts about France's future, doubts that were heightened in the face of the increasing cultural and economic power of the United States. Stuart Hall has seen the rise of heritage as a delayed reaction to the loss of France's colonial empire, coupled with evident demographic changes brought about by immigrants from former colonies (2005, 24–28).[11] This particular reading seems to be borne out by the fact that the rise of "immigration" politics in France occurred at precisely the same moment as the rise of heritage.[12]

A key difference between the two models of history and heritage is the way in which each frames local or regional identities. In the nineteenth century, the rural and the regional identities were encoded as an essential part of the national *past* but not the present or future. They are part of a past that is marching toward a new future. In conservative models of contemporary heritage, however, the national past is framed through the rural and regional (Lebovics 2004, 20; Lowenthal 1998, 79).[13] The regional pastoral identity functions as an emblem of national identity, a lost element of the national past that has to be retrieved. The valorization of such pastoral images, as Shanny Peer argues, constitutes a critique of the urban and the modern and therefore of "progress" (1996, 22). The regional pastoral is still encoded as part of the past, but it is perceived as lost, and it is this sense of loss that renders conservative heritage nostalgic.[14]

Heritage and Immigration

In some ways, it is not surprising that large-scale immigration would prompt a type of rethinking of the nation and national identity, particularly in a climate in which attitudes toward immigrants were already fairly negative. Ghassan Hage suggests that citizenship and nationality often function as two distinct categories within the modern nation (2000, 32–53). In such cases, citizenship becomes a political and juridical category of national belonging conferred by the state, and nationality becomes a cultural category of belonging, a type of cultural capital, conferred by the national group itself or by dominant classes within it. Hage argues that there are moments when nationality and citizenship are at odds with one another, particularly when a privileged or dominant class perceives that their capital is diminished and that therefore their position of dominance may be threatened (2000, 32). This often occurs, for example, when the state grants formal citizenship without the dominant community's acceptance. Therefore, if the nation is understood, as Stuart Hall suggests, as a system of cultural representation (1997, "Question of Cultural Identity," 292), then we could say that in such circumstances, formal citizenship has no signifying power and that it is heritage as well as language and custom, to which it is related, that function as signs of national belonging.

Such a split between citizenship and nationality does seem to be operative in contemporary France. Perhaps the strongest evidence of this is that "immigration" politics emerged only after large-scale immigration was already halted (Derderian 2004; Favell 2001; Hargreaves 2007, *Multi-ethnic France*).[15] The issue was not, as has often been pointed out, a massive influx of immigrants from outside of France but rather the presence of a visible population of French citizens descended from those immigrants (Withol de Wenden 1987; Silverman 1995; Favell 2001; Hargreaves 2007, *Multi-ethnic France*). In fact, although termed "immigration" politics, the focus of national identity debates post-1980 has not been immigration at all but rather the so-called *intégration* of immigrants and their descendants, or the terms by which immigrants and their descendants can (or cannot) be accepted by the majority culture as French (Kastoryano 2006; Noiriel 2001; Hargreaves 2007, *Multiethnic France*). These debates about integration have highlighted the supposed "inassimilability" of ethnic minorities, and they have turned on the question of heritage, since "collective memory . . . has been linked by French government and academic observers to the process of immigrant integration" (Silverstein 2004, 204). It is, in other words, the degree to which ethnic minorities conform to dominant-culture norms that determines whether or not they are perceived as nationals. Heritage may have (re)emerged as a means of excluding these new citizens from power and access by legitimizing the idea of an authentic culture, by allowing for the distinction between nationality and citizenship and linking the former, not the latter, to rights and privileges. Contemporary heritage is, in that regard as well, the opposite of its nineteenth-century predecessor, which was understood as fusing citizenship and national identity, as *including* rather than *excluding*.

This apparent split between nationality and citizenship that currently exists in France, however, is not entirely new. It can be argued that a similar split, derived from two different modes of imagining nationality, has existed in France since the nineteenth century. The first mode, which is known as universalism, theoretically defines nationality through citizenship, denying the legitimacy of cultural identities and subjugating all other identities to national identity, which this mode regards at purely juridical and political. The second mode is the idea of a "True France" that considers Frenchness to be an inherited identity that has its roots in the rural, Catholic past (Birnbaum 2001; Lebovics 2004; Beriss 2004, *Black Skins, French Voices*). The idea of the "True France" emerged in the post-Revolutionary period and was advanced by monarchists who regarded the republic as illegitimate. It denied any political basis to nationality, which it defined in purely cultural and ancestral terms. These two modes of constructing national identity are more interconnected than they might at first appear. Universalism, which officially refuses any specific cultural identity, is figured as a form of citizenship that is the product of France's unique and elect history. It is, therefore, in many ways nationalist, since it imagines France as divine and elect in much the same way as the concept of the "True France" (Balibar 1996, 193–94). Moreover, universalism's apparent "refusal" of any particular cultural identity is, in fact, the valorization of a specific, historically determined cultural identity, which means that universalism can and often does function as racism, particularly since it inscribes as acultural customs and norms that are specifically French (Balibar 1996, 192–95; Benantar 1996, 183–84).

In the current formulation of French National Heritage, there is evidence of the fusion of these two modes of thinking about the nation. National Heritage, for example, celebrates both the taking of the Bastille and the life of Joan of Arc (Le Goff 1988, 158). It emphasizes both the cultural unity of the nation and the cultural specificity of regions like Brittany and Provence. France is now imagined as the product of a total past, pre- and post-Revolution, national and regional, only it is a "total" past from which empire and immigration are largely absent.[16] This has particular consequences for France's ethnic minorities. First, as a result of the relative absence of the colonial past, there is no official "memory" of the processes by which France's ethnic minorities came to exist within the space of the nation. Secondly, this fusion of the national and the "universal" results in a narrative of citizenship that suggests that the "choice" of universalism is one that can only be made by those who have been historically formed to be capable of making it.[17] As a result, the only way that France's ethnic minorities could be imagined as legitimate members of the national community is through a reformulation or *decolonization* of the past. This reformulation would have to imagine history not as a line of events that unfolds in a single space across time but as a series of connections linking different spaces and different historical periods. It would have to imagine collective identity not as the consequence of rootedness in a single space across time but rather as the consequence of movement within and across various spaces over time. It could not, therefore, be linear but would by necessity be more prismatic in nature, imagining memory not as a downward, vertical connection to the events or ideas of the past but rather as an associative link that could unfold in any number of directions.

The Post-Colonial Heritage

Because it involves the institutional reproduction of a national collective memory, heritage is often assumed to be inherently nationalist (Citron 1987, 10; Lowenthal 1998, xiv; Hall 2005, 27–32; Vincendeau 2001, xix). That is to say, defining the nation through Heritage is seen, de facto, to exclude immigrants from the space of the nation because it is presumed to encode the nation an ethically and culturally homogenous community, closed to those who come from elsewhere or whose ancestors did (Citron 1987, 10; Birnbaum 2001; Weil 2005). That assumption has recently been challenged. G. J. Ashworth, Brian Graham, and J. E. Tunbridge, for example, argue that heritage has become increasingly multicultural as ethnic minorities within nation states have sought to "pluralise" the past and transform heritage into "many identities only some of which are associated with place" (2007, 4). I would go further: more than merely pluralizing the past that heritage embodies, advocates of multiculturalism have sought to restructure the relationship between past and present. The model they have progressively proposed is precisely the type of nonlinear, prismatic relationship that I have described. The emergence of this multicultural countermemory was first noted by Pierre Nora in his landmark work *Les Lieux de mémoire* (1993), a work that has often, perhaps paradoxically, been considered nationalist in nature. However, it is, I argue, cinema and not historiography that has been the central front in restructuring history and memory in the contemporary era. This process of restructuring is already evident in the first-wave heritage films of the 1980s. These films, contrary to the dominant interpretation, tend to undermine rather than reinforce conservative models of National Heritage because they are deeply ambivalent about the role ancestry, memory, and territory play in determining identity. The reworking of heritage in cinema is not, however, limited to the heritage film. It is a process that has shaped contemporary French films of all types, from action-packed blockbusters to experimental documentaries. Even the films associated with "Beur" cinema (films by young directors of Maghrebi immigrant origins) or the so-called *cinéma de banlieue* (films about life in the French suburbs in France's economically disadvantaged housing projects), films typically seen as rejecting or refusing any exploration of origins, have engaged with received narratives of nation and collective identity, and have functioned to close France's "colonial fracture," reinscribing the history of empire into the space of national history and memory.[18]

Contemporary French cinema has revealed that heritage is not de facto "tribal" in nature. Rather, its degree of inclusiveness or exclusiveness depends on its formulation, on who controls it, and on what it foregrounds and suppresses. This is particularly true in a nation such as France with a long history of colonialism, in which different versions of the past could either reinforce or completely undermine the power relations between the colonizing power and the formerly colonized and whose descendants now reside within the national space. What cinema has contributed to and what we are currently witnessing is not, as Nora once suggested, the death of collective memory in France (1997, 33). It is, rather, something of a rebirth, the opening up of French history and memory to spaces that already existed but were long forgotten or repressed.

Despite the differences among conventional heritage, National Heritage, and this new or post-colonial heritage, there are, however, also a number of similarities. All are rooted in the assumptions that there exist shared, collective identities and that all accept that these identities are historically constituted. All three models also tend to foreground local identities and to define belonging, whether national or transnational, through such local identities, and all three, therefore, regard identity, to varying degrees, as a product of "place." The National Heritage imagines that all members of the national community possess the identical memory of the same places, spaces, and events. The post-colonial heritage, however, imagines collective identity as an ensemble of memories, some of which are shared and some of which are not. Moreover, it suggests that even the moments, monuments, and events contained in National Heritage can be remembered differently. Identity in this model is not a line through history binding each individual to a single space. Rather, it is a kaleidoscope through which every individual is bound to any number of spaces. Immigrants and their descendants become, through this reconception of the past, not unassimilable foreign nationals but those who "have dwelled for many years, and long before migration, in the double or triple time of colonization, and [who] now occupy the multiple frames . . . of the post-colonial metropolis" (Hall 2005, 31).

Obviously, this struggle over heritage has implications for the distribution of capital, both cultural and economic in France. Those who espouse and support the National Heritage do so to maintain their own social and cultural dominance, as Ghassan Hage and Abdelmalek Sayad both suggest.[19] Similarly, those who espouse the (post-)colonial heritage seek to broaden access to economic and cultural capital and, therefore, to foreground and in some measure to shift what Hall refers to as the "system of structural inequalities" upon which France as nation is built (2005, 27). Reimagining heritage, therefore, is more than a way of reimagining the past. It is one way of redefining the power relationships between individuals and between individuals and the state.

Organization of the Study

Chapter 1 of this volume examines the National Heritage as it has been articulated in contemporary France, particularly in *Les Lieux de mémoire* (1981–97), edited by Nora. It explores the connections between this contemporary version heritage and that produced by the nineteenth century, particularly in the works of historian Jules Michelet. It argues that both versions of heritage are informed by colonial logic and suggests that the differences between the two versions can be explained by the changing relationship of the colonized to the nation state. It explores cinema's relationship to historiography and suggests that the cinema has functioned since the nineteenth century to transmit not only a specific version of French history but also its implicitly colonialist conception of historicity or historical time.

Chapter 2 explores the emergence of the French heritage film in the 1980s and 1990s. Focusing on such films as Daniel Vigne's *Le Retour de Martin Guerre* (1982), the Claude Berri diptych *Jean de Florette* (1986) and *Manon des Sources* (1986), and Régis Wargnier's *Indochine* (1992), this chapter investigates the way in which film narratives shape and reproduces collective memory. It argues that heritage films, in some respects, reinforce quasi-ethnic models of the nation through their narratives and their mise-en-scène, but it also suggests these films are deeply ambivalent about the role ancestry and territory play in defining either individual or collective identity. As a result, the heritage film is more problematic and more ambivalent than is typically imagined.

Chapter 3 looks at the emergence of the post-colonial heritage in French cinema, both in "mainstream" films such as Christophe Gans's *Le Pacte des loups* (2001) and Jean-Pierre Jeunet's *Le Fabuleux destin d'Amélie Poulain* (2001) and in Agnès Varda's experimental documentary *Les Glaneurs et la glaneuse* (2000). These films and others like them maintain certain characteristics of the heritage film but also begin either to recover the colonial past and the history of immigration associated with it or to point to its absence in national collective memory. And, more important, they also rupture cinema's implicitly historical function either by challenging the authority of received history, restructuring the conventionally linear model of historical time, or reconceiving of collective memory and identity in terms that are spatial rather than temporal.

Chapter 4 examines the problematization of heritage in the *cinéma de banlieue*. The analysis of Mathieu Kassovitz's *La Haine* (1995), Karim Dridi's *Bye Bye* (1995) and Abdellatif Kechiche's *L'Esquive* (2004) demonstrates that multicultural narratives do not reject the idea of collective (French) identity, nor do they necessarily affirm the cultural specificity of France's ethnic minorities. Rather, they tend to present ethnic minorities as alienated from the past by processes of marginalization that are and have been at work in the majority culture. These films attempt to recover the past by imagining identity in terms of space rather than time and by recovering historical spaces of commonality between ethnic minorities and the majority culture. These films also foreground the absence of such spaces of commonality in the current formulation of National Heritage.

Chapter 5 explores the post-colonial heritage in films by and about France's ethnic minority population, specifically, the Beurs. Analysis of Yamina Benguigui's *Mémoires d'immigrés, l'héritage maghrébin* (1997), Christophe Ruggia's *Le Gone du Chaâba* (1998), Bourlem Guerdjou's *Vivre au paradis* (1998), and Rachid Bouchareb's *Indigènes* (2006), shows that beur films have reinserted the history of colonialism and immigration into the national past. These films also attempt to restructure or redefine collective identity, linking it to local and regional rather than the national spaces. In so doing, these films work to divest heritage of its ancestral characteristics, foregrounding forgotten spaces of common history and memory that bind France's ethnic minorities and the majority population and conceiving of both memory and identity in terms that are either circular or prismatic.

One of the primary tensions between post-colonial heritage and the National Heritage is the place accorded the colonial past. Both forms reference and to some extent recover the colonial past. However, recovering that past involves more than simply remembering colonial history and the history of immigration it produced. It also involves recovering the complex processes by which imperialism and republicanism have coexisted in France and, therefore, uncovering many of the paradoxes of French nationality itself. For that reason, this study seeks to do more than simply demonstrate that progressively, since 1980, the post-colonial and the National Heritage have increasingly overlapped and that the post-colonial heritage has increasingly become the National Heritage. It seeks, rather, to understand the terms by which colonial history and the history of immigration have been adopted into the National Heritage. In the ongoing struggle between memory and countermemory, heritage and counterheritage, the dominant culture is always working, as Roberta Pearson suggests, to incorporate countermemory into itself in order to disarm it (1999, 180). The real question this volume attempts to answer, therefore, is this: has the nation simply co-opted multiculturalism by (re)inscribing the colonial past into the national past without interrogating the hierarchies upon which it was based? Has it, therefore, recolonized the formerly colonized within the space of the Republican nation? Or, rather, have those articulating the post-colonial heritage succeeded in recalling not only the fact of the colonial past but also the implications of colonialism on French conceptions of both citizenship and nationality? Have they, therefore, succeeded in making France post-colonial?

1

Constructing Memory: The History of Heritage in France

Heritage permeates contemporary French culture, from advertising to the film industry, from cinema to politics. Heritage is understood as a way of defining the national present through a particular vision of the past. It is seen as relying on glorious narratives about the past that justify seemingly nationalistic conceptions of the nation, and it also references particular cultural monuments, artifacts, historical figures, and historical events from the past to produce a conception of the nation as possessed of a superior culture and a superior history. In general, heritage privileges ancestry over citizenship, the rural over the urban, past over present. It is a way of conceiving of the nation as a cultural community, formed by common historical experiences. Heritage privileges collective memory, which it presents as the guarantor of national stability and integrity. French heritage assumes that modern France was created progressively over time through key transformational events, including the Roman conquest, the Hundred Years War, the Wars of Religion, and the French Revolution. It imagines that the memory of these events has been transmitted in an unbroken line across generations, starting from ancient Gaul. It embodies Ernest Renan's belief that the nation exists in the memory of the great things it has done.

Heritage, History, and the Colonial Past

Heritage is often read as a (post-)colonial or postmodern phenomenon. It has been understood as an attempt to detach nationality from citizenship and to privilege ancestry over citizenship in order to marginalize the post-colonial minorities who now reside in the nations that once colonized them (Hall 2005; Higson 2003; Lebovics 1992, 2004). In France, in particular, heritage has been understood as a return to certain nineteenth-century ideas concerning the nation and national identity. Herman Lebovics has grouped such ideas under the term "the True France," which holds that the French are a people in the cultural, if not the ethnic sense, of the term and which considers culture to be the foundation of national cohesion. Colonial subjects and their descendants are, according to this principle, permanently excluded from the space of the nation because they lack the appropriate heritage. The concept of "the True France" was central to thinking about the nation during the nineteenth century in general and during the Third Republic in particular. It was closely linked to the idea of "the Greater France" or to empire and to the colonial *mission civilisatrice* (Lebovics 1992; Conklin 1997; Sherman 2004), according to which France, as a result of its unique history, was obliged to spread its culture to "uncivilized" parts of the world. Colonialism, in this view, was not the domination or exploitation of the colonized. It was their salvation.[1]

Benedict Anderson argues that nineteenth-century conceptions of nation relied upon the belief that there existed fundamental similarities among the diverse members of a national group. Eric Hobsbawm and Terence Ranger similarly argue that from the nineteenth century forward, nations have depended for their legitimacy upon mythic narratives about the national past that propose deep, historical ties linking modern citizens to the ancient inhabitants of the same geographic space (1990). It was Renan who perhaps first articulated this particular understanding of the nation. His lecture "*Qu'est-qu'une nation?* (What is a nation?)" argues that the nation is a "spiritual" or intellectual principle, something that exists predominantly in the minds of its members (1996/1882, 52). The sense of common identity and common purpose that national identity implies derives, according to Renan, not from race but from history. The nation, in Renan's reading, is "a historical result" (1996/1882, 45), and what binds citizen to citizen is not ancestry but collective memory, "the possession in common of a rich legacy of memories" (1996/1882, 52).

On the surface, Renan's insistence that the nation is a historical rather than ethnic community seems to reject ancestral conceptions of national identity. By arguing, however, that the French nation is a historical result and by locating the origins of that nation in the ancient past, Renan imagines the nation in terms that remain essentially biological or ancestral. On the one hand, he conceives of the nation as something like a biological organism, which is born at a certain moment and then undergoes a process of development similar to maturation. On the other, he conceives of collective memory as a bloodline, uniform, stable, and transmitted across time. This biological characterization of memory is evident in Renan's assertion that collective memory is "received" (1996/1882, 52) rather than created. It is also apparent in his suggestion that the transmission of memory reproduces the past, affecting attitudes and behaviors in similar ways across time. This bears striking similarity to biological heredity by which individuals are shaped in the present by the genetic material they receive from their parents, grandparents, and great-grandparents.

If, however, this biological, evolutionary model of national history finds its most succinct expression in Renan's essay, the idea is not original to him. Much of the late nineteenth century's vision of history was influenced by biology. History in the nineteenth century was imagined as a vertical line of continuity connecting past to present. It imagined the nation as both stable and constantly changing in the same way that biological organisms or species may be seen to be both stable and changing across time. Such biological models of history and national development were particularly useful in France because they were able to correct what Richard Terdiman terms "the memory crisis" or the rupture in historical continuity produced by the political Revolution of 1789 (1993, 3). Biological models of history and memory resolved this crisis because they provided a model of continuity of which rupture was a vital part. In biology, both individual organisms and entire species are understood to undergo periodic transformation. These transformations, however, do not change the fundamental essence of either organism or species. Rather, these ruptures are seen as necessary to biological evolution. Conceiving of the nation in evolutionary terms was perhaps one way to insist that the France that had emerged from the Revolution was the same France that had preceded it (Matsuda 1996, 9). Moreover, applying an evolutionary model of history to the Revolution, specifically, it was possible to suggest that the Revolution was inevitable and "natural" and therefore to suggest that it was fundamental to national growth and development.

The emergence of this biological model of historiography is sometimes attributed to the influence of Darwinian theories of evolution, Darwin's *On the Origin of Species* having appeared in 1859 (Rosen 2001). It is clear that this biological, evolutionary conception of the nation and a parallel biological conception of memory were both active in the late nineteenth century. However, they did not originate there. The idea that the nation evolved through history and that it was defined and sustained by a type of inherited memory is found throughout the nineteenth century. Moreover, anxieties about the transmission and protection of *patrimoine* or national heritage were already present in the period immediately following the Revolution.

Colonialism, Climate Theory, and Narratives of the National Past

Loïc Rignol argues that biological, ancestral ideas of history were introduced into the nineteenth century by the early historians of the Revolution, most notably Augustin Thierry. Their function was to legitimize the new republic by reappropriating the logic of the royal genealogies that had guaranteed the stability and legitimacy of the monarchy (2002, 87). Theses genealogies had become fundamental to royal power during the reign of Louis XIV. At that time, Cardinal Bossuet and others suggested that the king's authority derived from God, and the integrity of the royal line became seen as a guarantee of the legitimacy of the monarchy and, therefore, the stability of the kingdom.

This type of genealogical logic, by which individual identity and legal standing become grounded in ancestry, is visible elsewhere in the seventeenth century. It was used, for example, to justify the practice of slavery in the Code Noir (1685), the legal tract detailing the status of slaves in the French kingdom. Slaves were legally residents on French territory and would normally, therefore, be classified as citizens. However, the practice of slavery required that slaves be accepted as French only for the purposes of governance. They were to be subjected to the authority of the king but were not themselves subjects. Moreover, slaves existed, according to the code, only in the colonies, not in metropolitan France. Officially, any slave brought onto the mainland of France was automatically emancipated.

The code made of the slave an absent presence. It granted the slave legal status but no legal standing. It also created a category of legal and national belonging that existed, by definition, only outside the space of the nation itself. It both acknowledged and denied the slave's humanity because it affirmed the Catholic Church's view that black skin was the mark of divine retribution, a sign from God that an individual was condemned to a condition of servitude (Hannaford 1996). If the slave's physical appearance seems to be the basis for his or her subjugation, the code makes it clear that it is his or her ancestry that determines his or her status because the condition of slave is a question of matrilineal inheritance. A person is a slave, in the logic of the code, because he or she has inherited that condition from his or her ancestors, specifically from the mother. This is a clear suggestion that identity and more particularly legal status or citizenship are a question of inheritance.

The eighteenth century reworked the seventeenth century's biological essentialism into a theory of culture and nations. Louis Sala-Molins comments that the philosophers of the Enlightenment were not much interested in slavery as a subject apart because they rejected the theological and hierarchical grounds on which it was justified (interview with Eric Pincus, 2002). Nonetheless, there is evidence in the writing and thinking of some of these philosophers that they were directly engaged in trying to resolve the philosophical problem slavery posed and that they were particularly interested in resolving the questions about collective and national identities that slavery raised.

Charles de Secondat, baron de Montesquieu's *De L'Esprit des lois* (1748), in particular, suggests the emergence of a type of mediational logic on the subjects of slavery, ancestry, residency, nationality, and citizenship. Montesquieu was, in general, opposed to slavery because he regarded the presumed inhumanity of the slave in Catholic theology and the Code Noir as unnatural. Nonetheless, in *De L'Esprit des lois,* he remarks that in warmer climates, people become lazy, and therefore, in such climates, forced labor might be justified for the good of the inhabitants of those regions. Montesquieu's position with respect to slavery is that it is essentially wrong, but in that in some cases, as a result of culture and ancestry, it is justified. While it is difficult to conclude from this that Montesquieu supported slavery, it is not difficult to see the emergence of a type of thinking that posited the superiority of certain nations or cultures and the inferiority of others.[2]

Montesquieu concludes in *De l'Esprit des lois* that these superior cultures have a responsibility to transmit their "superior" culture to those with an "inferior" culture.[3] The designations of "superior" and "inferior" are linked to what is perceived as the degree of technological sophistication achieved over time. Montesquieu, therefore, understood culture as the result of climatic influence over generations, a view that is primarily ancestral and that reflects the growing influence of climate theory in France's intellectual culture.[4] It also reflects the original logic of the Code Noir, which had presented slavery as a type of civilizing process that would ultimately lead to the slave's salvation (Hannaford 1996).

Climate theory was most fully developed in the George-Louis Leclerc, Comte de Buffon's *De L'Homme: histoire naturelle*, published in France from 1748 to 1804. It is also treated in numerous other works from the eighteenth century, including L'Abbé d'Espiard's *L'Essai sur le génie et le caractère des nations* (1743), Constantin François de Volney's *Voyage en Égypte et en Syrie* (1787), and various works by Voltaire and Denis Diderot, among others.[5] David A. Bell maintains that this theory not only influenced Europe's point of view on the cultures it colonized but also influenced Europe's point of view on the nature of cultures and nations in general. He suggests that the theory "seduced the French of the eighteenth century" (2001, 144) and became the primary filter through which they understood what today might be termed national identity. Climate theory profoundly influenced thinking about nationality and citizenship because it asserted that the Caucasian race, by virtue of its geographical location and climate, had developed civilizations superior to other races located in warmer climates and in particular to Africans. It also firmly linked culture and national identity because its definition of culture was tied to both ancestry and geography.[6]

Ancestral or biological conceptions of the nation and national memory find their first full expression in the nineteenth century and, specifically, in the historiography of Jules Michelet. Michelet's entire understanding of the history of France is informed by the theory of climates. Although he never directly references this theory in his works, its effects can be seen in many of his most basic assertions. He believed, for example, that civilization "evolved" as a result of history and geography. Moreover, he measured this evolution in terms of democratic and technological progress, a view that reflects climate theory's association between technological innovation and political and cultural sophistication.

Like his contemporary Thierry, Michelet was concerned with establishing continuity between the republic and the monarchy that had preceded it (Crossley 1993). He posited that this continuity lay in the development of democracy from the ancient Gauls to the Revolution and beyond, a trajectory that began with Gaulish resistance to the Roman occupation. This initial democratic impulse, according to Michelet, was progressively repeated and expanded until it reached its ultimate conclusion in the Revolution of 1789. In *Introduction à L'Histoire universelle*, for example, Michelet states, "[T]he genius of French democracy ... dates to the very origins of [French] history" (1834, 59) and that democratic principles were already evident in ancient Gaul in everything from the manner in which the Gauls chose their leaders to the tendency of the Druids to align themselves with the people and against the aristocracy. He finds similar evidence of democratic tendencies in later periods in French history, for example, that French resistance to English occupation during the fifteenth century constituted a repetition and expansion of Gaul's resistance of Rome. Michelet also argues that the Revolution of 1789, an event he considered preordained, constituted the ultimate repetition and expansion of both (1876, 2.191–93).

Michelet conceived of the nation in terms that are fundamentally biological. He regarded the nation almost as a living organism that had undergone change and development over time, and he considered each generation living in France to have received the actions and mindset of previous generations. This implicitly biological model is interesting, given that Michelet worked to divest French historiography of any overt notion that the French were a people in the biological sense of the term (Crossley 1993, 204). In contrast to Thierry, for example, Michelet emphasized the ethnic diversity of those living in France and repeatedly asserted that the modern French were not the biological descendants of the Gauls.[7] In *Le Peuple* (originally published in 1846), he seems, most notably, to go to great pains to discredit the idea that there is any biological component to Frenchness, claiming that the "genius" of the French nation lay in its complete rejection of ethnic identity (1974/1876, 217).

The biological elements to Michelet's histories are not limited to the linear, evolutionary narrative they propose. There is also a biological component to his belief that the past repeated itself in the present. The Revolution is presented in Michelet's writings as both the continuation of democratic tendencies that existed at the time of the Gauls and as the direct repetition of struggles for liberation including Gaulish resistance to Rome and French resistance to English domination. It was, in Michelet's reading, this combination of continuity and repetition that provided the forward momentum for the nation's evolutionary development.[8] Michelet's idea of repetition parallels biological models of evolution, and in his reading, the impulse toward democracy becomes something like a gene or trait transmitted across generations. Michelet was, therefore, proposing the existence of a type of transgenerational homogeneity of action or spirit in the French that has many of the characteristics of heredity.

If Michelet repeatedly asserted that the French were of mixed ancestry, he did not entirely abandon the idea of an ancestral past. He affirms in his work, for example, that the ethnic and cultural specificity of each of the ancient groups from which the French are descended had given way to a new, unified identity—French identity—because all of these people shared a common history. Michelet, therefore, recognized that the French are ethnically diverse, but he nonetheless insisted on their *cultural* homogeneity. He repeatedly referred to the Celts and Gauls collectively as "our ancestors, the peasants" (1974, 85) which suggests a common class and condition that supersedes the differences in their bloodlines. He also suggested that the Gaulish campaign against the Romans and France's later campaign against the English united these ancestors into a group with a recognizable collective identity, an identity forged in opposition to a common oppressor (1876, 2.177–78). Finally, and perhaps most importantly, Michelet argued that the French Revolution cemented this collective identity into a national identity, thereby fusing the diverse groups who composed the French nation into a single people (1974, 217). Michelet understands ancestry in experiential rather than in biological terms (Noiriel 2001, 138–41), which means he cannot be said to have argued for a biological or ethnic national identity as such. Rather, Michelet suggests, history functions to expand and reformulate such ethnic identities and to subjugate them to a greater national identity. However, since the historical events that created this fusion occurred, in Michelet's reading, more than two hundred years ago, his conception of national identity is nevertheless *implicitly* ancestral. Following Michelet's reasoning to its most logical conclusion, no one can really claim to be French if he or she did not have ancestors who went through this specific historical process.

If Michelet introduced into French historiography an implicitly ancestral conception of national identity, he also introduced the idea that national cohesion in the present depends on the shared consciousness or memory of the national past. For Michelet, history was primarily a type of memory, the resurgence or "resurrection," as he termed it in *Le Peuple*, of the past in the present (1974/1876, 73). The function of history, Michelet argues, is to bear witness to the past, to make it live again. In the 1869 preface to the *Histoire de France*, for example, Michelet criticizes the detached, analytical presentation of past events typically associated with history. He argues that the spirit or memory of past events reside in the artifacts of that past, "the living unity of the natural and geographical elements that constituted it" (1869/1845, 1:i). For Michelet, the role of historian is to channel and transmit these memorial traces and to fashion them into what Crossley calls "a narrative of national identity" (1993, 185). The memory of the past exists in objects, but it only lives in human consciousness and survives only through human transmission. The past, for Michelet, is more than simply a narrative or record of what had been. It is the lifeline or bloodline that connects past, present, and future.

It is possible to read Michelet's work, perhaps in spite of his own intentions, as a bridge between the hierarchical thinking of *ancien régime* and the civilizing mission of the Third republic. It was Michelet, David Caroll states, who first suggested that the French nation was the product of an internal civilizing process that prompted individuals to renounce ethnic and regional identities and to substitute them for a national identity (1998, 119). It was also Michelet who imagined that the fulfillment of France's destiny—the repetition of the Revolution—would come through the expansion of this civilizing process throughout the world (Carroll 1998, 121–26). Finally, and perhaps most interestingly, Michelet asserts that Africans were equal to but less developed than the French, repeating the logic of both the Code Noir and the *mission civilisatrice*, both of which hold that there is only one trajectory of development, that already undergone by Europe (1974/1876, 193–94).[9] It was part of France's historical destiny, in Michelet's view, to export democracy throughout the world, and if he rejects imperialism, he, nonetheless, supports the idea of the civilizing mission on which it was based, even suggesting that force and conquest might be necessary for France to fulfill that mission (Carroll 1998, 126).

Michelet's ideas about the relationship between the historical formation of France and France's civilizing mission helped to inscribe the colonial fracture into French historiography. The nation, according to Michelet, is the result of the interaction between history and geography. National identity is the collective memory of that specific history as it unfolds within a specific geographic space. If France is the product of a universal history that is understood as having brought democracy into the world, it is also a unique nation—the product of that universal history on a specific territory. According to Michelet's vision, France is called upon to repeat its universal history elsewhere in the world. However, when that history is reenacted in other geographic spaces, it produces new nations, new national identities; it does not produce new *French* nations or new *French* identities.

Therefore, the exportation of French civilization throughout the world functions as a part of French history—it is understood as part of France's destiny to "civilize" the greater world—but it also lies outside of French history because this exportation becomes part of the history of each new nation it creates. This is consistent with the conception of French history as both linear and circular, a conception that is already present in Michelet. Colonialism becomes part of the circular repetition of the democratizing project that is seen to have informed and shaped France's history. It also exists as a point on an ascending line that describes France's own move toward democracy and the realization of its mission to export democracy throughout the world. However, because the "civilizing process" once exported becomes part of a new line of historical development—a tangential line—the history of colonialism and the experience of colonization *are not* part of France's history. They form part of neither the circle nor the line. Colonialism, therefore, is both present in and absent from French history as Michelet understood it.[10] This present absence is, according to Suzanne Citron, the element that gives modern French historiography its coherence (1987, 181), and it is at the root of France's inability to accept post-colonial minorities as French (Wieviorka 2005, 117–23).

Now You See It, Now You Don't

Michelet's idea of history has much in common with contemporary heritage. Both view the present as dependent on the remembrance of the past, and in both cases, the function of remembering is to guarantee the coherence of national identity. Both also regard the past as redemptive, and both propose remembrance as a means of assuring the future. Michelet's histories, most notably *Le Peuple*, tend to foreground rural France and the rural peasantry, both of which figure prominently in contemporary heritage.[11] Michelet also locates history and, specifically, national memory in historic "sites" (primarily people, objects, and events) in much the same way that heritage does, and the two tend to privilege many of the same "sites," including spaces such as France's churches, events such as the Revolution, and historical figures such as Joan of Arc. Perhaps most interestingly, both Michelet's historical narrative and contemporary heritage simultaneously presume and deny the centrality of France's colonial past to the national past. In Michelet's work, colonialism is regarded as the fulfillment of France's own evolutionary development, but it is located outside of history. Heritage, on the other hand, is a reaction to decolonization that locates both empire and the end of empire outside the space of memory.

Many of those who have commented on the conflicted space represented by the colonial era in French national history and collective memory have cast this effect of absent presence or colonial fracture as the result of collective repression, a type of inability on the part of the French population to accept the loss of empire and particularly the loss of colonial Algeria. Anne Donadey, for example, argues that the relative absence of the colonial past from the space of contemporary heritage reflects what she terms the "Algeria Syndrome" (1996, 217). Borrowing from Henry Rousso, Donadey suggests that contemporary France finds itself at a point of obsession following the repression of an episode too traumatic to process. While I question neither the traumatic nature of the Algerian War nor the idea that the loss of empire was experienced as something like trauma, I suggest that the mechanisms of trauma do not entirely explain the way in which the colonial past is both constantly present and consistently absent from formulations of both the French national past and French collective heritage. Moreover, the colonial fracture has been in existence since the mid-nineteenth century and possibly since the seventeenth century, and it preceded the Algerian War or decolonization in general. This marked omission of empire also preceded the "memory" of colonization, since it was contemporaneous to the event. Given this, the failure to include empire in contemporary versions of the national past suggests not a crisis of *memory*—it is doubtful that anyone in France ever forgot there was an empire or that it no longer exists—but rather a crisis of *representation*. There is a gap between what is known and what can be said or represented. This gap is not the result of official (that is, governmental) censorship. Rather, it is a problem with inserting the colonial past into narratives about the French nation that obscure the existence of a colonial past and, perhaps more important, a problem with recounting the end of empire using a narrative of the nation that depends upon empire for its coherence.

Essentially, the end of empire constituted a rupture with the past that undermined the narrative of continuity designed to compensate for the rupture of the Revolution. It directly threatened the idea that a glorious past guaranteed a glorious future, and it shook the coherence of the narrative of repetition through which France had been defined. This rupture explains the complete turning away from the past that occurred during the Thirty Glorious Years (Ross 1996). But it also serves to explain why anxieties over the presence of French citizens who are also post-colonial minorities—citizens whose existence defies traditional historiography—have expressed themselves as a return to the past. It is not, as has often been suggested, that the rise of heritage in France is an effort to "forget" or ignore the end of empire. It is, rather, that the rise of heritage reflects the need to write a new past, to create a new narrative of French history that can account and compensate for the implosion of the old one.

This is not to say that heritage does not, at least in certain cases, attempt to reestablish the nineteenth century's paradigms of national identity. Looking at the rhetoric of the political right wing in France, it seems clear that the appropriation of heritage functions precisely to reinforce such older narratives. Christopher Flood and Hugo Frey posit that the right-wing version of heritage re-members empire, reinserts it into the national past and does so as a means of redeeming colonialism and reestablishing the old colonial myths (2002, 195–204). One prominent example of this type of re-membering is the February 2005 law on the teaching of French history; the law decrees that the colonial past could and should be included in the narrative of the national past and that it should be narrated in entirely positive terms.[12]

Contemporary conceptions of nationality in France are, however, much more a reworking of colonial-era thinking about the nation than a direct reappropriation. In the nineteenth century, it was held that the colonized were nationals but not citizens because the doctrine of the *mission civilisatrice* held that they were insufficiently "civilized" to be granted citizenship. The dominant contemporary view of nationality holds that ethnic minorities are citizens but not nationals because they are insufficiently "integrated" to be considered nationals. Contemporary heritage, therefore, at least on the surface, inverts the colonial-era's rhetoric (Wihtol de Wenden, *Citoyenneté, Nationalité, et Immigration*, 1987, 42–43). This inversion is evident elsewhere. However, it is true that both nineteenth-century conceptions of the nation and their contemporary counterparts are, in the words of Hue-Tam Ho Tai, "neither fully inclusive nor fully exclusive" (2001, 912), and both, therefore, seem to legitimize a system of structural inequalities that pushes ethnic minorities to the margins of the nation.

Heritage and *Les Lieux de mémoire*

Heritage is not, as is sometimes suggested, exclusively the domain of the right wing. François Mitterrand, who came to power in 1981, was as much responsible for the perpetuation of heritage as the right-wing governments that preceded and followed him. Mitterrand's *grands travaux*, a program of monument building commissioned and funded during his presidency, are an example of the type of "heritage work." These monuments, which include both the Pyramide du Louvre and the Grande Arche de la Défense, have been understood as classic heritage monuments, intended to counter a (perceived) loss of cultural cohesion, and brought about by the decline of national power and cultural prestige (Norindr, "Le Plus Grande France," 1996,

241). La Grande Arche de la Defense, for example, is a reinvention of the classical and neoclassical triumphal arch, a form that is more typically associated with monarchy and imperialism than it is to democracy and republicanism. The triumphal arches on which it was based may be found throughout France and are, for the most part, monuments commissioned either by the Romans, by the monarchy (specifically, Louis XIV) or by the emperor (both Napoleon and Louis Napoleon). The often celebrate military victories and are, therefore, commemorations of monarchy and empire and its triumph over resistance. The arch is, for that reason, a peculiar form to choose to embody a modern republic, as it represents the nation through the reappropriation of a reference to an antidemocratic and non-egalitarian tradition. Similarly, the Pyramide du Louvre is the reappropriation of an ancient, specifically, foreign form linked to pre-Christian religion and non-Western culture. It, too, suggests the colonial past because it borrows a specifically Egyptian form that suggests Napoleon's campaign in Egypt and because the original pyramids were associated with all-powerful rulers and were, at one time, believed to have been built with forced labor.[13] The borrowing of the pyramid shape in a clearly Western, postmodern reinvention implies the overwriting of ancient, pre-Christian cultures by French culture. However, since the French colonial campaign in Egypt was ultimately unsuccessful, the pyramid also evokes both empire and the end of empire and like the arch, it, therefore, points to episodes in the national past that are often omitted from official memory.

These two monuments demonstrate the way in which "the idea of nation in France continues to be constructed, contested and defended . . . against a broader system of colonialism that preceded it" (Norindr, "La Plus Grande France," 1996, 233). Moreover, their very construction, which was an effort at the postmodern reinvention of *patrimoine*, suggests that the nation of the present only exists through the repetition and reappropriation of the past. However, both monuments also embody a kind of history and memory that is neither linear nor strictly national. The forms these monuments reappropriate are not specific to France and can only be fully understood in transnational, transhistorical terms. Moreover, from the linear view of history, these monuments are problematic and conflicted. Panivong Norindr suggests they were intended as symbols of France's present and future greatness as guaranteed by its Europeaness (1996, 240–41). This would make of them embodiments of the idea that a glorious past portends a glorious future. However, as noted, the past they activate is not specifically national and not entirely glorious, and so it is difficult to read them unproblematically in this way. It is unclear what these monuments have to say about the relationship between past and present because the way in which that relationship is conceived depends upon which facets of the past are considered.

However they were intended, therefore, the monuments of the *grands travaux* activate a complex and multifaceted past whose full sense they do not quite capture. They cannot be read in linear terms, and they in no way imply a relationship of past to present that is either vertical or progressive. The relationship of present to past that they suggest is much more prismatic than linear. Moreover, each of these monuments, to a greater or lesser extent, actively and overtly builds the national past on the colonial past, something that traditional French historiography does not and perhaps cannot do. These monuments call for new forms of history and memory because they recall histories and events that lie outside the parameters of traditional French historiography.

The same may be said of what is probably the greatest monument to France to come out of the Mitterrand years, the seven-volume, collectively authored historical work *Les Lieux de mémoire* (1997). The work is a history of the nation through "an inventory of the sites where [the nation] has electively incarnated itself" (Nora, "Présentation," 1997, 15), and its publication is often regarded as one of the defining moments in the development of French National Heritage (Lebovics 2004, 6). Nora and his collaborators, including Georges Duby, Antoine Prost, Raoul Girardet, Jacques Le Goff, Jean Starobinski and Jean-Pierre Rioux have come to be seen as the guardians of the French national memory, and to this end, many of them were enlisted by the French government to help protect the sites of memory that they, themselves, defined (Greene 1999, 4).

In his introduction to the project, Pierre Nora describes *Les Lieux de mémoire* as an effort to create "an inventory of the sites where [the national memory] was electively incarnated" in order to combat the disappearance of that memory ("Présentation," 1997, 15). According to Nora, "traditional memory" has disappeared ("Entre mémoire et histoire," 1997, 27–35). As a result, Nora argues, "the national definition" has also ceased to exist. It is not, Nora explains, that an awareness of the national past has ceased to exist. Rather, personal, lived memory—in his view the cornerstone of memory—has been replaced by institutional forms of memory, and therefore, history, "the always problematic and incomplete reconstruction of that which no longer exists" has supplanted memory, "a phenomenon that is always current, a living link to the eternal present" ("Entre mémoire et histoire," 1997, 25).

Nora's insistence that the nation depends upon transgenerational memory is a direct appropriation of the nineteenth-century's linear conception of both national memory and the national past. Moreover, *Les Lieux de mémoire* can been read as borrowing from the same nostalgic, folkloric vision of the nation that underlies National Heritage. Steven Englund, for example, holds that *Les Lieux de mémoire* is permeated by nostalgia for a bygone national era (1992, 303). Perry Anderson comments that the volumes participate in "a self-indulgent heritage culture" that it ostensibly seeks to reject (2004, 7).

Naomi Greene suggests that the nostalgia in *Les Lieux de mémoire* derives from a sense of loss of a certain national cultural and religious homogeneity (1999, 157). Tai concurs, saying that despite Nora's declared interest in embracing polyphony and polysemy, *Les Lieux de mémoire*, nonetheless, represents French national identity as a stable entity, unchanged over time (2007, 910).

It is evident that nostalgia does play an important part in Nora's framing of the national past. First, by defining the nation through ancestral memory or, in Nora's terms, a lived connection to the past, *Les Lieux de mémoire* reproduces the linear structure of the past inherited from nineteenth-century historiography. Moreover, by insisting that the essence of the nation is memory, Nora also suggests that the nation's coherence is dependent upon the reproduction of the past in the present. Finally, by arguing for the existence of a breakdown in memory caused by a parallel breakdown of the nation, Nora positions his own age as fallen with respect to previous ages, and like Michelet, he proposes to redeem the present by resurrecting the past.

Nora's assertions about the decline of the nation depend upon the absent presence of the colonial past. While Nora asserts that in the present, institutional memory has supplanted personal memory, he bemoans the breakdown of certain institutions, such as the church, the school, and the family (Bell 1997). Nora seems to accept that these particular institutions, which he understands as surrogates of the state, guarantee and transmit both lived and personal memory. These institutions were deeply implicated in the colonial mission and were charged with transmitting Frenchness both domestically and in the colonies (Lebovics 1992; Conklin 1997; Bell 1997). Because these institutions still exist and function in France, Nora's insistence that memory is breaking down because these institutions are failing may be understood as an unspoken assertion that the failure of these institutions was a failure to maintain the empire and, therefore, that it is the loss of empire that has brought about the collapse of the nation. *Les Lieux de mémoire*, then, reproduces the same logic of absent presence with regard to the colonial past that characterizes nineteenth-century historiography. The memory of empire is present within the work, but its presence is a reminder of the absence of the empire itself.

Nora has, elsewhere, argued that collective memory should contain both positive and negative spaces in order to represent the nation in its most complete form. In the December 12, 2005, edition of *Le Monde*, for example, his editorial criticized France for failing to properly commemorate Napoleon's battle at Austerlitz; he called this absence of commemoration a failure of memory, a failure he cast as threatening the integrity of the nation. This failure of memory was due, in Nora's reading, to oversensitivity to colonialism. He categorized the failure as an unforgivable attempt by the nation to "cleanse" itself of unpleasant portions of the past, an attempt that threatened the integrity of the nation as a whole. Given Nora's passionate defense of the need to remember *everything* about the past and his parallel charge that France is oversensitive to the colonial past, it is worth noting that colonialism and empire barely figure in *Les Lieux de mémoire*. There is no entry on colonialism or empire in the work and almost nothing in any of the volumes that refers to either, with the exception of a single entry on by Charles Robert Ageron on the Colonial Exposition of 1931. That entry, interestingly, explores the commemoration or *memory* of empire, not empire itself, and it presents France's empire as the "crowning glory of the Republic" (Ageron, 1997, 493), in much the same way that it was presented in the nineteenth century. The same tendency may be seen in the few other entries in which the colonial past is obliquely referenced. Jacques Ozouf and Mona Ozouf, for example, write in their chapter, "*La Tour de la France par deux enfants* [A tour of France by two children]" that "colonial conquests came to show the world that France was great" (1997, 288). Empire, in both entries, is cast only in terms of its contribution to French national glory, not as a separate historical experience or reality. Moreover, the one-sided presentation of this memory of empire may be seen to exclude the experience of the colonized from the space of national memory while recording empire as a part of the national past. If, in the colonial era, the absent presence of colonialism legitimized colonization while locating the colonized outside the space of the nation, this absent presence in *Les Lieux de mémoire* seems to locate empire within the space of national memory while denying France's ethnic minorities any claim to that memory.

The content of *Les Lieux de mémoire* reinforces such a reading. For example, numerous essays relate to national/cultural institutions, particularly the school, including "*Lavisse, instituteur national* [Lavisse, teacher of the nation]," "*Le Tour de la France par deux enfants*," and the maps of France made by Paul Vidal-Lablache. These entries refer to the teaching of the nation through history or geography as it was practiced in the late nineteenth and early twentieth centuries. Asserting that the space of the school as it existed in the Third Republic is a site of national memory is equivalent to suggesting that all French citizens were themselves in elementary schools during that period or, more likely, that their parents or grandparents were. Anyone in the first group would possess this "site" of memory as a result of their own experience. However, there are very few left in France who can claim this as a site of personal memory. Those in the latter group would possess this site of memory through "hereditary" memory—they would know the school of this era, the book, and the maps because they have heard about them from someone who had direct experience. Those who are French but who are young and whose parents are not/were not French would, presumably, be excluded from this "site."

The same effect can be seen in other "sites" included in the text. André Burgière's essay, "*Généalogie* (Genealogy)," for example, describes that one aspect of Frenchness derives from the knowledge of an ancestral connection to the French historical past. This familial connection exists also in Armand Frémont's essay, "*La Terre* (The land)." The connection to the land is fundamental, Frémont states, because the land is for the French "the site of their daily history" (1997, 3056). What is more, the memory of farming the land is vivid to many in France who "retain the memory of grand-parents from Ségalas or from Armor who ate the black bread of daily misery as tenant farmers or as farm laborers" (1997, 3075). Again, what is implied is the existence of ties of memory that link to their descendants those who worked the land. In other words, memory depends upon a certain ancestry and a long-standing ancestral connection to the land.

Les Lieux de mémoire implies cultural homogeneity in other respects, as well. Several essays assume a tradition if not an active observance of Catholicism as a fundamental component of national identity. Philippe Boutry's essay "*Le Clocher* [The church tower]," for example, describes the church tower as "the architectural symbol par excellence of the memory of nearly two millennia of Christian life rooted in a territory, in the sentiment of belonging to a community" (1997, 3083). With this characterization of the church tower, Boutry links the church to traditional, rural life and mourns the disappearance of both. Thus, the presumed ancestral connection to village life is also an assumed religious affiliation that yet again excludes many from the space of the national memory. This set of assumptions and exclusions is replicated in the chapters "*La Cathédrale* [The cathedral]" and "*Catholiques et Laics* [Catholics and secular]" and on specific churches in the chapters "*Notre Dame de Paris*" and "*Le Sacré-Coeur de Montmartre.*"

While it is not the purpose of this volume to provide a detailed analysis of the component essays of *Les Lieux de mémoire*, it should be clear by this point that French work is predicated upon a particular notion of what it means to be French, a notion that comes very close to the ancestral model of national identity that is the legacy of the nineteenth century. A number of entries are specifically devoted to nineteenth-century theorists of the nation from Lavisse to Thierry to Michelet to Renan. Moreover, the entire focus on nation as memory is clearly rooted in the ideas of Michelet, in whose spirit Nora claims to have undertaken the work (Nora, "Entre mémoire et histoire," 1997, 43).[14]

If it is not entirely an elegy on the French national memory, *Les Lieux de mémoire* is, nonetheless, informed by uncertainty about the future of French identity. The need to assert the existence of a national memory, the need to validate the content of such memory, and the need to reinforce solidarity among those who claim to possess such memory suggest that Nora and others in France feel that French national identity may be disappearing as a result of the shifting composition of the nation itself. More than affirming the dynamic nature of the nation, however, the act of locating French identity in memory—in the past—is a way of responding to such shifts. A national identity that is figured in terms of common memory is, in some ways, rendered permanently untouchable by those who are French of immigrant parentage since there is no way for them to assimilate into the past. In that regard, it is not insignificant that both *Les Lieux de mémoire* and the National Heritage that informs it both emerged in the early 1980s, at precisely the same moment as a parallel preoccupation with "immigration" or, more precisely, with demographic changes in France's population brought about by (post-)colonial immigration.[15]

That being said, however, it is also true that *Les Lieux de mémoire* may be read, paradoxically, to undermine the same closed conception of the nation that it seems to construct. Specifically, in defining the nation as a community of memory, in cataloging and defining the sites that compose the National Heritage, and in fixing and transmitting those sites, *Les Lieux de mémoire* functions to keep alive the very memory it presumes dead. Moreover, anyone who can read the text can participate in the transmission of heritage because they can assume the national collective memory, at least as it is defined within the work. *Les Lieux de mémoire*, then, creates a type of lived connection to the very sites it has identified, whatever the background or ancestry of the person reading the work. And in so doing, it reopens the space of national memory to anyone who chooses to participate in it.

This implies a more fluid, nonlinear model of collective memory, one that does not rely on direct vertical transmission but that is, rather, open to engagement at different moments in time by individuals whose own histories may or may not coincide with that of French national history. This more fluid, nonlinear model is also evident in the relationship of past to present expressed by certain entries within the work. Ozouf and Ozouf, for example, characterize "*La Tour de la France par deux enfants*" as an old and new site of memory. They point to the book's reprintings in 1985 and in 2000 and 2004 and suggest that there are various and multiple connections of memory to the work that vary by generation. The chapter "*Le nom des rues* (The names of roads)" also argues for multiple layers of national memory. In addition to cataloguing the various national figures for whom French streets are named, the entry includes a commentary on the shifting attitudes towards those figures over time. Similarly, the entry "*The Collège de France*" discusses the illustrious names associated with the college, from Michelet to Michel Foucault, and "*Les Classiques scolaires* (Classic scholastic books)" explores literary classics taught in schools from the early nineteenth century to the late twentieth century. While these entries may be read as reflecting the circular view of the past—the repetition of the past in the present—they may also be read as articulating a new vision of the past and, specifically, of memory. What they suggest is that the memory of the past is not stable but, on the contrary, constantly shifting. It may, therefore, be viewed differently from different perspectives.

Les Lieux de mémoire, then, like the monuments of the *grands travaux*, offers a conflicted discourse on memory, embodying at one and the same time an open and a closed vision of the national past and of national memory. This is almost certainly the result of the fact that it reproduces the nineteenth-century's linear/circular model of the national past at a historic moment when that model is untenable. However, it also reflects the existence of competing conceptions of heritage and of the national past. In that regard, the text suggests that National Heritage, itself, is internally conflicted. Thus, like the monuments of the *grands travaux*, *Les Lieux de mémoire* points to the need for new models of memory and the past even as it reproduces old ones.

Perhaps most significant, even though *Les Lieux de mémoire* overtly validates the idea that there exists a direct, stable line of continuity from present to past and even though it figures memory as an embodiment of that connection, the organization of the text calls this linear model into question. For, however much Nora looks back to the historians of the nineteenth century, he has created a history of France that is radically different from theirs, not in substance but in structure. In place of the linear and circular narratives of the national past offered by Michelet and those who followed him, Nora offers a version of the past that is much less narrative and much less stable. While it is true that many of the entries within the work imply a vertical line linking present to past, the work as a whole has no linear coherence. Instead, it states that the national past must be conceived of in terms of spaces and places and of the echoes or ripples those spaces and places produce in the present. This is a direct reappropriation of Michelet's idea that the past inhabits the present in specific monuments, buildings, and artifacts, but it is also a rejection of Michelet's vision of the historian as medium, capable of channeling the past into a coherent narrative. Ultimately, *Les Lieux de mémoire*'s decidedly nonlinear, noncircular conception of memory and of the past constitutes more of a break with the nineteenth century than it does a continuation or repetition. *Les Lieux de mémoire* does not, it is true, fully or even partially embrace this restructuring of the past. In some ways, it seems to cast it as a part of the breakdown of memory it ostensibly seeks to reverse. Nonetheless, both the content and the organization of the text say that linear and circular narratives about the past no longer function. Moreover, the text as a whole posits new possibilities for structuring the past and for mapping national memory, even if it does not fully resolve the problems with existing narratives of the national past or existing conceptions of national memory.

Contemporary heritage is typically understood as a return to older, specifically, nineteenth-century modes of thinking about history, memory, and identity. Both ways of conceiving of the national past and its relation to the present were and are formed and informed by France's colonial history; however, there exist fundamental differences in the way the structure of the past was imagined in the nineteenth century and the way it is imagined today. As Michelet's histories demonstrate, the nineteenth century imagined the past as an ascending line of progress, in which the French nation enacted a preordained trajectory that took it from glory in the past to glory in the future. Each generation was imagined as inheriting the past from the previous generation, and the nation, therefore, was conceived of as evolving in much the same way as a species evolves over time. This model of history constructs national identity as the result of deep, vertical connection to a specific geographic space. This is an essentially if not overtly biological conception of identity, and the biological component derives as much from the linear structure imposed upon the past as it does from any specific content.

Cinema, like historiography, is an invention of the nineteenth century and, specifically, of the late nineteenth century. Like modern historiography, the cinema is rooted in a deep need for continuity in the face of rupture. Film is bound up, as Philip Rosen argues, with nineteenth-century historicity, and it reflects the nineteenth century's preoccupation with time in general and historical time in particular (2001, 140–43). This is reflected in film's tendency, from the beginning, to represent and re-present the historical past and in its anxieties about promoting its own re-representations as "real."[16] It is film's tendency to re-present or restage the past for the spectator that binds film to memory and particularly collective memory. Paul Connerton comments that the spectator who watches a historical film experiences the national past directly, as if it were lived, and in subsequent screenings, the spectator can remember this experience of the past and live it again as though it were eternal, a type of voluntary anamnesis. For this reason, historical films tend to function as what Etienne Balibar describes as "the imaginary [of the nation] which inscribes itself in the real" (1996, 93).

The cinema also tends to express the relationship of past to present—whether through history or memory—as both linear and circular, in the same way that Michelet imagined national history. Film provides a circular continuity with the past because filmic representation constitutes the repetition of the past or at least the representation of the past, in the present, a repetition that can be endlessly repeated. Moreover, as a result of classical narration and continuity editing—both common to French historical films—the cinema condenses time and action into a single, unified, linear narrative that implies linear continuity between the past as it is represented and the present in which it is viewed (Bordwell, Steiger, and Thompson 1985; Rosenstone 1998, 2006). Or does it? Does the rise of the French heritage film signify the reinforcement of older narratives of continuity concerning the national past, or does it reflect the same recognition of fundamental rupture expressed in *Les Lieux de mémoire* and the monuments of the *grands travaux*? What vision of the nation, of the national past, and of the relationship to that past is being represented in contemporary French cinema, and what are the consequences of this representation? In short, does contemporary French cinema cling to the continuities of the past, or does it, rather, articulate new versions of history, new conceptions of memory? And what are the consequences of filmic representation of the past upon present understandings of the nation?

2

Family Pictures: Ancestry, Nostalgia, and the French Heritage Film

*A*ndrew Higson first used the term "heritage film" to describe a type of nostalgic British cinema that emerged in the 1980s. Films such as *Chariots of Fire* (1981), *A Passage to India* (1984), and *Howard's End* (1992) and popular television drama mini-series such as *Brideshead Revisited* (1981) and *The Jewel in the Crown* (1984), were, according to Higson, backward-gazing pastiche texts that valorized the imperial past and reinforced notions of British cultural superiority. Such films, Higson argues, emphasized tradition and history and functioned to "turn their back on the industrialized chaotic present . . . [and] offer apparently more settled and visually splendid manifestations of an essentially pastoral national identity and authentic culture" (2003, 177). It did not take long for critics to recognize similar patterns in French historical films or costume dramas of the same period, many of which had been funded and promoted specifically for their capacity to valorize French history and culture.[1] French heritage films, these critics argued, were similarly nationalistic productions characterized by the meticulous re-creation of highly resonant periods and spaces of the national past (Austin 1996; Cousins 2006; Esposito 2001; Powrie 1996; Van Dijk 2002; Vincendeau 2001).

It is generally agreed that heritage films are historical-costume dramas that exhibit certain stable characteristics, among which are a traditional, linear narrative structure, an emphasis on particular historical periods, a tendency to center around so-called heritage properties, such as culturally prestigious literary texts, historically significant buildings, or culturally resonant landscapes and interiors and a tendency to generate heritage space—a nostalgic space of memory—rather than narrative space (Higson 2003, 177). According to Guy Austin, heritage films engage in "the artful and spectacular production of an elite, conservative vision of the national past" and function as "intimate epics of national identity played out in a historical context" (1996, 143). What distinguishes heritage films from earlier iterations of the historical film or costume drama, critics argue, is the tendency of heritage films to produce heritage space, a nostalgic space of memory, rather than narrative space (Higson 1993, 2003). This privileging of image over action encodes the past as detached from the present, as an emphasis on narrative would do, rather than intimately bound to the present. Heritage films, therefore, imply a fracturing or breakdown of the relationship of past to present rather than an assertion of continuity between the two.

Historical film production in France has occurred in a series of waves, the first of which coincides with the birth of cinema itself. The Lumière brothers Auguste and Louis made what might be considered the very first historical films including *Mort de Marat* (1897) and *Mort de Robespierre* (1897). These early films or scenes featured selected moments from the Revolution and functioned, in some ways, as animated paintings, reproducing celebrated moments of the Revolution in a manner similar to the nationalist paintings of artists like Jacques-Louis David.[2] They highlighted cinema's capacity to function as historiography by reviving the past and linked the nineteenth century's technological progress, of which cinema was a part, to French history's narrative of political progress.

This linkage of history and cinema had profound consequences for the development of film narrative. Most early films, like those of the Lumière brothers, consist of isolated scenes that are not situated within a broader narrative. Moreover, even those films that do attempt to convey a story often rely upon a tableau structure, rather than conventional linear narration.[3] Very early historical films like those of the Lumières rely upon the spectator's memory of history to give context to the film's subject. Progressively, however, historical films began to emphasize the progress of history itself, developing a linear narrative structure internal to the film that functions to convey both the progress internal to the events depicted and the broader notion of progress across time. Rather than relying on memory, historical films began to produce memory.

It is, in large measure, the historical film that gave modern cinema its overall narrative structure. Many of the earliest narrative films are historical films. These include Albert Capellani's *La Vie de Jeanne d'Arc* (1909), Louis

Feuillade's *Roland à Roncéveaux* (1910) and *Napoléon* (1912), Henri Andréani's *Le Siège de Calais* (1911), Henri Desfontaines and Louis Mercanton's *L'Assassinat d'Henri III* (1911), Gérard Bourgeois' *Richelieu* (1911), Georges Denola's *Charlotte Corday* (1909), Étienne Arnaud and Louis Feuillade's *André Chenier* (1911), André Calmettes and Henri Pouctal's *Camille Desmoulins* (1912), and Camille de Morlhon and Ferdinand Zecca's *1812* (1910). As the subjects of these films demonstrate, the early cinema tended to mirror or project the vision of the past articulated by nineteenth-century historiography, foregrounding those moments and events deemed formative by Michelet and his successors and implying among these events a linear narrative of national formation and development. These films privileged narration over everything, even historical accuracy (Vincendeau 2001, xviii). Their function was to transmit a specific version of the past, a certain structure of the past, not necessarily an accurate re-creation of the past. In many ways, therefore, film's narrative followed from the structure of history, and as the cinema developed, it progressively incorporated the structure of historiography, using a combination of emphasis and ellipsis to convey the illusion of the linear progression of time.

The second significant wave of historical film production in France occurred just after the First World War. Films from this period were made with the deliberate intention of rivaling Hollywood and protecting the French film industry at home and abroad. Hollywood had, just prior to the war, displaced French cinema as the dominant film industry. American movie studios had benefitted both from structural advantages they had developed over French cinema and from the economic devastation that was the result of the war in Europe.[4] Not only had Hollywood by that time supplanted France as the world's dominant film industry, it had also taken to making French historical films, which infuriated nationalists in France, who insisted that France and only France could accurately depict French history (Véray and Krohn 2005, 338). These films, which include Jean Kemm's *L'Enfant roi* (1922), Raymond Bernard's *Miracle des loups* (1923), Luis-Morat's *Jean Chouan* (1926), and Abel Gance's celebrated *Napoléon* (1927), were epic in nature and overtly patriotic, and they were produced in response to fears about the decline of French cinema but also, and perhaps equally important, to fears about the decline of France itself.

The third wave of historical film production in France coincided with the rise of the Front Populaire in France and also with cinema's transition to synchronized sound. Films from this era, which is often considered French cinema's golden age, include Gance's *J'accuse* (1930), Victor Tourjansky's *L'Aiglon* (1931), André Roubaud's *Danton* (1932), Bernard's *Les Misérables* (1934), Christian-Jacque's *Les Perles de la couronne* (1937), Claude Autant-Lara's *L'Affaire du courrier de Lyon* (1937), and Jean Renoir's *La Marseillaise* (1938). The fourth wave, which marked the peak of historical-film production up to that point, occurred following World War II. Films produced during this period include Marcel Carné's *Les Enfants du paradis* (1945), André Zwoboda's *François Villon* (1945), Pierre Billon's *Ruy Blas* (1948), Christian-Jacque's *Madame Du Barry* (1954), Jean Dréville's *La Reine Margot* (1954), and Sacha Guitry's *Si Versailles m'était conté* (1954) and *Si Paris nous était conté* (1956).

The postliberation historical films reveal a degree of internal ambivalence about the nature and structure of history that is absent from earlier waves. This was clearly a period of profound national change, during which the immediate past was seen as threatening. The films of the period tend to reinforce previously established conceptions of history and historicity and to glorify the past while avoiding and even discouraging any serious engagement with it. The films of Guitry, Christian-Jacque, and André Hunébelle, for example, are more diversion than history. They use the past as a means of entertaining their audiences and are less concerned with historical accuracy than with creating an object of visual pleasure. In that regard, they anticipate the present-day heritage film, which has also been read as nostalgic diversion. Other films, such as Henri Decoin's *L'Affaire des poisons* (1955) and Dréville's *La Reine Margot* paint the past in very dark tones, blending heritage with *film noir*, potentially as a means of warning against serious interrogation of history.

These films were produced, interestingly, at the same time as the rise of the detective film, or *polar*. Susan Hayward argues that the popularity of *polars* in the 1950s reflects France's "state of hermeticism in relation to her recent past" (1993, 147), an unwillingness on the part of the nation to deal with its role in the German Occupation. Indeed, *polars* are not classically narrative in the same way as historical films. They disrupt the continuity that is presumed to exist between past and present by figuring the past as a mystery, an unknown territory, whose relationship to the present must be doubted, interrogated, reconstructed. Therefore, even if, or perhaps precisely because, they do not deal with the historical past in any fundamental way, *polars*, nonetheless, articulate anxiety about the past, expressing a fear that the past is dangerous, that it cannot really be known. If they are a means of avoiding the past, however, many *polars* also constitute a nostalgic return to it. Many of the most popular among these *polars*, for example, were adaptations of the Maigret novels of Georges Simenon and were set in prewar France. These films included Carné's *La Marie du port* (1950), Decoin's *La Vérité sur Bébé Dongé* (1951), and Jean Delannoy's *Maigret tend un piège* (1958), and they conveyed, according to Nicholas Hewitt, "nostalgia for a 'real' France" perceived to be under threat (2004, 68). The unlikely coexistence of these two types of film—historical film and *polar*—therefore, suggests a degree of ambivalence about the past in the 1950s, a longing for a past feared dead or dying, and a simultaneous unwillingness or inability to confront that past for fear of what it might reveal.

By the end of the 1950s, pressures on history paralleled or rivaled those of the post-Revolution era. The Indochinese and Algerian wars of independence announced the end of the French empire and threatened the integrity of French national history. It was in this context that the New Wave emerged. In cinema, the New Wave is often seen to have announced "the explosion of new values and radical changes" (Lanzoni 2004, 199). It put a virtual end to the production of historical films, and the aesthetics to which it gave birth shattered the dominance of type of linear, narrative cinema that the historical film had done much to produce. Whether or not there were, as Colin Crisp maintains, underlying continuities between the *tradition de qualité*, of which historical films were a major part, and the New Wave, it is true that the rhetoric surrounding cinema became fundamentally altered (1997). High production values, seamless narration, continuity editing, and historical representation lost ground in a reordering of cinema that has been read as part of a broader reordering of France (Ross 1996, 160–64).[5] The New Wave, therefore, resolved the ambivalence toward history expressed by the cinema of the 1950s, and it did so by turning away from the past altogether, at least from any overt representation of the past.

Lynn Higgins suggests that New Wave filmmakers "incorporated into their films an awareness that the nature of their medium or apparatus shapes how the past can be shown" (1998, 30). While this may be true, it is also true that these filmmakers encoded this awareness without actually representing the past, at least in any overt manner. Films such as Alain Resnais' *L'Année dernière à Marienbad* (1961) or *Muriel* (1963) may have had, as Higgins relates, the past at their center, but this past was primarily encoded as an absence, a trauma that could neither be recalled nor represented.[6] The result was a crisis of history and cinema that presented itself as a crisis of history in cinema. The nineteenth century's narrative of the past could not function in a France without an empire. The impending end of empire disrupted cinema's capacity to re-present and transmit that narrative.

The Return of the Repressed

The heritage film constitutes the reemergence of the historical film more than twenty years after the New Wave supposedly killed it. In part, this is due to the intervention of the Mitterrand government, which regarded the heritage film as part of a project of *restoration*, an attempt to reestablish and promote an "authentic" national culture that it perceived as disappeared. Heritage films were intended as state-sponsored narratives that constituted a return to traditional values and to traditional film aesthetics, glorifying the French past for domestic audiences while raising French cinema's international profile.

In some respects, Mitterrand's project was a success, since the heritage film dominated French cinema of the 1980s and 1990s (Austin 1996, 143; Hayward 1993, 284; Powrie 1999, 2). As a result of heritage-film production, France had, by 2001, reclaimed its status as the number-two cinema in the world, drawing 184 million spectators to the box office in that year alone (Lanzoni 2004, 354–55). It is also fairly clear that heritage films constitute a direct reappropriation of a specifically French filmmaking tradition. This is evident in the sheer number of such films that are remakes of previous French historical films, including Andrzej Wajda's *Danton* (1983), which first made in 1913 by Henri Pouctal, and then in 1932 by André Roubaud; Jean-Paul Rappeneau's *Cyrano de Bergerac* (1990), first made in 1909 by Jean Durand and then again in 1945 by Fernand Rivers; Yves Angelo's *Le Colonel Chabert* (1994), first made by André Calmettes and Henri Pouctal in 1911, and then remade in 1943 by René Le Henaff; Patrice Chéreau's *La Reine Margot* (1994), first made in 1910 by Camille de Morlhon and remade in 1914 by Henri Desfontaines and again in 1954 by Jean Dréville, and Philippe de Broca's *Le Bossu* (1997), first made in 1914 by André Heuzé and remade in 1925 by Jean Kemm, in 1934 by René Sti, in 1944 by Jean Delannoy, and 1959 by André Hunébelle.

Like the early historical films, contemporary heritage films tend to cast well-known, well-established French actors ranging from Gérard Depardieu to Catherine Deneuve to Yves Montand.[7] Moreover, like both the historical films of the silent era and those tied to the *tradition de qualité*, heritage films rely on high production values. Such films also tend, like their predecessors, to foreground certain historical periods, among them the Revolution and the Third Republic, which suggests that like earlier historical films, they may be seen to replaying or representing official traditional versions of the national past. The question is, to what end?

The most widespread interpretation of heritage films is that they, like their predecessors, reproduce a well-established and widely held, conservative vision of the French national past. Austin states that they constitute an "authenticated spectacle, legitimized by claims to historical accuracy or cultural sources" (1996, 142). Maria Esposito suggests that they "use the past not only as a spectacle but as a means of shoring up notions of national identity in unstable, increasingly global times" (2001, 11). In many ways, the films do conform to these readings. They tend to privilege particularly resonant moments in France's history, and many of them are set in recognizable provinces with strong regional identities and feature landscapes that privilege the pristine beauty of rural France. They also posit a direct connection to the French past and a common memory of French historical experience as defining characteristics of *francité*, and in this respect they heighten what Susan Hayward maintains is French cinema's constant engagement with and participation in the construction of national identity by "reconstructing myths already mobilized by the nation" (1993, 15).

Most scholars who have studied heritage films also assert that the films' function is less to relate a specific story than to inscribe the spectator in the past the film re-creates. Russell Cousins, for example, says that audiences watching heritage films "experience the nation's formative past" (2006, 185). The audience, according to Cousins, comes to feel as if they themselves have directly lived the past, rather than simply witnessed it. This effort to reproduce and transmit the past is consistent with earlier historical films, and as with such forms, the result is a synthetic memory of the past transmitted in identical terms to all spectators. Esposito comments that heritage films also function as "*ciment identitaire*" binding audience members together, creating in them both a shared sense of belonging and a shared sense of loss (2001, 12–14). This, too, is consistent with earlier historical films, and it is also consistent with the broader project of heritage, which is to inscribe national identity as both the shared memory of the past and the shared desire to relive the past, a desire that the film itself satisfies. However, because the past as imagined by heritage films is, according to Ginette Vincendeau, aesthetically and ideologically conservative (2001, xix), the sense of national identity that heritage films manufacture may be closed to those whose ancestors were absent from it. Vincendeau also suggests that earlier historical films were more "narrative" than contemporary heritage films and the story mattered far more than historical specificity (2001, xviii). In the 1980s, this trend reversed, and the painstaking re-creation of particular historical periods took prominence over narrative. This, according to Vincendeau, renders heritage films innately nostalgic. They constitute the reappropriation of a vision of the past that no longer functions and a model of cinema that can be seen as outmoded and "mannerist."

Vincendeau's assertion that heritage films deemphasize narrative while privileging visual splendor and historical accuracy may be true. However, it may not function in entirely the way she and others outline, particularly since earlier historical films function to reinforce the model of history and historicity they promote. If, therefore, accurately re-creating and transmitting the past are concerns in contemporary heritage cinema, it is also true that the heritage film's retreat from narrative suggests a degree of ambivalence about the past, a recognition that traditional narratives of the national past do not hold, even if the desire for them, embodied by the films' visual images, still has force.

Heritage films, therefore, are more revisions of the national past than re-presentations of older narratives. This is borne out by so many contemporary heritage films that are overtly fictionalized reimaginings of the lives of real, historical figures or of major historical events. Unlike earlier historical films, which tended to be faithful either to received historical narratives or to established literary narratives set in the past, such films as Daniel Vigne's *Le Retour de Martin Guerre* [*The Return of Martin Guerre*] (1982), Ettore Scola's *La Nuit de Varennes* (1982), Patrice Leconte's *Ridicule* (1996), Benoît Jacquot's *Sade* (2000), and Laurent Tirard's *Molière* (2007) reinvent history and recast it in contemporary terms. Indeed, Austin says that such films attempt to "take control of French history, in particular, the founding moment of Republican France" (1996, 144). Films such as Scola's *La Nuit de Varennes*, Wajda's *Danton*, and Leconte's *Ridicule*, for example, reproduce episodes either from the Revolution or the period immediately preceding it. This suggests that heritage films seek to invent new historical narratives that can account for present realities, rather than to retell existing narratives in contemporary terms.

(Silver) Screen Memories

Heritage films do, there is no doubt, re-present the past. All of them are long flashback sequences, that transport the present-day spectator into a particular vision of the national past. Flashback, as a cinematic device, is already linked directly to memory and specifically to historical memory because flashbacks consist of "images of memory, the personal archives of the past" that give "large-scale social and political history the subjective mode of a single, fictional individual's remembered experience" (Turim 1989, 2). This creates a situation in which the spectator experiences the past through the subjectivity of a central character or characters, adopting that characters' experiences and memory as his or her own. This maps the past onto individual memory and implies a vertical line of continuity between the character in the past and the spectator in the present. This, as noted, is consistent with the representation of the past in earlier historical films.

One significant difference between many heritage films and their earlier counterparts, however, is the overt attempt within the space of the narrative to construct the past not as a character's *experience* but rather as his or her *memory*. The result is a type of double flashback, or embedded flashback, wherein the move into the historical past constitutes one layer of flashback—the historical flashback—that is followed by a move to a point even further back in time as a character within the historical flashback recalls events from a personal past; it is this second, personal flashback that structures the narrative. Films as diverse as Vigne's *Le Retour de Martin Guerre*, Alain Corneau's *Tous les matins du monde* (1991), Wargnier's *Indochine* (1992), Leconte's *Ridicule* (1996), and Tirard's *Molière* (2007) frame the main narrative sequence through this type of embedded flashback, and this heightens the already latent re-creation of the past as a collective flashback typical of historical films in general. On the one hand, this renders heritage films the *quintessential flashback*, in that their re-creation of the past is so complete that the present is entirely effaced from the narrative, an effect that forces a direct identification with the past through the present. On the other hand, it is also creates a degree of separation between present and past, because the past presented by the film seems more distant, more removed. While the spectator still participates in an act of collective remembering and re-membering, the past offered by the film is subjective—that of a character—and it is, therefore, often a newly constructed one. This use of an embedded past also gives the past the same type of linear/circular structure proposed by Michelet, since the character and spectator are tied by a vertical line, but the narrative itself is presented as a circle—moving from present to past to present. This raises the question of whether such films are reinforcing received histories or imagining new ones.

As noted, the common interpretation is that heritage films "re-member" the past as an attempt to counter anxieties about the disappearance of an idealized national identity (Austin 1996; Powrie 1996; Esposito 2001). Those who argue that this is their function point to their tendency to foreground regional identities, which might be read as reasserting older, more conservative paradigms of identity and affirming ancestral and historical connections to the land. Regional identities are, after all, often closely linked to the agrarian, preindustrial past and are highly evocative of an idealized national identity (Peer 1996). In heritage films, this connection between the *paysan*, or rural dweller, and regional identity is emphasized such that it is directly linked to France in periods prior to the rural exodus and urbanization. This has been read as an attempt to offer the spectator an alternative to the anxieties about crime, insecurity, and unemployment that are associated with contemporary France and particularly the multiethnic urban space.

Many heritage films also depict the past as problematic and interrogate or undermine the very privileging of the past in which they engage. Rappeneau's *Cyrano de Bergerac*, for example, explores the process of constructing the past in order to give it a certain meaning, and it questions the impact of constructed narratives about the past on the present. Angelo's adaptation of Balzac's *Le Colonel Chabert*, which centers on the return of a man presumed dead, problematizes both identity and inheritance and therefore seems to undermine many of the assumptions on which heritage is based. Corneau's *Tous les matins du monde*, often cited as the quintessential heritage film because of its use of classical music, its tableau shots that reproduce seventeenth-century paintings, and its use of literary and historical source texts, also explores and questions the ways in which the past impacts upon the present rather than simply celebrating the past. Josée Dayan's *Le Comte de Monte Cristo* (1998), a made-for-television adaptation of Dumas' novel, is also about a constructed past, and it, too, explores questions of ownership and inheritance rendering both identity and heritage problematic. Many of the better-known heritage films actually undermine their own nostalgic re-creations of the past while questioning the stability of such concepts as heritage and identity.

It is unclear whether heritage films reinforce conservative visions of nation and the national past or that they do so in order to exclude ethnic minorities from the space of the nation. Read through the filter of immigration and identity politics, heritage works would, indeed, seem to inscribe immigrants and their descendants outside the space of collective memory, since many of them would have no direct familial or experiential connection to the events or spaces privileged by such films. However, it is not entirely true that an emphasis on the past and the valorization of regional identities necessarily implies the exclusion of (post-)colonial minorities from the space of the nation, nor is it necessarily true that by replaying the past, such films reinforce conservative nationalism.

Foregrounding regional identities, for example, may actually undermine the idea that the nation consists of an ethnically and cultural homogenous group because the rise of regionalism is itself a (post)colonial phenomenon that points to the erasure of colonial history from contemporary constructions of the national past. Moreover, regional identities are a particular subset of distinct identities within the national space—a subset of identities that were once seen as marginal and peripheral but that are now central to dominant conceptions of national identity. If such identities have recently become iconic within the national space, they, nonetheless, maintain certain specific characteristics—languages, costumes, folklore—particular to them, and they, therefore, imply that other such identities may exist within the national space. Finally, the existence and persistence of such regional identities are nowhere inscribed in official histories of the nation, which tend to elide the histories of specific regions in favor of broader narratives of national development. By privileging regional identities, therefore, and by foregrounding the problematic nature of the past as it has been received, heritage films function less to valorize conservative, nationalistic paradigms of Frenchness than to draw attention to the failure of such paradigms and the historical narratives on which they are based to adequately account for the relationship between the national past and the national present.

Blood and Soil: *Le Retour de Martin Guerre*

It is, perhaps, those films that are *not* remakes of earlier historical films that provide the most insight into the way in which heritage, and particularly screen heritage, imagines and articulates the past. Many of these films, including Vigne's *Le Retour de Martin Guerre*, Claude Berri's *Jean de Florette* and *Manon des sources* [*Manon of the springs*] (both 1986), and Wargnier's *Indochine* (1992) frame their exploration of the past as family romance, making explicit historiography's implicit assertion that the nation is a community of blood. As a result of this familial framework, these contemporary heritage films directly explore the questions of ancestry and identity that permeate both heritage and history, and in doing so, they tend to question the validity of imagining identity in ancestral terms.

Vigne's *Le Retour de Martin Guerre* is one of the first true heritage films, although it was in production before Mitterrand came to power and did not, therefore, benefit from the targeted use of the *avances sur recettes* associated with many early heritage films. Despite that, the film had a relatively high budget and high production values, and it sought to meticulously restage the past in ways that previous films had not. The film is a fairly elaborate costume drama that re-creates the settings and practices of its specific historical moment. Vigne was so concerned about historical accuracy that he employed a consulting historian, Natalie Zemon Davis, in order to guarantee the authenticity of the production, and although the film was not filmed in Artigat, in the village in which the story takes place, it was filmed on location nearby.[8]

Le Retour de Martin Guerre established narrative and thematic patterns that would be repeated in other heritage films.[9] The film is set in sixteenth-century rural, southern France, and it has heritage—specifically, inheritance, bloodlines, identity, and land—at its center. The film tells the story of Martin Guerre, the son of a prosperous peasant family, who is marries Bertrande de Rosl (Nathalie Baye), the daughter of another prosperous peasant family. After several years of marriage, Martin disappears without warning or explanation. Several years pass without word from him, until one day, a man who looks like Martin and who claims to be him "returns" to the village. In reality, this "Martin" is a man named Arnaud, a comrade in arms of the real Martin. Arnaud (Gérard Depardieu) seems to recognize everyone in the village and in the family and knows all of the details of Martin's life. He is at first welcomed into the family, primarily because he is a more hardworking and more pleasant person than the son who disappeared. Bertrande, in particular, seems much happier with Arnaud than she was with Martin, and he is shown to be much kinder, more respectful, and more appreciative of her than was Martin.

Things change, however, when Arnaud seeks to collect his inheritance from the family, Martin's father having died during his absence. The family then turns against Arnaud, accusing him of being an impostor and bringing charges against him. Although Bertrande and other members of the family and village insist this is the real Martin, the uncle, Pierre Guerre (Maurice

Barrier), and several cousins seek to prove that Arnaud is an impostor. The matter is ultimately heard by the parliament at Toulouse. Arnaud is on the verge of being acquitted when, at the last minute, the real Martin returns, and Arnaud is found guilty of fraud and sentenced to death. Bertrande is pardoned, and her daughter with Arnaud is declared legitimate.

Like many heritage films, *Le Retour de Martin Guerre* is set during a privileged moment in French history, specifically, during the reign of François Premier. It can be considered both a historical film and a literary adaption because it recounts a real, historical event but also one that figures in French literature and folklore. Two contemporary, written historical accounts exist of the story of Martin Guerre. One of these is entitled *Arrest mémorable*, written by Jean de Coras, one of the judges who served at the Guerre trial in Toulouse. The other version of the story is entitled *Histoire Admirable*, written by Guillaume Le Sueur. It is the Coras version reportedly that was adapted for the screen by Jean-Claude Carrière.[10] The story also has also been transmitted orally as a part of French folklore, and it features fairly prominently in French literature, as it is referenced in a number of texts by Alexandre Dumas.

Apart from its cultural pedigree, *Le Retour de Martin Guerre* exhibits a number of visual, thematic, and aesthetic characteristics that render it nostalgic. The film is, for example, punctuated by tableau-like shots that evoke a sort of rural pastoral, from long shots of the village framed with the church at the center to numerous ensemble shots of peasants working the land (see fig. 1). Many later heritage films also utilize this type of picturesque cinematography, and it has become one of hallmarks of the heritage film, although it is notably absent from earlier iterations of the historical film. Thematically, also, the film has elements of nostalgia in that it seems, in many ways, to valorize traditional family values, projecting a conservative worldview that is also often associated with the heritage film. Numerous scenes in the film, for example, foreground marriage and childrearing. This apparent glorification of motherhood within the bounds of the traditional family is reinforced thematically when Bertrande is ultimately cleared of wrongdoing and her illegitimate child is legitimized in efforts to preserve the family structure. The end result is that both visually and thematically, the film tends, at least on the surface, to suggest that maintaining the traditional nuclear family and maintaining social stability are more important than individual choice, that the woman's place in the home is central to both familial and social stability, and that ultimately, therefore, the values of patriarchy must be maintained.

Like many subsequent heritage films, *Martin Guerre* is also structured through a type of double flashback, both personal and historical. The narrative is set in the historical past, which constitutes one level of flashback, but the film also tells its story through flashback, beginning at the "end" of

Fig. 1. A tableau shot of villagers working the land in *Martin Guerre* (1982).

the story that is told (the moment of Martin's trial) and then moving back in time to Bertrande's marriage to Martin, when the two were only children. From there, the film's narrative moves forward, depicting Martin's departure, Arnaud's arrival, Arnaud's welcome into the family, and, ultimately, the trial and conviction. There is another layer to this aspect of personal flashback, as the principal narrative is framed through the use of voice-over narration, and the spectator is given the impression that the entire story is being recalled by Jean de Coras, years after it occurred. This embedded flashback structure, as noted, merges the individual and collective acts of remembering because the narrative is presented as personal memory. At the same time, however, the film derives its authority from history in the form of the written text that de Coras wrote, a text that is directly referenced in the voice-over narration.

Le Retour de Martin Guerre also seems to merge individual and collective or national concerns through its focus on ancestry, heritage, family, and land. On the surface, the narrative appears to reinforce nationalistic and even xenophobic narratives of community and nation because it deals with the theme of insiders and outsiders, a theme that reproduces the dominant culture's concerns with immigration and citizenship. Although there is no one of non-European origin in the film, Depardieu's Arnaud may be read as a type of outsider or foreigner, particularly since he is constructed in a way that parallels the situation of contemporary immigrants. Arnaud is not from either the family or the village, but he seeks to take the place of someone who is, claiming the real Martin's identity, his wife, and his land. This, in many ways, parallels nationalistic narratives concerning immigration, which regard immigrants and ethnic minorities as illegitimate residents who have taken a place in the nation that rightly belongs to someone else. When, at the end of the film, Arnaud is revealed to be an impostor and is punished, this could be read as the film's assertion that the claim of outsiders (immigrants and ethnic minorities) to citizenship and nationality in France is similarly illegitimate and perhaps even criminal, an idea that is also in line with contemporary nationalism. Such an interpretation seems reinforced by the film's ending that ultimately restores the family, the bloodline, and the land to Martin, thereby reestablishing, or seeming to reestablish, orthodox models of family and community.

If, however, the film's surface narrative may be read as valorizing conservative, nationalist paradigms of nation and family, its treatment of issues like heritage and identity is much less straightforward. Although Arnaud is clearly an outsider in the most literal sense of the word, since he is neither a family member nor a villager, he is not immediately recognized as such and is widely accepted as an insider for most of the film. Because it is very near the end of the film before the villagers and the spectator realize that Arnaud is an impostor, uncertainty rather than certainty about identity characterizes the film. This suggests that the film does not reinforce heritage conceptions of ancestry and identity but rather questions the ability of anyone, even family members, to accurately judge a person's ancestry or identity.

The film's ambiguity with respect to Arnaud's true identity, therefore, renders conservative notions of heritage and identity problematic. Arnaud's success in convincing everyone, including the spectator, that he is who he says he is foregrounds individual capacity to integrate into "foreign" cultures and, therefore, undermines the very idea that identity is inherited. In this particular reading of the film, identity is presented as a combination of learned history and performance, as well as the sanction of both family and community. Arnaud's ability to pass for an insider, for example, depends on his conformity to family and village practice and his assumption of a certain set of "memories" that a true insider would possess. In this respect, Arnaud's integration into the family and the village parallels exactly the process of integration undergone by immigrants, which is a process of cultural learning. Moreover, as with immigrants, Arnaud's success in integrating is measured by his ability to be accepted as an insider by other insiders, which is, in turn, a factor of how well he has learned family and village history. This contradicts nationalist models of culture in that it posits that identity is performed in the *present*, not transmitted from the past. If culture and identity were, indeed, properties of heredity, then no outsider would be able to acquire sufficient cultural knowledge to be able to pass for an insider. Arnaud's success in doing just that implies that integration is not only possible, it is possible to such a degree that it may not even be recognized as such.

Beyond its problematic rendering of heritage and identity, *Le Retour de Martin Guerre* invites the spectator to question orthodox models of identity and family because it forces identification with Arnaud and Bertrande, effectively suturing the spectator into assuming their point of view. As a result, Arnaud appears as a superior version of Martin, not really an impostor or inferior version of him. Arnaud is also depicted as more hardworking and more likeable than the real Martin, and he clearly is better to Bertrande than was the real Martin. The presentation of Arnaud in the film is at odds with the historical record, which depicts Arnaud as a skillful liar and fraud who sought to profit from unknowing victims (Finlay 1998, 555). History, therefore, records Arnaud's conviction and execution as acts of justice. The film, however, depicts both as something much closer to tragedy. When Arnaud is unmasked as an impostor, the spectator does not derive any sense of satisfaction, nor does the film leave the spectator with the feeling that justice has been done or that order has been restored. Instead, the spectator is left feeling that outmoded models of community and family have been exploited by greedy and opportunistic family members. If, therefore, *Le Retour de Martin Guerre* is read as a sort of commentary on contemporary debates about immigration, the ending might actually suggest that immigrants bring a positive contribution to the national family and that their exclusion is due only to the unscrupulous exploitation of outmoded models of national identity.

The same sort of contradictory logic is apparent in the film's treatment of heritage and bloodlines. It is true that, ultimately, the bloodline is maintained and the "legitimate" heir of the family occupies and ultimately inherits the land. This would seem to suggest that identity in general and national identity in particular are the result of direct, ancestral connections to the land, which would render the film both conservative and nationalistic. It is also true however, that Arnaud's daughter is ultimately made into a "legitimate" member of the Guerre family by an order of the court, which means that, ultimately, the state turns an outsider into the ultimate insider. This undermines the idea of direct ancestry and heritage to some degree because it suggests that, in reality, it is difficult to tell in any meaningful way who is and who is not connected to the land by blood and even more difficult, especially with the passage of time, to accurately judge the nature of someone's ancestry. It also draws attention to the way the government and the state use and manipulate notions of heritage and identity to their own advantage.

Perhaps the most contradictory element of the film, however, is its treatment of the past and particularly the memory of the past. In its mise-en-scène and its production values, the film valorizes nostalgic re-creations of an idealized past. However, the narrative of the film functions to deconstruct such re-creations. One of the film's principal subjects is the resurgence of the past in the present. This interrogation of the past is figured through the "return" of Arnaud, who constitutes a fictive reconstruction of the past. It is also suggested by the return of the real Martin, the real past. Arnaud's arrival is something like a nostalgic re-creation of the past. He embodies not the return of the actual past but rather a fantasy of the past, a vision of what the past might have been. He is, as noted, the husband, nephew, and brother that the family would have perhaps *wished* Martin to be, rather than the husband, nephew, and brother who he was. In that regard, Arnaud resembles the nostalgic re-creations of the national past embodied by heritage and by heritage films.

In order to accept Arnaud as Martin, the family has to reconstruct and, in some cases, modify their recollection of the real past. In the same way, heritage films reconstruct the past for audiences, and the audience assumes the images of the film as a new "memory" of the past, even though this "memory" is often at odds with historical fact. Prior to the return of the real Martin, the film seems to justify the construction of idealized narratives about the past on the grounds that they are more palatable and perhaps more workable the real past. However, once the real Martin returns, that idea is completely undercut, and the family is forced to accept and confront the reality of the past, even if it is less than satisfactory to many of them than the fictive reconstruction offered by Arnaud. In this way, *Le Retour de Martin Guerre* questions the validity of National Heritage itself by suggesting that contemporary nostalgic re-creations of the past are just that—re-creations that will ultimately collapse under the weight of fact. Just as Martin's return forces an engagement with the actual past and conditions the resurgence of memories that Arnaud's acceptance had masked, *Le Retour de Martin Guerre* argues for France's need to engage with its past and to recover those elements of that past that heritage re-creations obscure. Although the film leaves the audience with the idea that this acceptance of the past is difficult, it also constructs it as necessary to the stability of the family, the village, and, by extension, the nation.

Thus, *Le Retour de Martin Guerre* offers a fairly conflicted view of heritage and identity. It valorizes rural, pastoral, peasant France and the more traditional values of the period in which it is set, but in the end, the spectator is left feeling unsatisfied by rural France and its values. The film suggests that outsiders or foreigners are threatening to the social order, that they are usurpers who take what rightfully belongs to insiders, but it also places into doubt the ability of insiders to distinguish who is an insider and who is an outsider, and it questions the motives of those who refuse to accept outsiders as insiders. The film valorizes bloodlines and an ancestral connection to the land while suggesting that it is difficult to know whether any such ancestral connection exists. Finally, the film seems to glorify nostalgic re-creations of the rural past, but it also suggests, rather forcefully, that such re-creations are untenable and possibly even dangerous, and it does so not by privileging visual aesthetics over narrative but by pitting the two against each other.

Blood and Water: *Jean de Florette and Manon des sources*

If *Le Retour de Martin Guerre* is a conflicted and problematic heritage film with respect to its treatment of history, family, and identity, it is far from the only such film. Berri's *Jean de Florette* and *Manon des sources* (both 1986) are equally conflicted films that offer similarly ambivalent interpretations of nearly identical themes. The Berri films are two of the most expensive French films ever made, with a combined budget of nearly 200 million francs (about US$40 million at the time). They boast impressive box-office records, due in large measure to an extensive marketing campaign that actively promoted what Phil Powrie terms their "loving recreation of a vanished or vanishing past" (Powrie 1996, 296). Part of the Berri films' connection to the past stems from the fact that they are remakes of works by Marcel Pagnol, specifically, his 1953 film, *Manon des sources*, and his subsequent novel *L'Eau des collines* [Water from the hills] (1962). The Pagnol texts were regarded as nostalgic during his lifetime, and this nostalgia is inherited and magnified by the Berri remakes. In addition, Berri's films, like many heritage films, also constitute a form of specifically cinematic nostalgia because, as Powrie remarks, Pagnol was a writer and filmmaker with close ties to French cinema's "golden age" (1996, 296). All of these factors combined to attract even those viewers who did not normally go to the cinema or who did not see French films when they did (Austin 1996, 158; Powrie 1996, 297). In France, 7.2 million viewers saw *Jean de Florette*, the most successful of the two films, a figure that makes it one of the top twenty-five French box-office performers of all time (Lanzoni 2002, 432). The films also performed respectably abroad, grossing nearly $9 million in the United States alone.

Jean de Florette recounts the story of Jean (Gérard Depardieu), a tax collector, who leaves the city to settle on a farm in Provence he has inherited from a relative of his deceased mother, Florette. The story opens with Jean's neighbors, the Soubeyrans, Ugolin (Daniel Auteuil) and Papet (Yves Montand), who are plotting to obtain the farm in order to grow carnations. Before Jean arrives on the farm, the Soubeyrans plug a spring they know to exist on the land. They pretend to befriend Jean, whose mother Papet knew, while secretly working to run him off. Jean, seized with romantic notions about the return to nature, proves to be far more tenacious than his neighbors had anticipated, and he works tirelessly to try to make a success of farming. However, he is killed trying to excavate a well, and the Soubeyrans succeed in obtaining the farm, displacing Jean's wife, Aimée, and his young daughter, Manon. The film ends with Manon's discovery that the Soubeyrans had blocked the spring on the property and that they had conspired from the beginning to take the farm away.

In the sequel, *Manon des sources*, a grown Manon (Emmanuel Béart) takes revenge on the Soubeyrans and the entire village of Les Bastides blanches, which she regards as complicit in her father's death. Manon finds the main source that feeds the village's fountain and springs and blocks it, enacting the biblical principle of "an eye for an eye" by depriving the village of water in the same way her father was deprived of water. Subsequently, Ugolin sees Manon and falls in love with her. She ultimately rejects him, and he kills himself in grief. Papet, already mourning the death of Ugolin, whom he believes to be the last of the Soubeyrans, learns that Jean, whose death he had engineered, was his son. The news is too much for him, and he dies. Both farms then pass to Manon, who marries the village schoolteacher and bears a son, the next generation of Soubeyrans.

Jean de Florette and *Manon des sources* were, like *Le Retour de Martin Guerre*, filmed on location in southern Provence. Like Vigne, Berri relied on historically accurate costumes, interiors, and outdoor sets, created on location in Provence "with all traces of modernity expensively disguised" (Cousins 2006, 188). Moreover, as Powrie notes, filmgoers were led to expect this historical accuracy and a certain degree of nostalgia before seeing the film because Berri touted both in the prefilm publicity (1996, 297). Like most heritage films, the Berri films have been read as nostalgic. They represent preindustrial, rural France during a period in French history that is removed from the present, but that is not so removed that the spectator would have no personal connection to it. What is more, the films are set in Provence, which, according to François de la Bretèque, is linked in the French cultural imagination to archetypal and folkloric aspects of the past (1992, 58).

Jean de Florette and *Manon des sources* have also been seen to privilege visual splendor over narrative. Russell Cousins, for example, argues that Berri condensed and streamlined the narrative of the Pagnol texts with the effect of rendering the village and villagers a "heritage backdrop" to the film (2006, 187). It is also true that like *Le Retour de Martin Guerre*, the Berri films utilize postcard-like cinematography, featuring panoramic landscape shots and tableau shots of village life, many of which function more to evoke a past that is presumed familiar and beloved than to specifically advance the narrative. Esposito argues that the privileging of the visual over the narrative serves to create an "idea of the past . . . [where] the nation is reduced to the visual signifier of a nostalgically projected Provence" (2001, 14). For those old enough to have lived during such a time, such images evoke a personal past. For those who did not experience such a life firsthand but whose parents or grandparents came from such villages, the scenes reenact the space of family history and memory, thereby emphasizing ancestry and continuity. De la Bretèque suggests that the films' visual emphasis on the village in particular functions to affirm social cohesion and collective identity (1992, 65–67).

If the narratives of *Jean de Florette* and *Manon des sources* are, indeed, subjugated to the cinematography, they, nonetheless, function as the frame through which the visual must be interpreted. In that respect, the narratives of the Berri films seem, at least initially, to reinforce the films' visual message, because ancestry, heritage, and identity are at their core. However, as the titles of the two films suggest, neither ancestry nor heritage nor identity is straightforward, and explorations of such issues often raise more questions than they answer. The titles of the two films suggest that Jean and Manon, respectively, are the films' protagonists. However, it could be argued that the real protagonists of the films are Papet and Ugolin Soubeyran. Therefore, the titles or names of the films cause the spectator to misread or misapprehend the films, and this foregrounds the type of misreading and misapprehension that structures the narrative. The title *Jean de Florette*, in particular, is emblematic of the issues raised by the films. Unlike *Manon des sources*, which came directly from Pagnol, *Jean de Florette* is unique to the remake. It is an unusual title, quite apart from its misleading nature, in that it defines Jean through his mother, although it is rare in France and the West in general, for a person to be so designated. Rather, we would normally expect to find the name of a place or the name of a paternal family following the "de" in Jean's name, a fact that highlights one of the central ambiguities in the film. Where *is* Jean from? Is he, as the villagers believe, from Crespin, or is he really from Les Bastides blanches, which he claims as his home? Moreover, the substitution of a maternal for a paternal name raises the question of *who* Jean is, or more particularly who his father is. Is it the man named Cadoret, whose last name he bears, or is it Papet Soubeyran?

The ambiguity surrounding Jean's name and his identity frames all of the action in both *Jean de Florette* and *Manon des sources*. The main narrative thread in both films concerns the interaction between the Soubeyrans and Jean and his family. The Soubeyrans, and Papet in particular, are driven to act against Jean precisely because they do not understand who he really is. Papet's principal desire is to guarantee the continuity of the Soubeyran line, and the primary reason he is willing to plot against Jean is that Papet (falsely) believes there are no other Soubeyrans besides himself and Ugolin. He is, therefore, willing to invest everything in order to assure Ugolin's ultimate success. An obsession with ancestry and heritage drives Papet, but it also ultimately costs him the closest blood relative he has, his own son.[11]

Similarly, the villagers of Les Bastides blanches are obsessed with keeping the village free from "outsiders." They are willing to ostracize Jean because they (falsely) believe him to be the son of an "outsider" and, therefore, an outsider himself. Their desire to discriminate against Jean, moreover, is made easier by the fact that he looks different than they do (he is a hunchback), and he behaves in ways they find strange. Like Papet, the village is motivated by a desire to maintain the integrity of its own line, or the purity of its population, but this desire causes them, inadvertently, to exclude one of their own. Ultimately, then, both *Jean de Florette* and *Manon des sources* do much more to undermine essentialized notions of ancestry and identity than they do to promote them, and this is true even if the cinematography leads one to believe otherwise.

What is more, *Jean de Florette* and *Manon des sources*, like *Le Retour de Martin Guerre*, explore the issues of ancestry and heritage through a dispute over the inheritance and ownership of the land, a dispute figured, at least superficially, as a struggle between insiders and outsiders. The dispute over the legitimate claim to the land can be read as a metaphorical rendering of the questions of citizenship and national identity, because citizenship is official or governmental authority to reside in or on a particular territory or land. Moreover, because Jean inherits his right to occupy the land, the film explores the question of whether citizenship is inherited, and in that respect, it evokes debates about immigration and integration in France, which are less centered on the origins and identities of those ethnic minorities who currently reside in France than on the origins and identities of their parents or grandparents.

The two primary modes of conveying citizenship—*jus sanguinis*, or the right of citizenship through heredity, and *jus soli*, the right of citizenship through presence on the land—are represented in this struggle between Jean and the Soubeyrans (Higgins 1996).[12] Jean possesses the land but is seen as illegitimate by the larger community. He has no apparent lived or ancestral connection to the land, made manifest by his ignorance of the spring. While it is literally true that he inherited the land, his status as an outsider renders this question of inheritance problematic, and the film initially seems to suggest that his inheritance of the land is an inheritance only in the juridical, rather than the more literal sense. The Soubeyrans, on the other hand, have no legal claim to the land, but they regard themselves as its rightful owners because their family has, for so long, lived on or near it. Therefore, although the Soubeyrans do not inherit the land, they feel they have a stronger ancestral claim to it than does Jean.

The film, then, creates a situation in which the legal right to occupy the land is at odds with what may be seen as the legitimate right to occupy the land. Moreover, this right or perceived right to occupy the land is bound up in a dispute about the nature of ancestry and continuity. The Soubeyrans and the villagers believe that the law wrongly considers Jean to have an ancestral tie to the land, because neither he, nor his mother, through whom he inherits, has lived there. This situation parallels the conservative view of contemporary France in which those with an ancestral tie to the nation, those whom Jean-Marie Le Pen calls the "true French," are "displaced" from the nation by those of foreign origin. What is more, in contemporary politics, just as in the film, having one or two generations of ancestors who are tied to a space is considered insufficient for staking a claim to that space. Instead, legitimate attachment to a space is regarded as the product of deep, vertical, blood ties to it.

At the end of *Jean de Florette*, the Soubeyrans obtain the land from Jean and become both the "legal" and "rightful" inhabitants. This seems to valorize blood ties over legal presence and to confirm right-wing, nationalist conceptions of nationality and citizenship. However, the films are not quite so straightforward, and a deeper reading of them reveals a fair degree of ambivalence concerning questions of identity, history, and heritage. First and foremost, the sequel to *Jean de Florette*, *Manon des sources*, ends with Jean's daughter, Manon, in possession of the land, a fact that reverses the resolution proposed by the first film. Lynn Higgins suggests that as a result of this revelation and reversal, the film resolves questions of origins and of legitimacy through Manon's son, "whose claim is legitimated through legal and blood inheritance and presence on the land" (1996, 103). For Higgins, the legitimate citizen is the one whose identity is guaranteed by both ancestry and residency, a construction that parallels the dominant view concerning French national identity.[13] However, if the revelation of Manon's true identity resolves the question of the ownership of the land, it greatly complicates any reading of the films as a commentary on citizenship or identity. The film resolves the conflict between the two different models of citizenship and identity not by combining them but by reframing the entire context in which identity is determined.

Jean de Florette and *Manon des sources* function in the same way as *Le Retour de Martin Guerre*—they cast doubt on the ability to know who has an ancestral connection to the land and who does not. Moreover, like the Vigne film, the Berri films center on the question of what constitutes an insider and what an outsider. If *Le Retour de Martin Guerre* ultimately suggests that *insiders* cannot really recognize *outsiders*, the Berri films suggest that insiders cannot really recognize *insiders*. Where Arnaud is an outsider taken for an insider, Jean is an insider taken for an outsider. In both cases, however, the real origin of the character is unknown or misread, and judgments about identity are made (inaccurately) on the basis of appearance, behavior, and a fictionalized version of history. The Soubeyrans and the villagers of Les

Bastides blanches believe they know Jean's lineage, but they are wrong. Their misjudgment is based on a misreading or misunderstanding of the past. They believe Florette left the village, married a man from Crespin, and the son she bore was, therefore, her husband's. This version of the past reflects what they learned, but it also constitutes a fictionalized version of the past that was created to cover over problematic realities. While it is true the villagers do not know Jean's full history—they do not know, for example, that Jean is Papet's son—it is, nonetheless, true that they have sufficient grounds for accepting him as one of their own. They simply choose not to.

It is not insignificant that the distortion of history that disguises Jean's true identity derives from an attempt to maintain conservative ideals of community and patriarchy. Florette leaves the village because she is unwed and pregnant and as such is threatening to traditional conceptions of social stability. Jean's return to the village, like Arnaud's arrival, constitutes a sort of return of the past, and it provides the villagers with the opportunity to confront the past and to "correct" it by accepting Jean as one of their own. Their refusal to do this is, once again, grounded in conservative notions of community, notions that refuse to accept an outsider as a legitimate member. This, in many ways, parallels the contemporary refusal to accept ethnic minorities in France as French. This refusal, like the refusal to accept Jean as a legitimate member of the village, is rooted in a failure to engage with the past. Jean's identity is misread because his history remains uninterrogated; ethnic minorities in France are perceived as outsiders because the realities of colonial history are ignored. Although colonial history is never directly referenced in either film, it quietly underlies the entire exploration of ancestry and identity in both films. Colonialism, for example, plays a direct role in what transpires between Jean and the Soubeyrans because the carnations Ugolin wishes to grow on Jean's land were brought back with him from France's colonies in North Africa.

If *Jean de Florette* and *Manon des sources* affirm the necessity of direct engagement with the reality of the past, they, nonetheless, caution against nostalgia. Jean, for example, seeks a nostalgic return to the past. His mother had come from Crespin but had moved to the city, a symbol of modernity that contrasts with the rural life in the village. Jean finds modern life unfulfilling and seeks to return to his rural roots in a gesture that mirrors the "return" offered by heritage. The film encodes this desire to "cultivate the authentic" in Jean's words, as both naïve and problematic, particularly since Jean's ownership of the land is a modern reappropriation, rather than a premodern return. Ultimately, Jean manages only a physical return to the site of the past, not the spiritual return he seeks, and even that type of return proves deadly. The

Berri films, therefore, like *Le Retour de Martin Guerre*, undermine heritage at the same time as they perpetuate it. They suggest that the past as received is a dangerous fiction based on lies and omissions, and they question the reliability of history in defining either individual or collective identity. The films call for a real engagement with the past, and they suggest that it is only through a full confrontation of the past that the community may remain intact. Finally, they suggest that the desire to escape contemporary reality and to return to a simpler, premodern past—the desire of heritage itself—is little more than a delusion and a dangerous one at that.

Imperial Heritage: Bloodlines and Citizenship in *Indochine*

Perhaps one of the most problematic heritage films is Régis Wargnier's *Indochine* (1992). While the film is typical of heritage works in its use of high production values and splendid cinematography and in its nostalgic re-creation of a bygone era of the French past, it is atypical of heritage in that it concerns an element of French history that was until very recently generally absent from the national memory—that of colonization and, more particularly, decolonization—with just a few exceptions. Despite this, *Indochine* exhibits many of the same thematic preoccupations as films such *Le Retour de Martin Guerre*, *Jean de Florette*, and *Manon des sources*. It is centered on questions of ancestry, of community, and of the relationship of the past to the present, and in that regard, it uses heritage to construct a discourse on national identity. Moreover, like the Vigne film and the Berri films, *Indochine* was shot on location (Malaysia rather than Vietnam), it features iconic French actors (most notably Catherine Deneuve), and it was a high-budget blockbuster ($20 million) that performed well at home and abroad.

Until recently, when events related to France's imperial history were taught, they were taught only from the point of view of the colonizers. A law passed in early 2005 even mandated that only positive aspects of colonization be taught.[14] With respect to cinema, a handful of films have dealt with the subject of empire or decolonization: Claire Denis' *Chocolat* (1988), which deals with colonialism in Cameroon, Brigitte Roüan's *Outremer* (1990), which deals colonial Algeria, and Pierre Scheondoerffer's *Dien Bien Phu* (1992), which treats Indochina. *Indochine*, however, was the most visible and successful of these films and the only one to gain an international audience.

The treatment of decolonization, whether of Algeria or Indochina, in films from the late 1980s and early 1990s is noteworthy, both because colonization remained at that time a relative *non-dit* and because the debates about immigration and identity that dominated French political discourse during those decades were closely linked to the history of colonization and decolonization.

As Pierre Birnbaum comments, many of those who argue most vehemently against the inclusion of the French of non-European origin also mourn the loss of the empire (2001, 238). Therefore, even those films from the period that deal with decolonization in Indochina or sub-Saharan Africa participate, to some extent, in the broader discussion about immigration and national identity. In Wargnier's *Indochine*, in particular, the subjects of immigration and national identity figure prominently. It may seem peculiar that debates about immigration and *intégration* should manifest themselves in a reexploration of the (de)colonization of Indochina. However, the highly charged nature of anti-Maghrebian sentiment in France demanded that the topic of decolonization be explored in another domain altogether. Thus, Indochina functions in Wargnier's film as a cultural screen memory for the loss of Algeria.[15]

Set in the 1930s, *Indochine* is the story of Eliane Devries (Deneuve), a second-generation French colonial who owns and runs a rubber plantation. The unmarried and childless Eliane adopts Camille (Lin Dahm Phan), an Indochinese princess, the daughter of deceased friends, and the two ultimately become involved in a love triangle with a French naval officer named Jean-Baptiste (Vincent Perez). When Eliane has Jean-Baptiste sent away to punish him for his relationship with Camille, Camille sets off to find him, and her journey across Indochina ultimately leads to a change in consciousness that will turn her into a communist. This change is precipitated by her eventual imprisonment (for having killed a military officer) and the murder of Jean-Baptiste, with whom Camille has a son named Étienne. Étienne is subsequently also adopted by Eliane, and the film ends with Eliane and the adult Étienne (Jean-Baptiste Huynh) witnessing the signing of peace accords between France and Indochina, an event that granted Indochina independence. Camille, who is a member of the Indochinese delegation, is visible in the distance in the final scene.

Indochine was one of the great triumphs of the French government's cultural project. The film was a success not only in France but also abroad, even garnering an Oscar for Best Foreign Film. The film has been read as a nostalgic meditation on empire, largely because of its privileging of the French point of view and because of the cultural prestige of the film's star, Deneuve. Panivong Norindr, for example, reads the film as reproducing the colonization of Indochina as a "feminized spectacle" composed of highly stereotyped images (1996, "Filmic Memorial and Colonial Blues" 126). Brigitte Rollet similarly argues that the film is constructed of stereotypes of colonizer and colonized and of postcard-like images of France's colonial heyday (1999, 39–40). Various critics have also pointed to Deneuve's offscreen role as a model for Marianne, the allegorical face of the republic, as evidence of the film's glorification of French colonialism (Austin 1996, 15; Norindr 1996, 127; Rollet 1996, 34).

While it is true that the film's treatment of colonialism is largely one-sided, it is also true that it is not entirely positive. Eliane is shown beating Indochinese workers, and the French are shown in various scenes engaging in acts of extreme cruelty. These scenes aside, the overall treatment of empire in the film is fairly nostalgic, since from the very beginning, the narrative is constructed to create a sense of regret and loss with regard to the colonial past. This overriding sense of nostalgia is, however, less a result of Deneuve's presence in the film than of the film's narrative structure and its visual composition. With respect to narrative, the film is structured as a flashback through which Eliane Devries revisits the colonial past, which happens to coincide with her own personal past.

Like other heritage films, *Indochine* uses picturesque long shots and panoramas that emphasize the splendor of the landscape as well as numerous medium or group shots of peasants working the land. The primary difference between Wargnier's film and those of Vigne and Berri, however, is that the countryside that is featured is that of colonial Indochina, not of France, and the peasants working the land are colonial subjects, not French peasants. The use of such heritage cinematography in *Indochine* renders the space of the colony another province of France, since it is figured in much the same way as Gascony in *Le Retour de Martin Guerre* or Provence in *Jean de Florette* and *Manon des sources*. This particular aspect of the film has been widely criticized. The combination of the first-person, flashback narration and highly nostalgic visual images have the effect, as Norindr observes, of exploiting "the identificatory of cinema mechanism of cinema on behalf of the colonizer" ("Filmic Memorial and Colonial Blues," 1996, 124). While this is certainly problematic with respect to historical objectivity, it has different implications for the construction of memory, specifically, the French national memory.

It is fairly clear that *Indochine* merges history with memory. Michel Guerin, Wargnier's historical consultant during the making of the film, acknowledged as much, quoted in the April 24, 2001, *Le Monde* as saying that the film was less a historical narrative than a document of national memory and this because the filmic image "has the force of evocation, of restitution of memory. It functions more to capture the imaginary than historical fact." Norindr concurs: "French colonial history becomes visible as Eliane's memories" ("Filmic Memorial and Colonial Blues," 1996, 124). Naomi Greene suggests that it is this presentation of the past through an individual character's personal memory, in particular, that renders the film inherently nostalgic (1999, 106). There is, however, another effect of casting colonial history as memory and, specifically, as the memory of Eliane. Eliane, as many critics comment, becomes a filmic representation of France, both because of her position in the narrative and because of the actress who plays her. By representing the history of colonialism through the personal memory of "the colonial Marianne" (Norindr, "Filmic Memorial and Colonial Blues," 1996, 124), history is transformed from purely personal memory into French collective memory, a space from which it had largely been erased.

This reinsertion of the colonial past into the space of national memory also functions to insert immigration, another nonsite of memory, into the collective past. This is so by implication, since the exclusion of those descended from immigrants is accomplished directly through a forgetting of the history of empire. Immigration is, however, also dealt with in the space of the narrative, if only superficially. Specifically, the film inscribes Eliane's remembering of the past as an act of transmission—she is recounting the past to Étienne—referenced by the film at three specific points in the narrative. Thus, Eliane's personal past and France's national past are transmitted not only to the spectator but also to a character within the narrative, a character who is of Indochinese origin but who has left Indochina to reside in France. Moreover, since heritage references the concept of collective identity as a product of collective memory, this act of transmission must be read as one that inscribes Étienne and those like him into the national space.

This act of transmission also links *Indochine* thematically to *Le Retour de Martin Guerre*, *Jean de Florette*, and *Manon des sources*. In all three cases, lineage, descent, and heritage are determined not by a child's father, but by his or her mother, and in the case of *Indochine*, it is actually decided through the (adoptive) maternal grandmother, making it doubly maternal.[16] Given that heritage, as I suggest, has its roots in the ancien régime, the rejection of paternity as a basis for identity could be read in all three films as a rejection of patriarchal forms of identity and belonging, of which national identity is one. *Indochine*, therefore, and many other heritage films are not only characterized by what Powrie terms a "crisis of masculinity" (1996), they are also characterized by a crisis of paternity, a crisis that suggests the breakdown and reformulation of received paradigms of both individual and collective identity.

It is not, however, only through the act of transmission that *Indochine* addresses questions of individual and national identity. These questions are also raised through the film's representation of adoption, the central metaphor *Indochine* uses for the act of colonization. This equation of colonization to adoption is established in the film's opening sequence. This scene begins with a white screen that clears to reveal a Vietnamese funeral. In voice-over, Eliane explains that it is the funeral of two Vietnamese nobles, whose daughter she has adopted. She ends by asserting that she and these two nobles, a prince and princess, had been inseparable and muses that in youth, one believes "the world is made of inseparable things: man and woman, mountains and plains, humans and gods, Indochina and France." Indochina, in this way, becomes represented as a child, not yet sufficiently mature to take care of itself, and France is figured as the adoptive parent, lovingly looking after the child until she can take care of herself. Such a rendering may be problematic with respect to a historically accurate treatment of colonialism, particularly since this representation of colonialism echoes but does not interrogate the concept of the *mission civilisatrice*; however, this particular metaphor for colonialism also asserts the existence of familial or ancestral ties between France and its former colonies. By framing the colonial past in essentially familial terms, therefore, *Indochine* functions to undermine the idea that immigrants from former colonies are fundamentally alien and inassimilable, as contemporary discourse tends to suggest, positing instead the existence of a common history, a family history that unites France and its former colonies.

Given the opening sequence, it should be of no surprise to find that Eliane's perspective is the only one given in the film. Camille and Jean-Baptiste, as well as all other characters, are presented only through Eliane's point of view. Moreover, Eliane is a completely omniscient narrator, able to recall and recount even those events she did not witness and to recount them as if they were her own personal memory. This detail reinforces the national/allegorical elements of her narration, because the national memory likewise takes upon itself the experiences and memories of innumerable individuals and transmits them, at least theoretically, to other individuals who have no direct connection to them.

This rendering of the national memory as a closed space is undermined, however, at that moment at which the film reveals that Eliane is recounting the past to Étienne. Since she is speaking to him about a past that is both hers and his and since her ultimate goal is to transmit the memory of the past to him, he also becomes included in the memorial space the film creates. This effect of transmission is reinforced visually in the film by a series of reverse shots that highlight the connection that exists between Eliane and Étienne and draw attention to the interaction between them. What is more, at the moment Étienne participates in this re-creation of the past, he is in Europe, and he affirms no connection either to Indochina or to his birth mother. Although it is true that he is in Geneva, Switzerland, and not in France, it is also true, as Eliane makes clear, that Étienne has come to Geneva from France, where he has been living since before he could remember.

If it is true, as Norindr states, that in many ways *Indochine* functions to suture the spectator into a colonialist perspective, it is also true that the film draws attention to this process of suture. Étienne's reception of Eliane's narrative, for example, inscribes him in the space of memory she creates, and it suggests the opening of that space for the (formerly) colonized or at least for their children. Moreover, Étienne's almost silent presence within the film suggests both the existence and the exclusion of alternative memories and points of view in the national historical narrative. The film, therefore, calls out for a new type of history, a history that cannot be rendered through Elaine's monolithic narrative.

What is more, Étienne's situation with respect to the question of citizenship and identity is significant. First of all, he has left Indochina, and he has no attachment to it. Secondly, he has spent the formative part of his life in France, a country he identifies as his own. Thirdly, he claims Eliane, widely read as an allegorical representation of France, as his mother, rejecting Indochina in the process. In this way, he seems to conform exactly to the demands of the republican model of citizenship, in that he has become fully integrated into France and claims France as his home. It is worth noting, however, that this inclusion into the space of the nation is not accomplished through a forgetting of origins, consistent with what is often termed the republican model of integration but rather through the *remembering* of those origins.[17]

Therefore, if *Indochine* valorizes, in some ways, current models of integration by insisting on the importance of a shared communal identity forged through the experience of the common past, it, nonetheless, breaks with such models in its formulation of the colonial past as part of the national past. Finally, and perhaps most interesting, Étienne is the French-Vietnamese son of a French-Vietnamese mother, doubly bound to France through his mother and his adoptive grandmother. Therefore, his status evokes, if it does not entirely conform to, the idea of the double *droit du sol*, the automatic citizenship afforded to those born on French territory to parents born on French territory.

This conflicted reading of colonialism and citizenship is heightened by another discourse introduced into the film by the opening sequence—Eliane's adoption of Camille. This adoption introduces a conflict between ancestry and cultural identity, because the act of raising an adopted child, particularly between two cultures, necessarily points to the competing influences of biology and environment. This conflict between ancestry and culture parallels debates about ancestry versus culture that have shaped contemporary France. By adopting Camille, Eliane seems to affirm the irrelevance of ancestry in determining identity, because presumably, she will raise Camille to be like herself, and cultural influence, rather than ancestry, will be determinative in forming Camille's identity. However, at the moment of adoption, Eliane suggests the inherent inferiority of Indochina with respect to France, an affirmation that implies that ancestry is determinative in constructions of identity, because, by this logic, no matter how Camille is brought up, she will never actually *be* French.

The question of ancestry versus culture reappears elsewhere in the film. Camille is expected to marry a man named Than, another Indochinese, in order to maintain the purity of both families' bloodlines. Camille refuses to comply, choosing Jean-Baptiste, a French man, over Than. Her choice reflects the preeminence of culture in forming identity, because she chooses a man who reflects the culture in which she was raised and not one who reflects her biological origins. Moreover, Than, who is himself French educated, aids Camille in seeking out Jean-Baptiste, which suggests that Than also regards culture as more important than ancestry. When his mother chastises him for his actions and orders him to apologize to his offended ancestors, he refuses, stating that such things are part of the past.

The question of ancestry versus cultural formation is never fully resolved in the film, at least not for Eliane or Camille. While it is true that Camille and Jean-Baptiste form a couple and have a child, this relationship leads to his death and her imprisonment, which would suggest that the mixing of cultures or bloodlines has devastating consequences. On the other hand, Étienne, a child of mixed race and heritage, identifies completely with Eliane, and she with him, and the film seems to suggest that this is more because of his cultural formation than his ancestry. What is more, culture, as the film presents it, is the product solely of environment and experience. It is a force in which ancestry plays no part.

Indochine, therefore, may seem to suggest that all identities are cultural, that they are transmitted and received. However, the construction of culture differs from the current use of the term in debates on national identity, particularly as they are expressed by the far-right wing (the Front National, founded in 1972 by Jean-Marie Le Pen). The right-wing construction regards culture as the logical consequence of ancestry, and, therefore, excludes a priori the integration of those of foreign origin into the space of the nation. *Indochine*, in contrast, affirms that culture and cultural identification are entirely the products of milieu. The film, therefore, suggests that the integration of immigrants into the nation is not simply likely, it is inevitable as a result of the shared histories of the formerly colonized and those who colonized them. In that respect, the film works to open not only the space of collective memory but also the space of national identity.

Rather than simply reproducing the logic of political nationalism, many heritage films foreground the contradictory thinking on ancestry and identity both in nineteenth-century historiography and in contemporary political debates. Heritage films often valorize certain aspects of the national past and rather forcefully suggest that the events and experiences of the past are a significant force in shaping identity in the present. However, the films also question the reception of the past and the ability to read the past in the present. Therefore, while they tend to validate the idea that bloodlines and cultural heritage determine citizenship, they also undermine such notions, opening up new possibilities for both history and identity. Moreover, these films also suggest that defining identity through heritage does not a priori prevent "outsiders" from becoming "insiders," nor does it necessarily mean that post-colonial minorities are permanently excluded from the space of the nation. After all, those who were and are imagined as foreigners by the nationalist paradigm of identity were, by and large, born and brought up in France and have gone through the same processes of acculturation as the dominant population.

For that reason, heritage films say relatively little about whether or not there exists a "true" French identity and a collective French memory. Instead, these films raise questions about the nature and content of the national past and the national collective memory and the relationship of both to the present. Cultural representations of the past—such as those offered by heritage films—open the door for identification with the national past on the part of those who have no direct connection with it. In this way, even someone who has not passed through such institutions as the French school system may assimilate into the national culture through the adoption of a certain set of "memories" created, for example, by watching heritage films.

Therefore, if heritage works are built upon a particular conception of history and identity, they also open the space of national identity more than they close it. Even if the historical film reemerged in contemporary France as the expression of an unconscious desire to create paradigms of history and memory that exclude those of non-European ancestry, they do not actually function to create that exclusion. Instead, such films create and reinforce a connection to the national past for anyone who chooses to embrace it. Moreover, heritage films' insistence on "pastness" as an essential characteristic of Frenchness invites the question of what should constitute the pivotal moments of the French past. This, in turn, draws attention to those periods of history that such works often leave out and those spaces of memory they ignore, spaces that could potentially create room for those in the national community who might otherwise be excluded.

This process of opening up occurs in both the structure and the narrative of such films. For example, the uses of both embedded flashback and voice-over narration function to disrupt the seamless, linear mode of narration traditionally employed by historical films. Hamid Naficy observes that "accented" or diasporic filmmakers often rely on similar techniques in order to disrupt the authority of dominant-culture assumptions about identity and origin (2001, 24). In such accented films, these techniques of disruption are used to open the door to the spaces, faces, and voices of exile, to foreground the existence of outsiders who might otherwise pass unseen. Through this type of disruption, heritage films blur the boundaries between insiders and outsiders and question the ways in which such categories are imagined and lived. For that reason, heritage, at least as it manifests in heritage films, is less a definitive discourse on nationality and identity than a step toward the broader redefinition of both.

3

Heritage and Its Discontents: Memory, History, and the Expanding Space of the Past

*I*n her study of nostalgia in French cinema, Naomi Greene asserts that contemporary France has been shaped by "a pre-occupation with the national past and the way it has been remembered" (1999, 191). In Greene's analysis, French cinema in general and the contemporary heritage film in particular have been characterized by a "landscape of absence and loss" that creates and sustains a nostalgic longing for the past. Greene's reading of the heritage film is close to the dominant interpretation, which holds that the authentic nation resides in the past and that heritage films tend to reinforce conservative notions that France is under attack by immigration and globalization. This reading of the heritage film, as argued in chapter 2, is somewhat problematic, particularly since French heritage films tend to engage with the past in ways that are fairly ambiguous. They are frequently ambivalent about the reliability of history and memory, and they often function as expressions of unease regarding past-oriented, nostalgic models of identity, both individual and collective.

As the heritage film evolved, this tendency to destabilize the past or at least existing narratives of the past became heightened. This is evident in such films as Patrice Chéreau's *La Reine Margot* (1994), Yves Angelo's *Le Colonel Chabert* (1994), and Jean-Paul Rappeneau's *Le Hussard sur le toit* (1995). Like first-wave heritage films, these works tend to feature well-known, high-profile actors and to rely on high production values. However, unlike earlier heritage films, they tend not to use a flashback structure, loosening the suture effect inherent in the earlier films. The cinematography in these later films also relies much more on the use of close-ups than on the postcard-like panoramas and long shots seen in earlier films. They tend to function more as individual histories than as depictions of a collective past. Perhaps more important, these films do not seem to glorify the past but, rather, to encode it as dark and unstable.

Despite divergences from the heritage paradigm, most critics and scholars have regarded these later films as merely new and different expressions of the nostalgia and nationalism that characterized the first-wave films of the 1980s. Ginette Vincendeau suggests, for example, that the visual and thematic darkness of such films reflects pessimism about the state of France and of French national identity at the time they were made (1995). Julianne Pidduck argues that these 1990s heritage films are, like their 1980s counterparts, an expression of nostalgia and a certain type of nationalism, an attempt to reinforce existing cultural myths that have been active since the nineteenth century (2005, 32–37). This interpretation would seem to suggest that these later films are informed by the same regret and sense of loss as the first-wave heritage films, despite the absence of any overt nostalgia in the films themselves.

Pidduck also observes that many of these later films, including Rappeneau's *Cyrano de Bergerac* (1990) and Chéreau's *La Reine Margot*, reproduce the ancien régime through the filter of the nineteenth century by adapting Romantic literary works (2005, 14–15). This is not unusual for heritage films, which are often literary adaptations. However, many of these later films are also *remakes* of films that were themselves adaptations of Romantic works. These late heritage films, therefore, are doubly removed from the stories they depict. As a result, they reference not only the original work and the historical period it recreated but also previous recreations of that period, both literary and filmic. The embedded nature of the meditation on the past inherent in such films suggests a relationship between past and present that is decidedly nonlinear. The past imagined and represented by such films is not the direct predecessor of the present. It cannot, for example, be directly recalled from the present. Rather, it can only be recalled through previous recollections and representations. The past that is recalled, therefore, is not really the past but a specular image of it, an image that can only be accessed and interpreted through previous and sometimes-competing representations of itself.

Chéreau's *La Reine Margot*, for example, re-creates the life of Marguerite de Valois through an engagement with particular interpretations of her life that were produced during various historical periods. Chéreau's film, therefore, not only engages what Pidduck has called the myth of "La Reine Margot" but it also points to the historical-myth–making process, because it consciously blends into its own historical recreation the ideas and representations of previous historical periods. At the same time, as Dudley Andrew suggests, the film uses the past as a mirror in which to contemplate the present, implying connections between the story it relates and contemporary issues such as ethnic cleansing or debates about *laïcité* (separation of church and state) (1995, 24). *La Reine Margot* imagines the past not a direct line between Renaissance France and the present, as traditional historiography imagines it, but, rather, as an associative link uniting Renaissance France, nineteenth-century France, postwar France, and contemporary France and at the same time the Wars of Religion, the Bosnian War, and Rwanda. The film does not, it is true, activate all of these spaces of the past. However, it does recall their existence to the spectator and assert a connection among them. *La Reine Margot*, therefore, like other late heritage films, begins to imagine history and memory in spatial rather than linear terms, in much the same way as Pierre Nora's *Lieux de mémoire*.

Not all late heritage films follow the pattern of Chéreau's *La Reine Margot*, however. Some, such as Rappeneau's *Cyrano*, Claude Chabrol's *Madame Bovary* (1991), Claude Berri's *Germinal* (1993), and Patrice Leconte's *Ridicule* (1996), are fairly straightforward films that do continue in the vein of the first-wave films. However, even these films depict the past in darker terms than their predecessors, a tendency evident in their subject matter as well as their cinematography. Other later films, including Benoît Jacquot's *Sade* (2000), Gabriel Aghion's *Le Libertin* (2000), and most recently Laurent Tirard's *Molière* (2007) are overt fictionalizations of the historical past that alter or invent portions of the lives of the people they depict. This deliberate play with historical fact is often presented as a means of exploring history's blank spaces, those moments in the lives of historical figures that history has left untouched. These films are, therefore, akin to the darker heritage films, even though they are themselves fairly light, because they posit that narratives about the past are essentially fictional creations of the present.

History's (Special) Effect: Gans's *Le Pacte des loups*

Perhaps the most interesting and at the same time problematic of these late heritage films is Christophe Gans's *Le Pacte des loups* (2001). Set in and around the town of Mende in what was the Gévaudan (now the Lozère), *Le Pacte des loups* recounts the story of the so-called beast of Gévaudan, a mysterious animal that attacked and killed at least a hundred people, mostly women and children, between 1764 and 1767. The beast, which was described as a wolf-like creature, was never captured or killed, although several people, including a local hunter named Jean Chastel and the master at arms to King Louis XV, Antoine de Beauterne, claimed to have killed it. Beauterne actually brought a large stuffed wolf back to Versailles with him as "evidence" of his success, and was feted as a hero despite the attacks continuing after he had supposedly slain the beast.[1]

Le Pacte des loups has much in common with typical heritage films. It is, for example, a historical film or costume drama that draws its authority from recorded history. It is set during a privileged period of French history—the period just before and during the Revolution—and it takes place in rural, provincial France in an area with a well-defined regional identity. It privileges visual spectacle over narrative, and it has very high production values. It was one of the most expensive French films ever made, at a budget of nearly $29 million. Moreover, like many of the big-budget heritage films, it was commercially successful, both in France and abroad. The film took in more than $70 million worldwide, including nearly $11 million in the U.S. market, which makes it one of the highest-grossing French films of all time.[2]

Le Pacte des loups was made as part of an agreement between Gans and producer Samuel Hadida to create a popular, commercially successful type of French film that could rival Hollywood in both the domestic and international markets. Its overtly commercial ambitions, along with its use of spectacular special effects and its tendency to blend traditional genres, have tended to obscure its heritage connections. Typically, it has been seen as a spectacular, action-packed, international superproduction on the model of *The Matrix* (1999) or *Crouching Tiger, Hidden Dragon* (2003), rather than a high-brow embodiment of French national culture (Molia 2007, 54). This interpretation notwithstanding, it is clear that *Le Pacte des loups* has more in common with the historical or heritage film than with any other type of film. The story it recounts, for example, may be considered a type of folk memory in much the same way as the story of Martin Guerre. People still talk of the beast of the Gévaudan in France, particularly in the Cévennes region, where there are monuments and a museum devoted to it and where postcards and other memorabilia depicting the creature are common.[3] These postcards and monuments play a significant role in the local tourist economy, and heritage and tourism, as already suggested, are closely linked. Also, indications are that the story has long been part of regional lore. Some of the houses in the area, for example, feature images or paintings depicting the animal, and the church at Saint-Alban-sur-Limagnole has a weathervane in the shape of the creature.

The memory of the beast and its attacks has also been preserved in writing. Newspaper accounts, for example, began appearing in the mid-eighteenth century and continued well beyond that period. Several accounts were published in 1764 and 1765 in both the *Courrier d'Avignon* and the *Gazette de France*, national paper published in Paris. Stories about the attacks were published in the *Journal de la Lozère* in 1795, *Journal des Chasseurs* in 1840, and *La Semaine des familles* in 1866, nearly a century later (Fabre 2001/1930, 181). The story of the attacks also appears repeatedly in literature. A melodrama relating the events in the Gévaudan was published by a Monsieur Pompigny in 1809, and a book-length account of events was published by Abbé Pierre Pourcher in 1889. Robert Louis Stevenson wrote about the beast for the English-speaking world in his 1879 work *Travels with a Donkey in the Cevennes*, and a number of more recent written accounts, includes *La Bête du Gévaudan* by Abel Chevalley (1936), *La Bête du Gévaudan* (1991) by Gérard Manetory, and a version in *Ce tant rude Gévaudan* (1985) by Felix Buffière. Thus, despite its absence from official histories of France, the story of the beast has a particular place in French popular memory, a fact acknowledged by Gans, who affirmed that he was familiar with the story of the beast before reading the film's script (2001).[4]

Because *Le Pacte des loups* is the retelling of events ignored by official history but transmitted through folklore, the film inherently questions the relationship of past to present and challenges the veracity and integrity of history. In the version of the story recounted in the film, Grégoire de Fronsac, an explorer and naturalist, is sent by King Louis XV to solve the mystery of the beast. Fronsac arrives in the Gévaudan with his blood brother Mani (Mark Dacascos), an Iroquois Indian whom Fronsac had saved from execution during his travels in New France (now Canada). Fronsac and Mani arrive in Mende at the home of Thomas (Jérémie Renier) and his grandfather the Marquis d'Apcher (Hans Meyer). The marquis recounts to Fronsac the details of the attacks and then arranges for Fronsac to meet with surviving victims at a hospital the marquis has established. Fronsac and Mani are later invited to a salon where they meet the various nobles and clergy of the area, including the Bishop of Mende; Sardis, the Curé at Saint-Albans (Jean-François Stévenin); and the Comte de Morangias (Jean Yanne); his wife (Edith Scob); his son, Jean-François (Vincent Cassel); and his daughter, Marianne (Emilie Dequenne). After a brief period of investigation and a sizeable wolf hunt, the king sends Antoine de Beauterne, his master of the hunt, to the Gévaudan. Beauterne kills a large but rather ordinary wolf and commands Fronsac to modify and preserve the animal it so that it can be publicly displayed. Fronsac reluctantly complies and returns to Versailles with Beauterne, on orders of the King.

Ultimately, Fronsac returns to the Gévaudan and lays a trap for the beast, but the monster escapes, and Mani is killed. Fronsac finds Mani's body and recognizes that he has been killed by bullets belonging to Jean-François de Morangias. Before he can act on this information, Fronsac is arrested and put in prison, where he is visited by Sylvia (Monica Bellucci), a mysterious prostitute he met at a local bordello. Sylvia appears to poison Fronsac, and he is pronounced dead and subsequently buried. Sylvia digs Fronsac up from his grave, revives him, and sets him loose to exact revenge, explaining to him that she is an agent of the Catholic Church who has been sent to put an end to a secret religious society that challenges the authority of both church and king. Fronsac avenges Mani's death and in the process solves the mystery of the beast, which, according to the film was a lioness brought back from Africa by Jean-François de Morangias. The king, in gratitude for Fronsac's service, offers him the opportunity to travel to Africa, and at the end of the film, Fronsac and Marianne leave France for Senegal.

Although *Le Pacte des loups* takes place in the mid-eighteenth century, it begins during the Revolution during the Reign of Terror. The film uses a framing narrative featuring Thomas d'Apcher, the son and now the marquis, to introduce the story of the beast. This use of a framing narrative or sequence is typical of heritage films, particularly first-wave heritage films such as *Le Retour de Martin Guerre* and *Indochine*. It creates a flashback within a flashback structure, whose effect, as suggested, is to impose a strong identification between the spectator and the past represented in the film. In *Le Pacte des loups*, however, the function of this frame is ambiguous. Although it provides the spectator a personalized subjectivity through which to experience the events in the Gévaudan, any strong identification created in this scene is ultimately undercut by the way in which the scene foregrounds the constructed nature of history.

Thomas's memoire about the hunt for the beast is presented in this framing sequence as an unauthorized history that challenges the authority of official history. Thomas risks being seized and executed in order to record this counterhistory, which he says will reveal the degree to which certainty "makes men blind." Thomas's narrative is a type of counterhistory that mirrors the counterhistory of the film itself. This is made clear through the use of the camera in the opening sequence, which begins with a descending vertical panorama of Thomas d'Apcher's castle. This vertical pan implies that the world in which Thomas now finds himself—the world of the Revolution—is a type of hell, an idea reinforced by the yellow flames from the torches carried by the mob on the ground. It also implies, however, a descent or a passage back through time, both from the present to the moment of the Revolution and from the Revolution to the time of the beast, particularly because the castle and Thomas are part of both stories.

The primary linkage in this scene, however, is the linking of the present moment to the Revolution. The Revolution becomes the filmic present that the secondary flashback will serve to elucidate and explain. This means that the real subject of *Le Pacte des loups*, as Raphaëlle Moine observes, is not the hunt for the beast but, rather, the Revolution itself (2007, 43). This is made clear by the structure of the second flashback in the opening sequence, the flashback from the Revolution to the time of the beast. In contrast to the initial, vertical, temporal passage from present to past, this flashback is expressed spatially, through an accelerated aerial tracking shot that begins at the castle and moves into the countryside where the attacks take/took place. This use of horizontal, rather than vertical, displacement suggests that the Terror and the attacks of the beast are part of the same story because they occupy the same physical space and essentially the same temporality, and it implies a horizontal rather than a vertical relationship between the two events.

This framing sequence destabilizes the authority of history, both official history and the counterhistory that Thomas offers in its place. This act of destabilization is encoded in the vertical pan that begins the scene. The camera is positioned so that it films from a low angle, which is a characteristic shot in expressionistic genres such as film noir but not in historical films. Moreover, the camera is titled slightly off its axis, producing a Dutch (oblique) angle shot, which decenters the point of view offered by the film and draws attention to the presence of the camera. This is a classic film-noir camera angle, and it is designed to produce an emotional response—specifically, a sense of unease—rather than the effect of realism. The use of this type of shot in a historical film, particularly in the opening scene, ruptures the identification that should normally take place between the spectator and Thomas, drawing attention, right from the beginning, to the fact that the spectator is watching a film or a representation and undermining any illusion that the spectator is reliving the past. Moreover, by relying on a horizontal rather than a vertical linkage of events separated in time, this sequence undermines the implied causality between past and present and proposes instead an associative link, or a link of equivalences. This effectively undermines the conventional structure of history.

Although the camerawork in the opening shot evokes film noir, most of the other elements in the scene suggest the historical film or costume drama. The sequence, therefore, anticipates a wider tactic of generic bricolage or genre bending that occurs throughout the film. It also introduces one of the principal blends evident in *Le Pacte des loups*, that of the historical film and the detective film. The blending of these two particular genres suggests that *Le Pacte des loups* is more an investigation of the past than a simple re-presentation. As noted in chapter 2, the detective film and the historical film are the two principal film genres that involve the re-creation of the past. Historical films restage the past as though it were taking place, and the narrative presented is intended to pass, therefore, for reality. This type of film posits that historical reality is knowable, stable, and transmissible, and it functions to reinforce or naturalize whatever version of past events it offers. The detective film, on the other hand, presumes that the past as it has been received is problematic. Its re-creation occurs as a corrective to previous, false recreations. When the crime is solved, a new narrative about the past is established that supplants and corrects the old version. Detective films, therefore, may posit the past as knowable, but they also foreground the unreliability of memory and the potential to manipulate history. In blending the two genres, *Le Pacte des loups* points to the force of re-creations of the past—to their capacity to pass for history—while foregrounding the essentially fictive nature of such recreations and potentially calling for revisions to them.

The detective film is not the only genre blended into the historical melting pot of *Le Pacte des loups*. The film also includes incongruous elements from the martial-arts film, the action film, the porn film, and the western. The repeated intrusion of these other genres into an essentially historical film disrupts the film's historical re-presentation and repeatedly draws attention back to the fact that the spectator is watching a film. *Le Pacte des loups* also repeatedly disrupts the classical, linear sequencing of time associated with the cinema. For example, the body discovered shortly after Fronsac and Mani arrive in the Gévaudan actually belongs to a woman not killed until they have been there for some time (Gans, "Production Notes" 2001).[5] In another scene, Fronsac comes back to the Gévaudan after having returned to Paris with Beauterne, but a temporal ellipsis prevents the viewer from knowing when this occurs. These disruptions also function to erode any sense of historical realism and to undermine traditional notions of historicity.

Various other disruptions in *Le Pacte des loups* undermine the historical illusion. The repeated use of *mise-en-abyme* reminds the spectator that he or she is watching a re-presentation of the past that is built on other representations (see fig. 2). At the dinner scene in which Fronsac meets the local aristocracy, for example, the dinner guests are seated in front of a wall featuring a mural. The mural, painted in red and black, depicts figures from an earlier age, seemingly the medieval period or the Renaissance. The dinner guests, who are themselves a representation of an earlier historical period, are also dressed in red and black. The fundamental similarity between the two sets of images foregrounds the representational or fictional nature of each and suggests that all representations of the past are in some measure reworkings of previous representations.

In addition to foregrounding the representational nature of history, *Le Pacte des loups* functions to question its accuracy. This is evident in the way in which the film remains faithful to the historical records in some circumstances but overtly fictionalizes in others. A case in point is the film's cast of characters, which is a blend of real historical figures, fictionalized historical figures, and purely fictional figures. Antoine de Beauterne and King Louis XV are real

Fig. 2. Use of *mise-en-abyme;* Jean-François de Morangias (Vincent Cassel) in red and black, shot against a mural in red and black in *Le Pacte des loups* (2001).

characters whose involvement with the beast is recorded in either in literature or in official accounts from the period. Grégoire de Fronsac (Samuel de Bihan) was a real eighteenth-century explorer and naturalist, however he had nothing, as far as history is concerned, to do with the attacks in the Gévaudan. Mani is a pure invention, created as a vehicle for Mark Dacascos (Dacascos 2001).

This blending of fact and fiction also extends to elements within the film's narrative. If, as suggested, *Le Pacte des loups* is a counterhistory built on other histories, it is also, to a large degree, a counterhistory constructed of histories that are encoded as fictions. A key example of this is Antoine de Beauterne's "hunt" for the beast. According to the film, Beauterne is sent by the king not to kill the beast but to bring back an animal that could be presented as the beast. The king, according to the film, (rightly) believes that the beast is part of a revolutionary plot designed to overthrow the monarchy. His solution to the plot is to narrate it out of existence, both by suppressing a book used to foment rebellion and by creating a story that the beast has been caught and killed. Beauterne's role is to create the illusion that the creature is dead, undermining any sense that there is disorder in the kingdom and undercutting any sympathy for the revolutionaries and their plot. This illusion, however, requires some evidence to legitimate it, and this evidence comes from Fronsac, who is ordered to transform whatever animal Beauterne manages to kill into something that could be displayed as the beast.

This episode, like much in the film, is a blending of what is recorded in the historical record, the beliefs that have grown up around the events in the Gévaudan over the years—and pure invention. It is true, for example, that Antoine de Beauterne killed a wolf and that the wolf was displayed as the beast. However, nothing in the historical record suggests either that the beast was part of a treasonous plot to overthrow the king or that Beauterne's wolf was transformed in an effort to counter such a plot. Both ideas, however, are grounded in the real history of the Gévaudan, which was long a hotbed of religious and political dissent. They are also consistent with conspiracy theories about the beast that have been circulated since the time of the attacks. If, therefore, the film's version of events in not "true" in the sense that it is not a version sanctioned by official history, it is true in the sense that it reflects an interpretation of the events that has been consistent over time. The film, therefore, positions its fictional history as the counterhistory to the "official" (but equally fictional) version of events authored by the king. The difference between the two versions is not that one is true and the other is not; after all, both are fictions created by the film. It is, rather, that one derives from the will of the ruling power and the other derives from the beliefs of those who are ruled.

Numerous other fictional histories are incorporated into the film. Jean-François de Morangias creates a false history about having a "maimed" arm to detract suspicion from his involvement with the beast. He claims that he lost his arm in Africa in an encounter with a wild animal, when in reality his arm is intact and hidden via a special corset made for him by Sardis, the Curé of Saint-Albans. This "fictional" history, like that of the king, is created by those in power and functions to maintain existing power relations. It is also, like the story of Beauterne and the king, an invented history that is not corroborated by the official historical record. Moreover, whereas the spectator is fully aware that the king's story concerning the killing of the beast is a fiction, the illusory nature of the story of Jean-François' arm remains unknown to the spectator for much of the film. This calls into question the spectator's ability to discern fact from fiction, which, in turn, highlights the cinema's capacity to generate (fictional) historical narratives. Another fictional history involves Fronsac's apparent death and resurrection. The prostitute Sylvia gives Fronsac a potion that makes him appear dead, and she spreads the story that he has died. Because Sylvia is ultimately revealed to be an agent of the Catholic Church, this history is also in some sense authored by powerful interests. It also remains unknown to the spectator until it is revealed toward the end of the film. Finally, Fronsac attempts to create a false history. During his introduction to the aristocrats of the Gévaudan, he displays a furry trout he claims to have found in Canada. Fronsac's false history is probably the least "successful" of all of these false histories, perhaps because he operates from a position of relative powerlessness. Jean-François de Morangias recognizes that the trout has had fur attached, and he immediately unmasks it as a hoax.

These "fictional" histories, like the use of *mise-en-abyme*, suggest that all histories, including the film itself, are composed of fictions that are accepted as real by those who consume them. They also form the building blocks from which the film's counterhistory, putatively authored by Thomas d'Apcher, is formed. These fictional histories implicate the cinema in the creation and perpetuation of historical myths since all of them are part of the ostensibly real version of history advanced by the film. It is also interesting that each of the fictional histories that compose the narrative depends, like the film itself and historical films in general, upon "special effects" for its success. The king's story about the beast being slain, Jean-François' story about being maimed, and Sylvia's story about Fronsac's death all draw their sense of "authenticity" from a visual effect or trick. The king's false history relies on the display of Fronsac's false beast. Jean-François' false history depends upon his hidden arm. Sylvia's false history derives its realism from the semblance of death she is able to induce. These fictional histories function as metaphors for historical films, which are also essentially fictive narratives about the past that use illusions to convince the spectator of their authenticity. Moreover, since all of the successful fictional histories within the film are authorized or sanctioned by a particular powerful interest, they suggest that historical films and the versions of history they re-present are used by those in power to maintain existing power relations, a critique that has been leveled at historical films in general and the heritage film in particular.

This brings us back to the question of history and what, if anything, *Le Pacte des loups*, may be trying to say about it. It seems fairly clear from the elements of film noir, from the play with real historical events, and from the fictional histories woven throughout the narrative that *Le Pacte des loups* constructs history as pastiche, and that functions in the postmodern sense to reveal the ideological processes that underlie the act of representation (Hutcheon 1989). Pastiche functions specifically to draw attention to the fact that those in power (re)write history for their own purposes, and to point out that the "false" histories generated as a result are generally accepted as real, unless their authors choose to unmask them. Moreover, because the story of the beast is linked, from the beginning, to that of the Enlightenment and Revolution, the film's critique of history specifically implicates the history of the Revolution and therefore, the national history on which it was built. The eighteenth century as depicted in *Le Pacte des loups*, for example, is highly evocative of previous filmic representations of that period. The dinner-party scene recalls a similar dinner party at Madame de Blayac's in Leconte's *Ridicule*, the hunt for the wolf evokes the battle scenes of Rappeneau's *Cyrano*, and the scenes from the Terror that open and close the film evoke Andrzej Wajda's *Danton* (1983).

This overt referencing of previous re-creations of the past suggests that there is no lived historical memory, only an internalized image created by other images. This implies that even counterhistorical narratives, such as the film itself, are merely reworkings of other narratives. Even the film's destabilization of history is, in part, achieved through references to other films. The shots of the wolf in the film, for example, recall Neil Jordan's *Company of Wolves* (1984), as do the eeriness and surreal quality of overall imagery. The blending of costume drama and detective film evokes Jean-Jacques Annaud's *Name of the Rose* (1986), as do the tone and the combination of gothic and crime film to make a philosophical and political statement. The merging of soft porn, horror, and action, as well as in the specific use of a bordello as a principal setting, brings to mind Robert Rodriguez's *Dusk till Dawn* (1996).[6]

The critique by *Le Pacte des loups* of the history of the Revolution is also rooted in the presentation of the character of Fronsac and particularly the fictional history Fronsac attempts to create. In the film, he appears to embody the ideals of the Enlightenment and the Revolution as they are typically understood. He believes in liberty, equality, and fraternity, as demonstrated by his acceptance of Mani as his brother and his concern—not shared by the aristocrats, the king or the Church—for the welfare of the peasants of the Gévaudan. He also relies on reason and the scientific method to interpret the world around him. In typically rational fashion, Fronsac displays his furry trout in order to offer a commentary on the situation in the Gévaudan, in order to suggest that the beast of the Gévaudan does not really exist, and that things in the Gévaudan are not as they seem. The irony in Fronsac's exercise is that it is *he* who cannot see things for what they are. The aristocrats who appear to be so concerned about the attacks are the beast's master, but Fronsac fails to recognize this. For all his analysis and reliance on reason, therefore, Fronsac is not, as he believes himself to be, an enlightened character. He is, rather, perhaps the least enlightened character in the film.

It is also true that Fronsac has a history of being the unwitting agent of undemocratic outside forces, be they the colonizing armies in New France or the king and the Church in the Gévaudan. He never manages, in the course of the film, to convince anyone else of the merits either of democracy or reason, and most important, he neither solves the mystery of the beast nor resolves the attacks. Instead, he simply functions as the agent of someone else's resolution. In rewriting the history of the Revolution through Fronsac, therefore, *Le Pacte des loups* essentially undoes traditional historiography. The narrative of the Revolution the film offers is not one in which democracy overturns monarchy, and reason overturns religion. It is, rather, one in which the Enlightenment becomes the window dressing through which existing elites, including the king and the Church, may act on the public without being seen. Thus, the Enlightenment, according to the film, is the ultimate disguise, the one in which the powers in France may cloak themselves in order to convince the world of revolutionary change. Indeed, this may explain the dominance of the motif of disguise in *Le Pacte des loups*. Everyone, from Fronsac to the beast, appears at some point in disguise. The film seems to suggest that narratives about the Revolution are themselves disguises, designed to mask the reality of the past.

If at the end of Fronsac's intervention, the aristocrats of the Gévaudan are thwarted and the peasants saved, the king and the Church nonetheless remain in charge. The Revolution that seemingly overthrows them is presented, by the logic of the film, as a continuation of what was begun in the Gévaudan—an attempt by discontented regional powers to overthrow the national government.[7] The Revolution, then, becomes not the founding moment of a republican nation or an act by which diverse regional identities fuse into a single national identity. It becomes, rather, the expression of regional discontent with an existing national structure and the ultimate triumph of the aristocracy over the king. If this understanding of the Revolution has been lost, it is, the film suggests, because it has been deliberately buried. The story Thomas d'Apcher scrambles to write, then, becomes the "real" history of the Revolution. The film, however, disrupts even this "alternative" history of the Revolution by presenting it, too, as an essentially fictional narrative, built on other fictional narratives. *Le Pacte des loups* does not, therefore, attempt to tell what the Revolution "really" means. It simply points out that any narratives or histories that profess to relate its meaning are fictional accounts masquerading as fact and serving one or another powerful interest. While this particular reading or representation is not new, what is new is the way in which *Le Pacte des loups* specifically implicates the cinema in the creation and perpetuation of history's fictional narratives.

At several points in the story, as noted, reality and history are altered through the use of "special effects." This use of "special effects" within the narrative points to and perhaps explains their use outside of the narrative—the special effects of the film. Just as with those internal to the narrative, essentially two types of special effects are used in the film—those that succeed or that are transparent to the spectator (like Sylvia's "poisoning") and those that fail, or that are recognized by the spectator (such as Fronsac's alteration of Beauterne's wolf). Special effects in the first category include the use of special makeup to create the effect of blood and wounds or the special effects that produce the illusory existence of the beast. These effects are "transparent" or invisible in that they enhance the realism of the film, and they pass largely unnoticed or unseen as effects by the spectator. The second type of effects used in the film—those that are "opaque" or apparent to the spectator—include the use of stylized slow- and accelerated-motion shots as well as the appearance that characters can hang in the air or fly. These opaque effects jar the spectator, disrupting the film's carefully created historical world and undermining, at least temporarily, its illusion of reality. They effectively draw the spectator's attention back to the fact that he or she is not observing the historical past as it unfolds but a re-creation of it.

What distinguishes the transparent from the opaque special effects, however, is not merely the ease with which they are detected by the spectator. Those effects that are transparent are for the most part related to mise-en-scène and tend to reinforce the apparent reality of the fictional world in which the film takes place. Those effects that are opaque, on the other hand, have to do with editing or enhancement that takes place postproduction. They tend to disrupt the film's verisimilitude at the level of narrative, and, specifically, they interrupt or undermine the unified, linear sequencing associated with filmic realism and, in particular, historical realism. Most historical films combine realist mise-en-scène with seamless narration and continuity editing in order to reproduce the effects of both history and historicity. As suggested, these films imply a linear, causal relationship between events in the narrative and between the past as represented in the film and the present in which the film is viewed. By maintaining the illusion of *history* but disrupting the illusion of *historicity*, *Le Pacte des loups* unmasks the process of transmission engaged in by historical films. The film first convinces the spectator that he or she is witnessing the past and then reminds the spectator that neither the past nor the present exist in cinema, that filmic time is an illusion, susceptible to manipulation. This draws attention to the power of cinema to re-create and transmit the past while blocking any such transmission.

Gans asserts that one of his primary motives in making *Le Pacte des loups* was to re-create an eighteenth-century France that never existed outside of the minds of tourists (2001, interview). It might have been more accurate to say that the eighteenth-century *Le Pacte des loups* creates is one that does not exist outside the cinema. The film ultimately produces a specular image of the eighteenth century, an image that is itself the product of previous images and representations. This specular recreation is informed by what Nora calls the "historiographic consciousness," or the critical reappraisal of the national past that defines the contemporary era ("Entre mémoire et histoire," 1997, 25). This reappraisal is not an attempt to replace existing narratives about the national past with new narratives made in their image. It is, rather, an attempt to conceive of the past in entirely new ways. This type of engagement with the past is antithetical to memory, according to Nora, because it regards the past *as past* and as problematic. *Le Pacte des loups* offers, however, another way of understanding this reappraisal. Rather than simply overturning the idea of a lived, communal connection to the past, one can, as the film does, attempt to re-member that connection.

Le Pacte des loups, for example, constructs the past in terms that are decidedly nonlinear. There is no unified narrative about history put forth in the film. Instead, what the film provides is a type of mapping of the various associations concerning the past that exist in contemporary culture. The eighteenth century the film re-presents, for example, is one marked by oppositions—libertinage and religious fundamentalism, aristocracy and the peasantry, reason and faith—oppositions that may not account for the reality of that century but that do correspond to the contemporary period's vision or memory of the eighteenth century. Moreover, because *Le Pacte des loups* conceives of this memory as essentially representational and particularly cinematic in nature—it is in many ways a type of memory created by the cinema—it opens up the space of "national" memory. The film builds a community of memory similar to the one implied in heritage films. However, this community comprises film spectators everywhere. The more cosmopolitan the spectator, the more he or she is able to assume this memory, which is itself an ensemble of images taken from films worldwide.

The version of history implied by *Le Pacte des loups* is, therefore, both national and postnational and both colonial and post-colonial. The film, for example, brings the question of the colonies into the narrative of the national past. Fronsac and Mani both came from Nouvelle France, and both remember that space within the context of the narrative. This alone suggests that the colonial past is part of both the history and memory of France. However, very subtle but very significant references to the colonies are also elsewhere in the film. The "beast" came, according to the film, from Africa. This suggests that the colonies exert an enormous influence over the events in metropolitan France, events that ultimately led to the Revolution. When Fronsac, at the end of the film, moves toward Senegal, it points to the continuation of colonial practice beyond the Revolution, making colonialism not merely a part of the history of the ancien régime but also of the republic. The film's inclusion of the colonies within the narrative seems, at one and the same time, to suggest the opening of history and memory to the colonial past and the continuation of existing processes of repression. For if the colonies make themselves felt in the film, neither Nouvelle France nor Senegal is actually ever shown. There are characters that have been to both spaces, and there are references to both within the film. Nevertheless, both remain completely outside of the frame. The film, therefore, visually references French history's colonial fracture. The colonies are an absent presence, in much the same way as they are in conventional French history.

This effect of fracture is heightened by the fact that from a purely visual perspective, the film's primary character is not Fronsac but his Native American companion, Mani. The film devotes a disproportionate amount of screen time to Mani relative to his place in the narrative. Moreover, whenever Mani is in the frame, he tends to dominate, to be at its center. Despite this position of visual dominance, Mani is all but absent from the story. The spectator knows relatively little about him, about his life, his history, his motivations, his thoughts. More important, nearly all that is known is told by Fronsac. Where Mani is concerned, Fronsac functions as the voice of history. This may be the most important element of the critique of history offered by the film. For if Fronsac acts, within the context of the narrative, as the agent of the Enlightenment, in the film's margins he functions as an agent of empire. In both the prehistory in Nouvelle France and the posthistory in Senegal, he embodies the idea of France's *mission civilisatrice*, a force of domination and suppression wielded in the name of liberty and equality. Fronsac's narration or absorption of Mani's history into his own story metaphorically renders the way in which colonial histories absorb the histories of those they colonize, rewriting and suppressing those histories and ultimately denying colonial subjects the right to speak for themselves. Moreover, Fronsac's failure to fully record or understand either his own history or that of Mani's points to France's inability to accurately understand either its own past or the past of those it has colonized. Ultimately, *Le Pacte des loups* fails to fill in the historical blanks of the colonial past, but it does point out that they are there. In that respect, it repeats Nora's gesture in *Les Lieux de mémoire*—proposing a reformulation of French history that it never fully achieves.

Problematic: Past to Present in *Le Fabuleux destin d'Amélie Poulain*

Christophe Gans's *Le Pacte des loups* reproduces and then undermines the space of history in order to enlarge it. However, it is not the only film to do so. As Gans himself suggests, Jean-Pierre Jeunet's *Le Fabuleux destin d'Amélie Poulain* (2001), released the same year, also works to both foreground and question history and memory. There are a number of similarities between the two films. *Amélie*, which grossed nearly $200 million internationally, was also one of the best-performing French films of all time. It was, like *Le Pacte des loups*, a generically hybrid film with striking visual images that was both critically acclaimed and condemned, garnering four Oscar nominations and four César awards but also setting off a polemic from critics who saw the film as inherently nostalgic, conservative, and even nationalist.[8]

Amélie recounts, in highly allegorical and "fabulous" fashion, the story of Amélie (Audrey Tatou), a waitress who lives in Montmartre. Isolated as a child, Amélie has difficulty connecting to others until the chance discovery of a box someone had hidden more than forty years previously in her apartment prompts her to become involved in the lives of those around her. These various interventions ultimately lead her to love with Nino (Mathieu

Kassovitz), a sex-shop and carnival worker who collects discarded identity photos. *Amélie* is sometimes regarded as a late example of the *cinéma du look*, a postmodern style of filmmaking that recycles images from film, literature, and popular culture. Influenced by advertising culture, films of the *cinéma du look* privilege visual spectacle over narrative substance. Although there are realist elements to the *cinéma du look*, it is more surreal in the way it plays with received expectations and in its highly focused, intense visual images.

Heritage films, as already suggested, tend to privilege visual spectacle over narrative, with the difference that they produce meticulously detailed, seemingly realist images of the past. The images of the *cinéma du look* are also spectacular. However, they are overtly recycled and, therefore, antirealist because they point to the representational or fictional nature of cinematic images. *Amélie* exhibits characteristics of both heritage films and the *cinéma du look*. Like *look* films, *Amélie* is a pastiche built of images taken from popular culture. It references or evokes numerous other films, for example, ranging from Marcel Carné's *Hôtel du Nord* (1938) to François Truffaut's *Jules et Jim* (1962), and it, therefore, imagines the past as a space of memory created through the cinema in much the same way as *Le Pacte des loups*. *Amélie* is also reminiscent of the *cinéma du look* in its attention to color, framing, and the general impact of the visual. However, the same elements that connect *Amélie* to the very postmodern *cinéma du look* also connect it, seemingly paradoxically, to the nostalgic and often backward-gazing heritage film. In that respect, *Amélie* tends to reproduce the space of heritage in order to call attention to the mechanisms involved in its construction.[9]

Nostalgia, especially nostalgia for the France of the 1930s and 1940s, is a defining characteristic of heritage films. Claude Berri's remakes of Marcel Pagnol's films, for example, have been read as doubly nostalgic for their recreation of a lost era and for their references to 1930s French cinema. Jeunet's *Amélie* is similarly nostalgic, and it also seems to reference the France of the 1930s and 1940s. Jean-Marc Lalanne and Didier Péron (2001), Patrice Girod (2001), Michel Rebichon (2001), and other critics have observed that *Amélie* evokes the Parisian photographs of Robert Doisneau, photographs that date to the 1940s. What is more, the overall image of Paris as it appears in *Amélie* is in many ways a composite of filmic representations of the city from that same period. The use of crane shots to capture Paris, for example, evokes René Clair's *Sous les toits de Paris* (1930), and Andrew observes that some shots in *Amélie* directly echo ones in specific films by Carné. The most notable of these is the scene in which Amélie skips stones on the Canal Saint Martin, where Arletty and Louis Jouvet argued in *Hôtel du Nord* (2004, 41). Tatou, in general, is dressed and shot in *Amélie* in a manner that recalls Arletty. This is particularly so when Amélie's very short hair is (inexplicably) done in an updo or wrapped in a scarf, both of which are styles Arletty often wore. Isabelle Vanderschelden also notes that the character of Amélie was originally called Garance, after Arletty's character in Carné's *Les Enfants du paradis,* which suggests that the similarities between the two are not entirely coincidental (2007, 37).

References to other French films are in *Amélie* as well. The overall whimsy of the film and the predominance of the color red are evocative of Albert Lamorisse's *Le Ballon rouge* (1956).[10] Jeunet has also stated that he more or less borrowed the title of the film from Sacha Guitry's *Le Destin fabuleux de Désirée Clary* (1942), and the use of voice-over narration in *Amélie* recalls Guitry's film. Moreover, as Andrew observes, *Amélie*'s opening scenes reference Guitry's *Le Roman d'un tricheur* (1936) both through the use of voice-over narration and through the use of personal anecdotes (2004, 41). *Amélie* also borrows from the films of the *Nouvelle Vague* or New Wave, most particularly the films of Truffaut. The use of Montmartre as a setting, for example, evokes Truffaut's *Les 400 coups* (1959), and Jeunet has acknowledged the influence of Truffaut's films, *Les 400 coups* in particular, on *Amélie.* He has pointed out, for example, that Claire Maurier, who plays café-owner Suzanne, also played Antoine Doinel's mother in Truffaut's film, and he has suggested that specific scenes in *Amélie* replicate scenes from Truffaut's film, among them a scene of pigeons flying (Jeunet, 2002). Other elements of *Amélie* also point to Truffaut's work. Amélie, like Antoine Doinel, looks to the cinema to escape the world, and in the scene where she is in the movie house, she is watching a clip from a Truffaut film, *Jules et Jim* (Jeunet, 2002). One of *Amélie* flashback scenes involving the character Dominique Bretodeau (Maurice Bénichou) involves humiliation at school, which also recalls Antoine's humiliation at school in *Les 400 coups.* And like Truffaut, Jeunet filmed outdoors, on location, something he had never previously done.

In addition to references to French cinema in *Amélie* are also a number of literary references, a characteristic that also links *Amélie* to the heritage film. Carné's scripts were, for the most part, written by the poet Jacques Prévert, whose works Jeunet reread before filming (Vanderschelden 2007, 37). Allusions to other French writers in *Amélie* include the observation by Thomas Sotinel in the April 25, 2001, *Le Monde* that Jeunet's presentation of many of the film's characters through a list of likes and dislikes evokes a technique used by writer Georges Perec. The film also contains a number of references to French art, specifically, impressionist art. Raymond Dufayel (Serge Merlin), one of the tenants in Amélie's building, is obsessed with Auguste Renoir's painting *Le Déjeuner des canotiers* (1881). Jeunet includes a shot of the Pont des Arts in the film, a scene that is the subject of another Renoir painting. Several scenes shot in Amélie's apartment, particularly those showing red wallpaper, evoke the work of Henri Matisse, specifically, the painting *La Desserte* (1908). The numerous still-life shots in the film recall the paintings of Paul Cézanne. The reference to the painting of Auguste Renoir within the film may also be seen as references to French cinema, since Renoir has already figured prominently in a number of French films. Bertrand Tavernier's heritage film *Un dimanche à la campagne* (1984), for example, is structured around several of Renoir's paintings. Jeunet also seems to reference Jean Renoir's film *Une partie de campagne* (1936) and the Pierre-Auguste Renoir painting of *La Balançoire* (1876), which the film restages when Amélie pushes her teddy bear on a swing.

Amélie also mimics the heritage film in its use of highly picturesque imagery. The film is composed of numerous postcard-like shots of the city, and even in medium shots, identifiable monuments or characteristic landscapes are often visible in the frame. For that reason, film critics Lalanne and Péron have described *Amélie* as "a moving post-card," and the first few shots of the film are presented as postcards of recognizable Parisian landmarks, such as the Eiffel Tour and the Sacré Coeur. Andrew argues that in constructing his film around the monuments, shops, street corners, and cobblestoned streets of Paris, Jeunet was borrowing "the iconography of poetic realism" (2004, 38), which would again suggest the recycling of previous filmic images. These images also reflect the iconography of the heritage film, with the sole difference being that the landscapes and images in the foreground are those of the city and not the countryside. Rather than distancing the film from heritage, the choice of Paris amplifies *Amélie*'s heritage quality because there is probably no greater heritage site in France than its capital.

It is not simply mise-en-scène but also substance that ties *Amélie* to the heritage film, however. Many critics, for example, have observed or criticized the use of stereotyped, stock characters in the film. Such characters once again evoke the French cinema of the 1930s (Vanderschelden 2007, 37). Pagnol films and their remakes, for example, rely heavily on stereotyped characters, as do many of the heritage films that have recognizably provincial settings. François de la Bretèque suggests that heritage films in general "reactivate a number of archetypes or stereotypes with their origins in folklore or literature" (1992, 63). Thus, the use of character types is again doubly evocative of heritage, both a specifically filmic heritage and a folkloric one. *Amélie* was branded an overtly racist and nationalist film by many French film critics precisely because it uses such characters. Serge Kaganski, editor of the journal *Inrockuptibles*, calls *Amélie* "a Front National of the cinema" and criticized the nostalgic and somewhat fantastic view of Paris the film presents. In a May 31, 2001, article in *Libération* (a national newspaper published in Paris), Kaganski also suggests that the absence of Africans or Arabs from a film set in a part of Paris where both are numerous as evidence that the film is racist and engaging in the same type of filmic nationalism of which heritage films have sometimes been accused. It is true that with regard to passers-by in the film, there is no one of non-European origin, absent three black youths in one of the metro-station scenes. However, it is also true that the grocer's assistant, Lucien, is played by the popular comedian Jamel Debbouze, who is of Moroccan origin, a fact that seems to contradict Kaganski's assertion.

Kaganski and those who, like him, regard *Amélie* as presenting an ethnically cleansed vision of Paris argue that the casting of Debbouze as a nonspecific grocer named Lucien is an act of effacement or white-washing of his non-European heritage. Others, including Alec G. Hargreaves, have suggested that Debbouze as Lucien may be an example of transparent casting, a gesture that reflects something like the opposite of racism (2006). I argue that such casting constitutes neither. Rather, it represents both an acknowledgment of France's multiethnic reality and a questioning of whether the image of France offered by contemporary heritage reflects that reality. Moreover, I suggest that Lucien's position in the film is key to understanding the film's overall presentation of Paris and, by extension, of France.

First of all, it must be observed that casting an actor of Moroccan origin as a character with a French sounding first name does not necessarily imply an erasure of his origins but perhaps a reflection of reality, because there are people in France with North African last names and "French" first names.[11] Moreover, the fact that Lucien has no last name does not set him apart from the other minor characters in the film. On the contrary, many if not most of the minor characters also lack last names, and Lucien's missing last name, therefore, makes him blend in. Despite the absence of a last name, it is probably obvious to the average French spectator that Debbouze is of Moroccan origin, and it is, therefore, difficult to imagine that there is no transference of this knowledge onto the character of Lucien. Vincendeau suggests that film audiences, in general, tend to merge actors with the characters they play, particularly when viewing established stars (2000, 7). Debbouze was well known in France as a Beur comedian and actor long before he appeared in Jeunet's film, and, in several scenes, Debbouze incorporates characteristics associated with his comedic persona, particularly his speech patterns and gestures (Vanderschelden 2005, 66). Debbouze's injured, unusable left hand, another signature of the actor, is inscribed into the film by the various camera angles used to frame him, although no explanation is ever given for this injured hand within the context of the narrative. The issue of the hand remains unresolved unless the spectator draws on existing knowledge about the life of Debbouze, who lost use of that hand in an accident. Thus, *Amélie* more or less forces the spectator to conflate Debbouze with Lucien in order to resolve a question that the film itself refuses to address.

Debbouze as Lucien is not the only example of ambiguous casting in *Amélie*. Mathieu Kassovitz, who is also very well known in France, plays the role of Amélie's love interest, Nino Quincampoix. Kassovitz is of Jewish Eastern European origin, and his own filmmaking has tended to foreground both his origins and the ethnic diversity of Paris in general. Yet, in the film, he plays a character with an almost stereotypically French name. Dominique Bretodeau, another very stereotypically French character within the film, is played by Maurice Bénichou, who was born in Algeria. While this is perhaps less well known to the spectator, it is of interest since it points to a pattern in Jeunet's casting. Finally, it is fairly clear that Jeunet originally intended to cast British actress Emily Watson as Amélie, which would have added a further layer of diversity to the mix.[12]

The significance of such casting within the space of the film is a puzzle that the spectator must figure out. It is doubtful that it constitutes a denial or negation of the city's ethnic diversity, since Jeunet could have made different choices than to cast at least two and possibly three actors who were known to be either not French or to be French of Jewish or North African origin. Rather, these casting choices point *within* the film to a diversity that lies *outside* of it. The casting of those of foreign or immigrant origin as stereotypical French characters invites speculation on the reality of the city's population, even if the film does not directly comment on it. *Amélie* works to suggest that it is impossible to know what someone's origin is merely by looking at them because the film consistently undercuts the idea that people can be judged by their appearances.

The characters in *Amélie* are also almost all defined by their personal pasts—or at least that is what they believe. Amélie, for example, is a girl who must learn to overcome the isolation and solitude of her past. This is made clear not only by the details of her history but also by the way in which the past acts directly, almost like a character, in the narrative of her life. The film begins, as the voice-over narration in the opening scene indicates, with the resurgence or intrusion of the past upon the present, a resurgence that presents a puzzle that Amélie must work to solve (see fig. 3). The past that reemerges in the film's opening sequence is not, it is true, Amélie's personal past. It is, rather, that of Dominique Bretodeau, a person completely unknown and seemingly unconnected to Amélie. Bretodeau's past emerges in the form of a box hidden in Amélie's apartment, and this box provides a connection between the two characters, a connection that had long been there but that had remained hidden. It is in trying to resolve the mystery of Bretodeau's past that Amélie comes into contact with most of the other characters in the film, characters who are also, to some degree, prisoners of their past. This suggests that the past—the way it is remembered and perceived—is one of the principal subjects of the film, a suggestion reinforced by the framing of the shot in which Amélie discovers Bretodeau's box. The camera, in this scene, shoots from behind the wall where the box is located, and Amélie is framed outside the wall by the hole made when a loose tile was removed. The composition of this shot suggests that the point of view through which the spectator witnesses the action in this scene is actually *that of the past*. Moreover, because this scene occurs so early in the film, it functions to force identification between the spectator and the past, not merely between the spectator and Amélie. This means that it is the movement of the *past* through Montmartre, rather than Amélie's personal movement, that we follow as the film unfolds.

This trek with and through the past leads Amélie both to overcome her own past and to help others overcome theirs. In her first encounter, she returns the newly discovered box to its owner, Dominique Bredoteau. Dominique, in some measure, also returns the past to her. Because he and his family once lived in the same building she now occupies, they are able to reveal to Amélie a great deal about those who live there. Thus, her encounter with Dominique leads Amélie to another with her landlady, Madeleine Wallace, someone who is held captive by the idea that her long-dead husband never loved her. Just as she does for Dominique, Amélie frees Madeleine by transmitting the past to her, and just as with Dominique, she does this by returning to Madeleine something she had "lost."

In place of the missing or hidden box of memories, what Amélie "returns" to Madeleine Wallace is a letter from her dead husband. This letter, according to Amélie, has been lost in the mail for forty years. Like Dominique's box, this letter constitutes a sort of anamnesis, a resurgence of the past on the present. The case of Madeleine Wallace, however, is also very different from that of Dominique Bredoteau. For if Amélie returns an authentic past

Fig. 3. Amélie (Audrey Tatou) uncovering the past in the form of a box hidden behind the wall in *Le Fabuleux destin d'Amélie Poulain* (2001).

to Dominique, what she "returns" to Madeleine is an invented one. In order to correct Madeleine's belief that she was unloved, Amélie takes the letters Madeleine received from her husband when he was alive—dry, mundane, factual letters—and cuts and pastes them into a passionate love letter. This past is not, therefore, exactly Madeleine's, but it is not a wholly imagined past, either. It is, instead, a pastiche, the facts of the past rearranged to convey a new message. This letter may be a metaphor for the film itself, which is also a reconstitution of the past.

Images, not words, form the basis of another of Amélie's interventions with one of her neighbors. Like Madeleine Wallace, Raymond Dufayel is a prisoner of the past. Dufayel is an artist, a painter, but he is unable to actually create anything new. Instead, he endlessly repaints Renoir's *Le Déjeuner des canotiers*, attributing his fixation on his inability to accurately capture or understand the figure of a young woman in the painting. Dufayel, unlike Madeleine, is physically and not merely psychologically trapped, as he suffers from a brittle-bone condition that prevents him from leaving his apartment. As with Madeleine, Amélie resolves Dufayel's problem by fabricating or creating a solution. She secretly commandeers a video camera Dufayel uses to observe her (because she resembles the girl in the painting), and she turns it on the outside world transmitting to Dufayel the present he cannot himself see. However, the images she provides him are, like the letter she makes for Madeleine, largely composed of other images—they are pastiche images put together to form something new. By presenting these reconstituted images to Dufayel, she convinces him to reinvent Renoir's image rather than merely reproduce it—something he does by repainting Renoir's painting in an abstract-expressionist style.

It should be clear from these examples that the transmission of the past, whether real or reimagined, is central to the narrative of Jeunet's film. The specific form the past takes and the function it has vary from person to person. In nearly all cases, however, the past, in whatever form, is something that must be overcome. Amélie, too, eventually overcomes the solitude of her past by entering into a relationship with Nino. Nino, who has been obsessed with reconstituting the abandoned photos of others, moves forward by entering into a relationship with Amélie. Amélie moves Joseph past his obsession with Gina by inventing a new past in which Georgette is interested in Joseph. She also moves Hippolito past his history of scorn and rejection by inventing a past in which his work is admired.

Like the character of Amélie, the film that shares her name reinvents the past by appropriating and reworking existing images. It is this recycling of older images of Paris, for example, that gives *Amélie* its ambiguous temporality. The film, like the character, offers not the real past nor the real Paris but images of Paris and the national past that have been cut and pasted from older images. This aspect of the film is what has led to its being called nostalgic because it has been interpreted as the expression of a desire to return to some idealized moment in the city's and the nation's past. However, this reading seems problematic, given that the existence of a clear parallel between Amélie's fictional re-creations and the version of Paris offered by the film of which she is a part. Like Madeleine's letter, the film is a fiction, a representation made by fusing other representations, including films, fairytales, paintings, and texts. The film, therefore, cannot be nostalgic precisely because the Paris it depicts never existed. If it never existed, it cannot be recovered, and nostalgia, by definition, is the expression of a desire to return to something that once existed but has since been lost.

Returning for a moment to the evocation of the films of Marcel Carné in *Amélie*, Carné, unlike other Parisian filmmakers such as Truffaut or Louis Feuillade, filmed the city on soundstages, not out in the streets. His Paris, therefore, was also a fiction, his own creation. Jeunet, it seems, studied the sets Alexandre Trauner created for Carné and had his production crew study them as well (Vanderschelden 2007, 37). It is these soundstages that Jeunet reproduced in *Amélie*, but he did so not by using or reproducing Trauner's sets but by filming on location, by taking the *real* city and making it conform to a *fiction* from the past. Because the real city does not resemble this fiction, Jeunet was forced to modify it, and this process of "modification" is visible in the space of the film—it draws attention to itself. Thus, *Amélie*'s restaging of Carné does not function to valorize Carné's image of Paris. Rather, it functions as an assertion that *that* Paris—the image of Paris to which many people cling—is a fiction, a distortion of the real.[13]

Does *Amélie*, then, like *Le Pacte des loups*, suggest that *any* engagement with the past is problematic? It seems not. If, in most cases, the past in *Amélie* functions to confine or trap characters or even the spectator, there is one case in which the sense of confinement derives from a disjuncture between past and present, and in this case, the remedy is precisely an engagement with the past. Dominique Bretodeau, the first character in whose life Amélie intervenes, is not trapped by his past. He is, rather, trapped by its *absence*, and what frees Dominique is the recuperation of the past. At the moment Amélie returns the box to Dominique, he literally relives his past, as a wave of memory washes over him, and it is this recovery of a past from which he had been alienated that brings Dominique out of isolation.

Through Dominique, *Amélie* calls for a rejection of idealized, fictional images of the past and a reengagement with the reality. This is a call that reinforced through the film's reproduction of the photographs of Robert Doisneau. Doisneau was one of a group of left-wing, humanist photographers, including

Henri Cartier-Bresson and Willy Ronis, who photographed Paris in the 1940s and 1950s with the aim of capturing the lived reality of the working classes, or the *classes populaires* (Hamilton 1997, 94). As part of their project, these photographers shot all parts of the city, including the *banlieue* and the *bidonvilles*, or shanty towns. Many of the photographs taken by Doisneau have become iconic emblems of France and Frenchness. However, the photographs elevated to iconic status are not, for the most part, from the Paris project. Rather, many of the best-remembered and most widely circulated images are staged photographs that were taken for popular magazines and, specifically, magazines in the United States. Doisneau's photographs, therefore, point to a tension between the memory of Paris that exists in the popular imagination—as expressed in those staged photographs—and the real Paris of the past that has been forgotten. By recycling Doisneau's images of Paris, *Amélie* foregrounds the artificiality of such idealized images and calls for the engagement with the real past—as suggested by the lost or forgotten images of the banlieue and bidonville.[14]

There are other places where the film points to a disconnect between the stereotype of Paris circulated in filmic and photographic images and the reality. For example, there are moments in the film in which a compressed zoom is used to focus in on the character of Amélie. The use of that shot is particularly interesting because it is closely associated with Mathieu Kassovitz. Kassovitz rather famously used that shot in *La Haine* (1995), a film that foregrounds both the ethnic diversity of Paris and the failure to adequately recognize and accept that diversity. Moreover, the specific function of that shot in *La Haine* is to focus in on the protagonists, a multiracial trio consisting of a black Frenchman, a Jewish Frenchman, and a Frenchman of North African origin. The use of the compressed zoom in *Amélie* evokes the use of it in *La Haine*, primarily because it is used in the same way. Thus, the shot becomes a marker within the film for an ethnically diverse city that lies outside of it, an ethnically diverse city that was represented in Kassovitz's film but that is absent from Jeunet's. Similarly, the film's presentation of Montmartre as ethnically homogenous, when it is widely known to be ethnically diverse, draws attention not only to the absence of diversity in *Amélie* but also to the absence of diversity in films about Paris in general, particularly because *Amélie* is largely composed of images from such films. Read this way, *Amélie* calls into question not the reality of Paris but the false images of the city that exist in many people's minds. Jeunet has repeatedly said that what he created in *Amélie* was not a nostalgic image of a Paris that has been lost but the image of a Paris that does not and never has existed (Jeunet 2001).[15]

Ultimately then, *Amélie* represents the collective image or memory of Paris as constructed and artificial, a stereotype that is at odds with both the real past and the real present. This is apparent in everything from the unimagin- ably clean Parisian streets, to the postcard-like images of a city that seems trapped in a perpetual past, to the digital enhancement of color in the film. It is also apparent in the numerous references to impressionism scattered throughout the film. Impressionism is not realist in its impetus. It does not try to represent the world as it is but to record an impression of the world, to capture the essence of the way it is perceived. *Amélie* is similarly impres- sionistic, recording *the idea of Paris* that exists in the contemporary world.

This brings us back to the character of Lucien. Lucien is a character whose name reveals nothing about his identity, and, in fact, he is the only significant character in the film about whose origins and personal history nothing is revealed. This draws attention to itself and has caused those inclined to view the film as racist to charge that Lucien's presumably foreign origins have been erased from the film, whitewashed like the image of Paris the film presents. I suggest that rather than effacing Lucien's origins, this act of suppression func- tions to foreground them, or rather to foreground their absence, particularly because the issues of the past and of origins are so central elsewhere in the film. This, in turn, invites the spectator to wonder about Lucien, about his family, about his childhood, about his fascination with Princess Diana, about his interest in painting, and several other details concerning his life that are never explained. The spectator, therefore, is invited to imagine a history for Lucien in much the same way as Amélie and Nino imagine histories and identities for the people in the photos Nino collects. In imagining Lucien's past, it would be difficult not to think about that fact that he is played by an actor of Moroccan origin, and this invites a reimagining of Paris that is open to the presence of those of Moroccan or other origin, a past that exists in reality but does not exist within the space of the film. Rather than valorizing a stereotyped image of Paris past, therefore, *Amélie* functions to deconstruct such an image. The film foregrounds stereotyped visions of French identity only to point to their fabulous, which is to say, fictional nature.

Beyond simply challenging the content of the past, however, *Amélie* also functions to challenge its structure. The film, like *Le Pacte des loups*, works to undermine any perceived vertical connection between past and present and to propose a series of horizontal connections that link individuals in the present. If *Amélie* is nostalgic or retro, it is as Isabel Vanderschelden suggests, vaguely so—its precise temporality is unclear. We do not, therefore, have a sense of connectedness between our present and a particular moment in the past precisely because we cannot identify which moment of the past we are ostensibly watching. Similarly, the flow of narrative time in the film is ambiguous. It is difficult, for example, to know precisely how many days of Amélie's life are represented in the space of the narrative. Time in the film seems to have stood still, to have become irrelevant. Ultimately, therefore, it is movement rather than time that drives the film. As suggested, we follow the movement of the past through the film, and we specifically follow its movement through *space*. This substitution of space for time implies a new, relational or horizontal model of temporality, rather than the typical ancestral or vertical one, a model that conceives of past and present in terms of interaction rather than in terms of descent.

Harvesting and Gathering: Heritage in Varda's *Les Glaneurs et la glaneuse*

Le Pacte des loups and *Amélie* both function to simultaneously reproduce and undermine conventional images of and narratives about France and its past. Agnès Varda's *Les Glaneurs et la glaneuse* (2000), on the other hand, does not merely call for the creation of a new heritage, it actually moves toward its creation. *Les Glaneurs et la glaneuse* achieves this not by reinventing or restaging the past but by reinterpreting it. The film uses cinema to create a spatial rather than a temporal mapping of the past in order to explore the forgotten or hidden connections that exist between the real and the ideal, the center and the margins. A documentary shot on digital video, *Les Glaneurs et la glaneuse* is a film about gleaning, the long-held tradition and right in France of recuperating the fruit, vegetables, or crops left over after the harvest. Through its interrogation not only of the traditional forms of gleaning but also of the modern variations that act takes and through its exploration of the types of people involved in the act of gleaning, the film foregrounds France's traditions and its rural and artistic heritage, while creating a space wherein even the most seemingly marginal citizen becomes connected to all of these.

From the time of its opening at the fifty-third annual Cannes Film Festival, critical attention has been focused on the film's exploration of waste and excess in modern society (Rosello, "Agnès Varda's," 2001, 30). While waste and excess are certainly major themes in the film, the focus on waste has tended to obscure the film's treatment of heritage. Despite the fact that *Les Glaneurs et la glaneuse* is a documentary, it strongly resembles those narrative films grouped under the rubric of heritage. First and foremost, *Les Glaneurs et la glaneuse* foregrounds rural France and privileges the French provincial landscape. Specifically, the film represents the rural as the quintessential site of heritage, and it presents the rural as a space of tradition and community. What is more, the film visually reproduces the shot composition of heritage films through its alternation of picturesque long shots that emphasize landscape and ensemble or medium shots that suggest harmony between people and the land. The film also includes nostalgic, postcard-like tableau shots that emphasize continuity and tradition in a specifically rural space, shots reinforced by its picaresque structure, which presents areas of France ranging from Arras to the Jura to Arles. In many respects, *Les Glaneurs et la glaneuse* recalls the classical tour de France as recounted in G. Bruno's book *Le Tour de la France par deux enfants* (1877), a connection that links it doubly to heritage.[16]

Varda's film, like many other heritage films, continuously foregrounds and references French cultural heritage through both architecture and art. It begins with a meditation on a painting, specifically, Jean-François Millet's painting *Les Glaneuses* (1857), from which the film derives its title. This particular painting is referenced, described, or shown in various places throughout the film. Millet's painting, however, is not the only work of art featured. The film also foregrounds another painting of gleaners, Jules Breton's painting *Les Glaneuses* (1854), which predates the Millet, as well as a number of other paintings, most notably by Vincent Van Gogh. Finally, *Les Glaneurs et la glaneuse* evokes paintings in the film's shot composition and its mise-en-scène even when it does not directly represent them. Varda often "re-creates" famous paintings by filming scenes that resemble them, and she consistently and repeatedly foregrounds the art and architecture of every region she visits. Art and, specifically, painting therefore, shape *Les Glaneurs et la glaneuse* in the same way that they structure narrative heritage films such as Bertrand Tavernier's *Un dimanche à la campagne* (1984) and Alain Corneau's *Tous les matins du monde* (1991).

Art, high culture, tradition, and the act of gleaning are all woven together in Varda's film, and this is apparent even in the first sequence. As the film opens, the camera presents a close-up of the Dictionnaire Larousse and then focuses in on the volume E-G, which contains the entry on gleaning. A hand, presumably Varda's, removes the volume from a shelf and opens it, flipping through pages and eventually stopping on the definition of the word "glaner," to glean. In voice-over, Varda reads the Larousse's definition of "glaner," which is "to gather after the harvest." The camera cuts to a close-up of the page. Visible in the frame is a black-and-white reproduction of Millet's painting *Les Glaneuses*. The camera then cuts to an extreme close-up of the definition of the word "glaner," specifically, the part of the definition that cites Millet's painting. A cut brings a long shot of the interior of the Musée d'Orsay and then to a series of medium shots of various people looking at or photographing Millet's painting in the museum.

This opening sequence emphasizes the privileged position of Millet's painting and art in general in French cultural heritage. It also suggests a connection among Varda's film, Millet's painting, and the broader French heritage. The Larousse, for example, may be considered a heritage work because it is probably the authoritative dictionary in France and because language is considered one of the central elements of French cultural heritage. What is more, the page of the Larousse featured in the film contains a reproduction or representation Millet's painting, which is also a significant part of the nation's cultural heritage. The Musée d'Orsay is an excellent example of nineteenth-century architecture, the site of a former royal residence, the d'Orsay Palace, and one of the earliest train stations to be built in France. It was transformed from a train station into an art museum, and it is now the official home of many of the better-known works of French nineteenth-century art. Most interesting, this transformation from train station to museum was one of the projects undertaken as part of François Mitterrand's *grands travaux*. All of this makes of the d'Orsay one of the preeminent heritage spaces in France.

In its initial sequence, *Les Glaneurs et la glaneuse* evokes a number of different *lieux de mémoire* and, like narrative heritage films, uses them to point to and valorize France's cultural heritage. The film, however, does more than simply reference these spaces. It references and appropriates these works and sites of memory to inscribe itself in the space of heritage. This is done, principally, by the way in which the film presents itself as a re-production or re-presentation of the Millet painting from which it takes its name. *Les Glaneurs et la glaneuse*, just like Millet's *Les Glaneurs*, features people in the act of gleaning. The film in many ways is a reproduction of the painting in contemporary form. It is, therefore, like many heritage films, a remake or an adaptation of a previous heritage work. Varda effectively takes what was paint and canvas and remakes it into a digital image.

While the film's gesture of reproduction or imitation may seem obvious, its significance is less so. Millet's painting performs a specific social function in its representation of gleaners in a field. The women featured in the painting came from the lower classes, and constituted, at the time they lived, some of the most marginal and marginalized of France's inhabitants, being both women and poor. Through his painting, Millet moved these women from the margin to the center, taking them out of the space in which they existed and placing them in the space of official or high culture. Over time, this gesture became magnified, as the painting featuring these marginalized citizens became assimilated into the space of official culture. Thus, women who were marginalized when they lived become icons of heritage, part of society's center. Their likeness hangs in one of the museums dedicated to French culture, and they embody a rural pastoral vision that is central to contemporary constructions of Frenchness. Millet's painting, therefore, may have reproduced or valorized an existing notion of heritage by foregrounding rural France, but it also enlarged that space, inscribing into it those who were previously excluded. *Les Glaneurs et la glaneuse* functions in the same way, moving the homeless, immigrants, gypsies, and the mentally ill away from society's margins and towards the center. For that reason, the film is more than a reproduction of Millet's image. It is also a reproduction of Millet's gesture.

The act of gleaning is not incidental to this process. Gleaning, as the definition implies, involves taking what has been discarded and recuperating it or giving it value. It is an act of redemption in both the literal and figurative sense. The film presents gleaning as a communal, national, traditional act, so participating in gleaning is, to a certain degree, participating in the space of heritage. This suggests that it is part of the nation's tradition to bring in those who are excluded, and this could be read as an argument that accepting and integrating "outsiders" has long been part of French heritage. Moreover, Varda also presents herself as a gleaner (see fig. 4). She repeatedly links filmmaking and gleaning, filmmakers and gleaners, specifically by including or gleaning shots, scenes, and footage into her film that filmmakers are normally expected to cut or throw away. This includes numerous shots of her hand in front of the camera and one of her camera lens dangling while she shoots. However, Varda gleans not only footage but also those in that footage. By filming the marginalized, she recuperates and redeems them, placing them, through her film, at the cultural center.

The recuperation or redemption of the marginalized is accomplished through a double gesture—it is both active and passive. By participating in the act of gleaning, those in *Les Glaneurs et la glaneuse* are participating in a heritage that is presented as inclusive. By being filmed in the act of gleaning,

Fig. 4. Agnès Varda posing as a gleaner in *Les Glaneurs et la glaneuse* (2000).

they become part of a work of art, literally becoming heritage. Gleaning, therefore, becomes a metaphor for a type of social and cultural integration. It is both the expression of a desire for inclusion and the mechanism by which one may be included. Belonging is no longer about ancestry or lineage but about participation in a process that binds the individual to the community through history, tradition, and the land.

This association between gleaning and integration is established through the progression of images in the film. *Les Glaneurs et la glaneuse* first explores traditional, rural forms of gleaning and then passes to images of modern gleaners, many of them in an urban setting. Following the opening sequence, which ends with the scene in the Musée d'Orsay, the film cuts to a long shot of an older woman standing in a field in front of a traditional *mas de provence* (a traditional farmhouse in Provence). The woman, who speaks in a marked regional accent, talks about the act of gleaning and defines gleaning as "*l'esprit d'antan*" or "the spirit of the old days." She talks of how she used to glean, and as she does, the film intercuts old black-and-white film of women gleaning, film that dates presumably to the silent era of the late nineteenth century. The woman, of course, represents the traditional gleaners, such as those in Millet's painting, and the film footage constitutes yet another nineteenth-century image of women gleaning. The parallel use of Millet's painting of women gleaning and then the film of women gleaning creates, in a classic use of montage, a parallel between the two images. Moreover, Varda's image of women in a field, which is placed in between the other images, connects *Les Glaneurs et la glaneuse* to both the painting and the black-and-white film, establishing a diachronic chain of reproduction from the Millet painting to Varda's film.

Following this scene of gleaning is one set in a café where various people of different generations discuss gleaning and their experience with it. This sequence, like the opening sequence, links the act of gleaning to France's rural heritage and through it to the broader, past-oriented construction of French identity. In place of heritage works, like the dictionary or the painting, the film foregrounds images of people who evoke this heritage-based identity: the woman in the field in front of the *mas*, different generations drinking in a café. These people and places, located in southern France, a regional strongly associated with the rural pastoral component of current models of French-ness, link the act of gleaning to both the spaces and the people pictured and convey the idea that gleaning is quintessentially French and rooted in a long French history, an impression reinforced by the woman's assertion that the act of gleaning constitutes the "spirit of old." Moreover, the film later reaffirms this idea of gleaning as a specifically French tradition and right by featuring a lawyer, Maître Dessaud, who cites the history of the legal foundation of the right to glean in France.

If these sequences confirm that *Les Glaneurs et la glaneuse* re-creates the space of heritage, it is other sequences, linked to those already described, that work to expand it. As a transition from early scenes that present gleaning as an act of tradition, the film cuts back to Millet's painting as Varda comments, in voice-over, that "if gleaning belongs to another age, the gesture remains unchanged in our society of plenty." This statement is an assertion of continuity, an affirmation that the act of gleaning links the present to the past. In this way, the act itself becomes a site of memory, and those who participate in it become members of the broader community, linked to a common past through the continuation of a tradition. This suggests that memory, too, is an act of gleaning. Through memory, that which might otherwise be forgotten or discarded is redeemed or maintained, that which was at the periphery is brought back to the center. This implies that all of those who remember the past are also gleaners, and it binds these "traditional" inhabitants of France to the less-traditional inhabitants who glean in modern spaces. It is also an expression of a new conception of heritage, one that is spatial and relational rather than familial. The people in *Les Glaneurs et la glaneuse* are connected by a shared behavior that they have "inherited" by choice rather than by a name or trait they inherited by blood.

The next sequence features a series of images of urban waste and garbage, with a hip-hop song that discusses gleaning. Again, the use of montage draws the urban into the space of heritage by creating a connection between urban garbage and what is left behind in the field after a harvest. This similarly suggests that the urban and the rural are tied together and that gleaners in both spaces are connected through their common act. Varda comments on this sense of direct connection between urban and rural, tradition and modernity by affirming in voice-over, "In the city and in the country, yesterday and today, it is the same gesture of gleaning." The film reinforces this sense of connection in a subsequent scene in which a lawyer, Maître Espié, discusses the legality of urban gleaning, a scene that parallels the earlier legal discussion of more traditional forms of gleaning.

The remainder of *Les Glaneurs et la glaneuse* explores the idea that gleaning is the embodiment of France's cultural heritage and that, therefore, anyone who gleans is a member of that heritage community. The film repeatedly uses this idea to link marginalized populations to those who occupy a central position in the space of French heritage. In one scene are various people gleaning potatoes. While this includes those who conform to stereotype of French people, it also includes a black woman and a man who may be of North African origin. As volunteers for the charity *Les Restos du Coeur*, both gather potatoes to feed the homeless. What unites them is both their mutual participation in a communal act of gleaning and their mutual difference from the stereotype of the rural peasant or even the French citizen. Varda makes no comment about the origins of either the man or the woman, and they become, like the others who gather potatoes, simply figures in a sort of rural pastoral commentary on contemporary France.

These scenes function to enlarge the space of heritage, to modernize it. They also expand the connection established in the film's opening sequence between gleaning and art. The film foregrounds urban artists who make their art from things they find left on the curb or in the trash. Some of these artists, like Louis Pons, are well known and well established. Others, like a man of Russian origin who built a palace of trash, are less well known or at least less respected. Through the inclusion of such artists, the film again links gleaning to official culture, specifically, art, and it again includes a diverse group of people in the heritage space it affirms. Moreover, by linking the specifically urban act of urban gleaning to high culture, *Les Glaneurs et la glaneuse* opens a space for others who glean in an urban setting, be they poor, homeless, or merely *brocanteurs* (people who collect things). Through the juxtaposition of artists with those who glean food, whether from markets or trash bins, the film creates equivalence between the two, suggesting that the person who lives on what others throw away is as central to the culture as the one who makes art from what others throw away.

The exploration of urban gleaning in *Les Glaneurs et la glaneuse* also affirms the communal nature of gleaning. Even if gleaners often seem to be working alone, the film suggests they are acting on behalf of or in the interest of others. This suggestion takes many forms. Some of those filmed gathering potatoes for charity literally are working to feed others. Others, like the artists, are gathering to create something intended to be shared. One of the most interesting examples of this communal side of gleaning may be found in the sequence depicting Charlie, a man of Asian descent, and Saloman, a man of African origin. Charlie and Saloman live together, making a living, at least in some measure, from what they glean.[17] It is Saloman, in particular, who gleans, and he is filmed in the act of doing so. He gleans food, including bread, meat, and fish from markets and supermarkets, and he also gleans televisions, refrigerators, and appliances, which he repairs, from the street. Saloman's act of gleaning is communal in that he shares what he finds with Charlie. But it is also communal in the larger sense because both Charlie and Saloman often share their food with their neighbors. Finally, Saloman's gleaning and repair of broken appliances are also communal because he takes what was cast away, makes it useful again, and returns it to the community from which it was rejected. His act also recalls the function of the film itself, which is to return to society that which it has cast aside.[18]

Another person filmed in the act of gleaning is a man name Alain. Alain is first filmed gathering discarded vegetables at a market near the Gare de Montparnasse. He lives only on what he finds, making him one of the most dedicated gleaners in the film. Moreover, despite the fact that he has an advanced degree, Alain lives in a homeless shelter, sells magazines whose proceeds support the homeless, and in the evening gives free literacy classes, primarily to African immigrants. Alain's actions, from selling the magazine to teaching reading, are individual and communal. Like Saloman, he gleans alone, but unlike Saloman, the wider community benefits from his actions. What is more, like Saloman's act of repairing discarded appliances, Alain similarly returns to society that which it rejects, specifically by transmitting the (written) language to those newly arrived in France and who are often refused by the society at large. Alain, therefore, like Varda herself, transmits heritage, in his case through the language, and he uses this transmission to inscribe the marginalized in the space of the nation or at least of national culture. Moreover, it is, in large measure through Varda's representation of Alain, that the film conveys the idea that gleaning, in the broadest sense, means precisely this sort of act.

Charlie, Saloman, and Alain all function in the film to enlarge the definition of gleaning to make it mean not simply the act of gathering food or objects that have been rejected or discarded but also to mean the creation of a communal space in which those who have been rejected are similarly recuperated. Other points in the film also emphasize this. Varda's own repeated insistence that she is a gleaner and that her camera is the tool she uses to glean repeat the idea that people may be brought from the margin to the center in much the same way food that has been discarded may be recuperated. Moreover, the film includes a scene with psychoanalyst Jean Laplanche, who presents psychoanalysis as an act of gleaning by explaining that his interest in psychoanalysis was to "attempt to locate the Other, in a position of priority with respect to the subject." Laplanche's act of gleaning, then, echoes that of the film in that it is an act by which individuals regarded as alien or other, those who are refused by the center or Subject, are assimilated into the center. Finally, the film seems to point directly to the idea that this is a theme of her film by ending Deux ans après (2002), the sequel to Les Glaneurs et la glaneuse, with footage from a demonstration against the Front National. Through Laplanche's theory, through the acts of individuals like Alain and through the film's diverse images, gleaning is redefined from the act of gathering food into the act of incorporating the Other into the Subject or of moving those who are marginalized into the center.

Ultimately, then, Les Glaneurs et la glaneuse functions to create an alternative or enlarged space of heritage, one in which everyone who gleans is included. Through this alternative heritage, the film constructs a vision of France that is, as with the traditional model, rooted in the rural, in a long-standing past, and in tradition but that, unlike the traditional model, is conceived of as evolving. As a result of this evolving space of heritage, everyone, from gypsies, to immigrants, to homeless youths, to artists, to lawyers, to psychoanalysts, is bound together into a community, presumably a national community, through their shared gestures of gleaning. Although this gleaning has many forms, the film inscribes all of them as a corrective act against the excesses and waste of modern society, a waste and excess that, according to Mireille Rosello, is less the "result of cracks in the harvesting system . . . [than] the redefinition of what is acceptable, good, first-rate" (2001, 31). In numerous sequences, the film connects waste and excess to the refusal of society to include or accept individuals such as immigrants or gypsies, by suggesting that it is greed and greed alone that leads society to deny the right to glean and to refuse many of those who are gleaners. Moreover, just as the numerous gleaners in the film challenge society's definition of what is acceptable and what must be rejected, so does the film itself call for a redefinition of who is acceptable and who must be rejected from modern society and, specifically, French society. Thus, *Les Glaneurs et la glaneuse* challenges the construction of heritage, even as it valorizes its existence. It places the marginalized, those who lie outside of modern society's culture of excess, at the center of tradition and heritage, and it places those at the center of this culture of excess outside of the space of heritage.

In so doing, the film also proposes a new model of memory, a new relationship of present to past. If the nineteenth century proposed that memory is a passive connection tying an individual directly to a specific moment of the past, that it resided in objects and spaces or sites, *Les Glaneurs et la glaneuse* suggests that memory is active and participatory and that it resides in the community created by participation. If the nineteenth century produced a model of memory that regarded the connection of past to present as linear and unitary, the film proposes a prismatic memory, in which a single act, a single space, a single gesture may resonate in different ways for different people. Memory, according to the film, is a form of gleaning. It is a sweep in all directions, an attempt to recover that which lies at the margins of consciousness, an effort to bring it back to the center. *Les Glaneurs et la glaneuse* conceives of heritage in similar terms, not as the reappropriation of the nineteenth century's rigid, hierarchical worldview but a multicultural gesture that creates a place for all in France. The vision of heritage articulated through the film regards diversity not as a threat to French culture but as the logical outcome of a French tradition that has, historically, sought to recuperate and redeem rather than to exclude or cast aside.

Agnès Varda's *Les Glaneurs et la glaneuse* (2000), Christophe Gans's *Le Pacte des loups* (2001), and Jean-Pierre Jeunet's *Le Fabuleux Destin d'Amélie Poulain* (2001) are three radically different films, united by a common engagement with the past and particularly the national past. All three films engage, whether directly or indirectly, the question of memory and specifically the question of how the collective or national past has been remembered and inscribed. Through this engagement, all three films seek to problematize the notion of national heritage, pointing either to spaces and events from the national past that have selectively been omitted or rewritten or to hidden continuities between past and present. Moreover, all three films engage with the past in order to call for a revision and expansion of the idea of heritage, one that includes those whom the traditional model of heritage would seem to exclude.

These films interrogate the content of the current construction of the national past and of national memory. However, none of them ever directly challenges the existence of the national past, nor do they really directly challenge the idea that the national past has shaped the national present. Instead, they attempt to redefine the content of the national past and to reimagine the relationship of past to present. In that regard, these films, and the broader cultural discourse they embody, do not constitute a challenge to prevailing constructions of French identity. Instead they constitute an evolution of that construction, an evolution that seeks to construct a past that better accounts for the national present.

4

Memory's Blind Spots: Immigration, Integration, and the Post-Colonial Heritage

Sociologist and author Azouz Begag asserts, "[A]ll the sociopolitical issues related to the incorporation of French people of Maghrebi origin into mainstream society connect up with constructions of their collective memory. Without memory, one cannot claim to be fully part of a society and its History" (2006, 56).[1] Begag's assessment runs directly counter to the dominant interpretation of such "problems" of integration. Where the dominant interpretation has been that religion and cultural practice block the integration of France's ethnic minorities, Begag poses the problem in terms of collective memory. His statement is interesting because although it challenges conventional wisdom concerning the integration process, it does not challenge the fundamental assumptions about the basis of national or collective identity.

Begag, for example, borrows directly from the dominant culture the idea that shared history and memory are central to national identity. However, if both history and memory are typically regarded as fixed, stable, and, in some respects, hereditary, Begag suggests, through his use of the word "constructions," that both are produced by the culture itself and that they are, therefore, neither fixed nor stable. Moreover, in suggesting that it is the "construction" of the collective memory of France's ethnic minorities that is at the root of the problem, Begag shifts the responsibility for integrating minorities away from immigrants themselves—where it is often placed—and instead places it on the dominant culture. The problem for immigrants, he states, is not the content of their collective memory, but it is the way that the majority culture imagines or *constructs* that memory. Begag reinforces this suggestion by avoiding the official term "*intégration*" and substituting the term "incorporation." Where French political rhetoric and cultural discourse have tended to construct *intégration* as a process by which immigrants make themselves acceptable to the dominant culture, Begag emphasizes a mutual process of inclusion that by extension relies on a *mutual* construction of both history and memory, one that recognizes the existence of common spaces of memory that have, for the most part, been ignored or overlooked (2006).[2]

Begag's comments concerning both memory and identity are of interest less because they constitute a radical break with France's vision of its own identity than because they constitute nothing like a break with that vision. That is to say, he does not at all challenge the idea that collective history and memory define collective identity. On the contrary, he upholds the basic premise upon which French national identity is currently built, namely that national, collective identity is the product of a specific remembering of a specific past. In asserting the centrality of cultural memory to what he terms "Beur" cultural production, however, Begag does break with much of the existing scholarship on such texts, which has tended to regard such literature as the expression of a collective identity crisis rooted in the absence of memory (Rosello 1993, 15).[3] For Begag, the past and the memory of the past are not absent from Beur literature and cinema. They are, rather, at their core, and such texts, therefore, are less about the absence of cultural identity or the inability to reconcile two conflicting cultural identities than they are about the process by which two different cultural identities, two versions of collective memory, become one.[4]

Begag is not alone in pointing to the centrality of the past in texts by French authors of Maghrebi origin. Assia Djebar, another novelist concerned with the shared colonial past and the legacy of that past, similarly insists on the importance of a common collective experience. Djebar, who became a member of the Académie Française in 2006, chose to speak during the occasion of her induction on the subject of the shared heritage that exists between France and Algeria, a theme she has explored in her own writing. She points, in that speech, to the shared space of colonialism, which she calls "a wound recently reopened through memory" and suggests that it was this shared space that had conferred upon her the French language, in which she speaks and writes (2006). For Djebar, colonialism, however problematic, created common spaces of history and memory between the histories and memories of the French and those they colonized. Using the heritage model that asserts that commonalities of history and memory are what define collective identity, it may be concluded that, to some extent, France and its former colonial subjects in some respects share in a single, if multivalent identity.

Leïla Sebbar, who was one of the first writers to produce overtly multicultural narratives in France, also explores the way in which the colonial past shapes the present. Her novels, including *Fatima, ou les Algériennes au square* (1981), *Shérazade, 17 ans, brune, frisée, les yeux verts* (1982), *Les Carnets de Shérazade* (1985), *Le Fou de Shérazade* (1991), and *La Seine était rouge* (1999), foreground the forgotten spaces of history and memory that are shared by all of those living in contemporary France, regardless of origin. Sebbar characterizes her work as an attempt to counter an absence of memory on the subject of immigration, but interestingly, the historical past is only indirectly referenced and rarely re-presented in her work (McCullough 2003, 120).[5] More often than not, the past is figured as an absence that the characters in her novels strive to reconstruct. This, in many ways, provided the paradigm for the engagement with the past that characterizes many if not most French multicultural narratives.

Anne Donadey has suggested that Sebbar mixes Western and Eastern cultural references, high culture and low culture, the written and the visual in order to create a mosaic of history and memory (2001, 120). I say that Sebbar's construction of memory, or rather heritage, is that of a prism in which a single past can be experienced and remembered in a number of different ways. This type of mosaic or prism structure emphasizes both the elements held in common by everyone living in France, regardless of origin or age, and also points to differences in memory, differences that stem from the origin and age of the person who remembers. This project to reconstruct or re-member unifying spaces of history and memory is perhaps most evident in Sebbar's 1999 novel *La Seine était rouge,* which recounts the events of the so-called Battle of Paris, on the night of October 17, 1961.[6] On that evening, Paris police rounded up, arrested, and killed an unknown number of Algerian workers and students who demonstrated against a curfew imposed on them by Paris police. The novel tells the story of that night through various characters of diverse ages, ranging from students to journalists to the demonstrators who experienced the events directly. In so doing, the novel points to the repression of the event in the broader cultural memory, but it also points to the fact that this repressed site of memory is held in common by those of the majority population and those of North African origin. Traumatic as it is, it is a common site of memory marking a significant, if troubling moment, in the shared history of France and Algeria and, more important, those of Algerian origin in France. Moreover, it points to the presence of North Africans in France well before the contested period of the 1980s.

Another of Sebber's novels, *Shérazade,* explores the diverse heritage or *patrimoine* that is both the cause and the consequence of France's current diversity through the trope of interracial romance. The overlapping histories of France and the Maghreb are embodied in the relationship between Shérazade, a young "Beurette," and a pied-noir man named Julien. The romantic relationship suggests that the colonial past constitutes an enduring, if problematic connection between France and its former colonies. However, Sebbar also suggests that this colonial history prevents the dominant culture from accepting those of Maghrebi origin as French since the majority culture cannot forgot the colonial origins of those of Maghrebi descent in France, but it also refuses to remember the colonial past as part of its own history.[7] The novel also engages in a fairly detailed mapping of the city of Paris, and Paris is, in many ways, the cultural capital of France and one of its greatest heritage sites. However, Paris in Sebbar's text is more than the repository for the stereotypical emblems of French culture, such as painting and architecture. It is a mosaic city composed of numerous kinds of heritage, many of them closely linked to its current diverse population. Moreover, because every character in the novel is defined through his or her connection to the city, it may be seen that the city shapes identity in much the same way as Provence shapes the identities of the characters of Marcel Pagnol.

Many other Beur authored texts, including those by Nina Bourraoui, Mehdi Charef, Tassadit Imache, and Mounsi (a pen name, meaning "for order"), express the idea that the so-called French of French roots and their (post-)colonial cocitizens share a common past and a common heritage.[8] The same is true of so-called Beur or banlieue films by filmmakers such as Farida Belghoul, Yamina Benguigui, Rachid Bouchareb, Mehdi Charef, Karim Dridi, and Abdellatif Kechiche.[9] These novels and films assert fairly clearly the existence of both similarities and differences in the personal and collective pasts of the French of North African origin and their majority-culture counterparts. Moreover, many of these texts seem to participate in the same redefinition of national heritage that characterizes late-heritage or postheritage films. The interaction of heritage and postheritage works and Beur novels and films has produced a reworking of the national past and national heritage that foregrounds the processes by which both history and collective memory have been constructed as well as the uses to which they have been put. The resulting redefinition of the past is not, as it is sometimes seen, a refusal of collective memory or collective/national identity. Nor is it the death knell of heritage or collective memory, as Pierre Nora suggests. It is rather an attempt to decolonize heritage, to point out that French history and the memory of that history have long been informed by colonialism and the colonial past.

It may be surprising that those interested in creating a multicultural or post-colonial identity would work through the space of heritage, particularly because heritage often regards ancestry as the basis of identity. Heritage, however, is only implicitly or metaphorically ancestral. It actually defines collective identity not through bloodlines but through the possession in common of certain experiences and memories. The implied racial and ethnic components of the dominant version of heritage, therefore, stem, as Begag points out (2006), from a particular *construction* of French heritage, not from the logic of heritage itself. For that reason, minority authors and filmmakers who have engaged with heritage have tended to recast collective memory, (re)inserting experiences and memories common to those of various ancestry and therefore privileging shared experience over ancestry, reimagining both heritage and collective identity in nonancestral terms.

Late heritage or postheritage films, as suggested, engage in a similar process of reworking, but it is multicultural or Beur or banlieue novels and films—many of which emerged at approximately the same time as the first-wave heritage films—that began the process. Despite that, the relationship of multicultural narratives to heritage has not always been recognized or understood. This is partly because such multicultural narratives, unlike heritage narratives, rarely engage the past directly. They are, for example, rarely set in the past, and they only infrequently represent or reference the past. They have, therefore, typically been understood as the antithesis of heritage, read as calling into question "certain hegemonic (white, middle class, republican) understandings of Frenchness" (Tarr 1997, 59).

While there are a number of differences between late heritage or postheritage and multicultural texts—one is rural, the other urban, one is set in the past and the other in the present—the two types of text are, nonetheless, engaged in much the same process of memorial construction or reconstruction. Like heritage narratives, multicultural narratives assume the centrality of the past in shaping present-day France, and they often explore the nature and content of the past, even if they do so in ambiguous ways. Paul Silverstein argues that such narratives rewrite "the immigrant past in order to understand the intercultural present" (2004, 193). Despite this engagement with the past, few multicultural narratives, be they historical, literary, or filmic, conform overtly to the heritage paradigm. Nor do they reproduce or reference the collective past as it is imagined by current models of national heritage or identity. Nonetheless, multicultural narratives, like late-heritage narratives, tend to point to the missing spaces of history and memory in the national past and, specifically, to the histories of colonialism, immigration and/or "*intégration*." Moreover, like late-heritage narratives, multicultural narratives tend to break the linear, progressive model of the past that defines conventional historiography. Instead of imagining time as a continuous line, these narratives imagine it in terms of rupture, where the past becomes an absence, a space that cannot be retrieved. Multicultural narratives also share some characteristics with early or conventional heritage narratives. Like these heritage works, they tend to define identities through a connection to smaller, local communities, rather than through a more abstract connection to the nation itself.

If films such as *Le Retour de Martin Guerre* (1982) or *Jean de Florette* (1986) imagine identity through the prism of village life, multicultural narratives foreground the banlieue, the bidonville, or other urban spaces. What the two types of narratives have in common, however, is the assumption that collective identity derives from a connection to a local, rather than a national space, an idea that has its roots in regionalism. Regionalism, which was once regarded as antithetical to and incompatible with nationalism, now features fairly prominently in French heritage. The recent revalorization of regionalism is, in many respects, a post-colonial phenomenon because it is as a result of the (post-)colonial challenge to the concept of a uniform, homogenous national identity that regionalism reemerged in France (Lebovics 2004; Sherman 2004). The emphasis on the (sub)urban, therefore, as the defining space of identity is in some measure a multicultural reappropriation of the logic of regionalism. It borrows from regionalism the idea that the collective identity is primarily local, but it also implies, as does contemporary regionalism, that national identity is not homogenous and that the nation can and does recognize difference.

What I term multicultural narratives are not always authored by those of Maghrebi or even non-European origin, despite the tendency to classify many of these narratives as beur. A number of writers, filmmakers, musicians, and scholars of various origins have worked to open French cultural memory to episodes and histories it has tended to forget. Because space does not permit a detailed analysis of all of these works and because those of Maghrebi origin finds themselves at the center of cultural and political debates about what it means to be French, my focus is on those narratives that explore the convergences of the "French" collective memory and the collective memory of those of North African origin. My interest, however, is not necessarily in the identity of the author or filmmaker but rather in the way in which specific narratives explore the identity of the French of non-European origin and, specifically, the French of North African origin. However authored, these narratives tend to suggest that if Frenchness is defined through history and shared memory, France's post-colonial citizens are indeed French. For despite the fact that France has worked to suppress the memory of the colonial past and of the way in which immigration has formed France's population for at least the past century, those two spaces do, nonetheless, exist.

Hidden Histories: *Cinéma de banlieue* and the Heritage Connection

Literature and, specifically, the so-called Beur novels articulate the reality of France's ethnic diversity and the need to recuperate a past and a heritage that explain and include this diversity. Beur and banlieue cinema, which emerged slightly later, have also been seen to engage in this exploration of identity and heritage, and as with literature, the central role of the past in this exploration has often been overlooked. The terms "Beur" and "banlieue," like the term "heritage film," are somewhat problematic in that they do not necessarily describe a coherent genre or movement but rather a handful of characteristics common to a certain number of films produced during the 1980s and 1990s. The term *"cinéma beur,"* or "beur cinema," was coined in 1985 by the French journal *Cinématographes* to describe films by and about the French of North African origin that began appearing on the French film scene in the early 1980s (Tarr 2005, 2). It refers to films directed by and focusing on the Beurs and as such focused more on the ethnic origins of the films' characters and directors than on form, aesthetics, or any other aspect of filmmaking style. The term *"cinéma de banlieue,"* on the other hand, which emerged a decade later, is used to describe films that are set in France's (sub)urban areas and that focus primarily on the experiences of adolescents or young adults, regardless of the origins of the director or the characters depicted. It describes primarily gritty, urban realist films, many of which have elements of the *film policier* (detective film). Although the terms are sometimes used interchangeably, they focus on different elements of the films in question. Films such as Bertrand Tavernier's *L.627* (1992) or Thomas Gilou's *Raï* (1995), for example, could be classified as banlieue films, although their directors are not beur. A film such as Rachid Bouchareb's *Indigènes* (2006), on the other hand, may be classified as a beur film, but it is not a part of the *cinéma de banlieue*. Together, however, these labels draw attention to the two principal frames through which ethnic minorities are viewed in France—that of race and of space—and both are central themes in both Beur and banlieue films.

The banlieue has, in recent years, been at the forefront of debates about integration in France, but the relationship between the *cinéma de banlieue* and the heritage film is not widely recognized or understood. A fairly substantial number of films by directors of various origins may be considered under the rubric Beur or banlieue cinema. These include Claude Berri's *Tchao Pantin* (1983), Bouchareb's *Baton Rouge* (1985) and *Cheb* (1991), Mehdi Charef's adaptations of his novel *Le Thé au harem d'Archimède* (1985), Gérard Blain's *Pierre et Djemila* (1987), Tavernier's *L.627* (1992), Anne Fontaine's *Les Histoires d'amour finissent mal en general* (1993), Mathieu Kassovitz's *Métisse* (1993) and *La Haine* (1995), Malik Chibane's *Hexagone* (1994) and *Douce France* (1995), Karim Dridi's *Bye Bye* (1995), Mahmoud Zemmouri's *100% Arabica*

(1997), Kechiche's *La Faute à Voltaire* (2001) and *L'Esquive* (2004), and most recently Laurent Cantet's *Entre les murs* (2008). These films, in general, are set in the present in France's urban centers or the banlieue, and they do, for the most part, feature ethnic minority protagonists, although they are not unconcerned with the past.

The media coverage concerning the October 2005 riots demonstrated the degree to which the banlieue is figured in the contemporary French imagination as an ethnic enclave in the midst of an otherwise-tranquil society, a space of lawlessness and violence that threatens to erupt and disrupt the perceived stability of the nation in which it is found.[10] The intense political and media focus on France's working-class, (sub)urban areas would suggest that there has been some fundamental change in the nature of these urban areas, something, no doubt, related to the shifts in population brought about by (post-)colonial immigration. The banlieue has long been perceived as a marginal space that lies both inside and outside the wider society of which it is a part. It has, as Kiran Grewal observes, "long been spoken of in ominous terms: a site of the 'dangerous classes' who pose a threat to French society and social order" (2007, 44). The *cinéma de banlieue* engages directly with the prevailing perception. This would seem to suggest it is a new type of cinema, reflecting contemporary attitudes toward a uniquely contemporary space. The newness of the term "*cinéma de banlieue*" reinforces this suggestion, implying that the films grouped under this rubric are marked by a coherent set of particular stylistic or thematic characteristics that distinguish these films from anything previously produced. In reality, nothing could be further from the truth. Just as the current stereotypes concerning the banlieue and its inhabitants recycle and rework earlier stereotypes of the same space, so, too, does the *cinéma de banlieue* recycle a type of cinema about the urban working classes, a type of film that has existed almost from the beginning of cinema itself. In many ways, therefore, the *cinéma de banlieue* is as grounded in the past as the heritage film.

Probably the earliest narrative films to foreground both the urban working classes and the space of the banlieue were the silent-era crime serials of Louis Feuillade. Feuillade was for many years the head of production at Gaumont, and he produced a number of commercially successful film series, including *Fantômas* (1913–14) and *Les Vampires* (1915). These films were often shot on location in Paris, something that was unusual at that time. Moreover, they focused on the experience of the working classes and therefore included working-class neighborhoods in their depiction of the city. Feuillade figured these working-class areas as centers of crime and instability and suggested, through his films, that the characters who inhabited them posed a direct threat to the city's more affluent residents as well as to the society as a whole.

While he was, no doubt, reflecting the attitudes of the elites of the day, he was also projecting forward, establishing a filmic topos that holds to the present day.[11]

Following Feuillade, filmmakers such as Jean Renoir and René Clair filmed the working classes and the banlieue. Renoir's films, including *Nana* (1926) and *La Bête humaine* (1938), offered gritty, realist depictions of the Parisian lower classes that remained relatively consistent with the image of these areas Feuillade had painted, even if the characters in the Renoir films were more complex than those in Feuillade's. Clair's *Sous les toits de Paris* (1930) offered a more light-hearted, whimsical view of these areas, presenting the working classes as picturesque and quaint but not threatening. His film, despite its popularity, did little to undermine the basic association between the urban working classes and crime and violence. In the 1930s and 1940s, working class (sub)urban films figured prominently in French film production. Filmmakers associated with poetic realism, among them Julien Duvivier, Pierre Chenal, and Marcel Carné, presented stylized portraits of the working-class areas of Paris, many of which have become iconic. These films also depicted these areas as violent and desperate, however, because they were strongly influenced by naturalism, they tended to feature characters who were more tragic than threatening, and these two aspects carried forward into later representations.

If the 1950s are better known for the glossy, escapist, studio-driven costume dramas disdained by the filmmakers of the New Wave, the darker, more sober world of the lower classes was not abandoned. Jacques Becker carried the influence of poetic realism forward. His classic noir film *Touchez pas au grisbi* (1953) is a visually stunning depiction of the Paris of gangsters and criminals. Jean-Pierre Melville also emphasized both the urban lower classes and the criminal or socially marginal in his films. Melville's *Bob le flambeur* (1955), for example, recreates a Montmartre strikingly similar in ambiance to the Montmartre of Carné or Feuillade. It was, however, the filmmakers of the New Wave, themselves influenced by Becker and Melville, who reinvigorated French urban cinema. François Truffaut, Jean-Luc Godard, and Agnès Varda, for example, all reprised Feuillade's habit of filming the (sub)urban and doing so on location. The "New" in "New Wave" suggests a complete break or a reinvention of cinema, and indeed, the New Wave is often understood as just that. If, however, the New Wave filmmakers broke with the aesthetics of the studio that had shaped the filmmaking of many of their immediate predecessors, it is also true that this "break" constituted in many ways a return to an even-older paradigm of filmmaking.

Keith Reader argues that the New Wave has very little in common with the *cinéma de banlieue*, apart from low budgets and the mutual engagement with contemporary social problems (1998, 105). There is however much to link the two types of film. Both, as suggested, draw from a tradition of urban film-making with deep roots in French film history, and both may be regarded as a rejection of a type of studio film aesthetics that dominated their respective periods. The New Wave was seen as a refusal of the swashbuckling historical films of the 1950s. The tendency to use handheld cameras, to film on location, and, in Godard's case in particular, to minimally edit or script the films was a direct rejection of studio production techniques. The gritty neorealism of banlieue films constitutes, for many, an implicit critique of the opulent melo-drama of contemporary costume films, and the sober depiction of the present functions as an antidote to the nostalgic rerendering of the past. This choice of present over past is seen, in turn, as constituting a refusal of the nationalist identity politics that heritage films are presumed to endorse.

Despite these similarities, it is also true that there exist fundamental dif-ferences between the films of the New Wave and the *cinéma de banlieue*, differences that are rooted in the way each type of film engages with the past. In the films of the New Wave, the present dominates, and the past is a virtual nonentity. The characters in the films seem to have no past or at least no past that is directly referenced. Moreover, the past has no evident influ-ence on the behavior or destiny of the principal characters. In some cases, most notably Alain Resnais' *L'Année dernière à Marienbad* (1961), the past is figured as an absence that can never be recovered. This marks a departure from earlier versions of the urban film, in which the past was often a central component. In both noir films and the films associated with poetic realism, the past is a driving force in the narrative, a force from which the protagonist and other principal characters are often trying to escape. In appropriating the urban form but divesting it of this framework, the filmmakers of the New Wave may have been trying to break with the past altogether at a historical moment—the moment of decolonization—when the past had become par-ticularly problematic.

The *cinéma de banlieue*, in contrast, often engages directly with the past. If banlieue films seem, as Carrie Tarr suggests, to privilege the present over the past, they do so in order to draw attention to a disconnect between past and present that characterizes contemporary France. In so doing, banlieue films often frame the problems of the present as the consequence of an ear-lier erasure of the past, perhaps the very erasure the films of the New Wave attempted to achieve. In particular, banlieue films tend to present France's ethnic minorities as subjects without a past, unaccounted for by history and unable to identify either with French cultural heritage or with the cultural heritage of their parents or grandparents (Tarr 2005, 189). Despite its relative absence, therefore, it could be argued that the past is one of the principal subjects of banlieue films. Read superficially, banlieue films often actually suggest that ethnic minorities do not "fit" in France precisely because they lack a heritage connection to French culture. A closer reading, however, suggests that these films often rework or expand the space of heritage in order to include those who are seemingly excluded.

Probably the best-known and most commercially successful of the banlieue films was Mathieu Kassovitz's *La Haine* (1995).[12] *La Haine* was the second major feature film by Kassovitz, who had attracted a certain amount of critical attention with his first film, *Métisse* (1993), a Spike Lee influenced, socially charged romantic comedy. *La Haine* was made on a budget of approximately $2.5 million and achieved reasonable success in France, finishing among the top-twenty films of the year (Vincendeau 2005, 6). It also had some success internationally, most notably in the United States, where its release was underwritten and promoted by actress/director/producer Jodie Foster.

La Haine is a "day in the life" film that follows three urban youths, Vinz (Vincent Cassel), Hubert (Hubert Koundé), and Saïd (Saïd Tagmahoui) and explores the violence and isolation that often characterize life in the banlieue. It was inspired, according to Kassovitz, by the 1993 death of Makomé M'Bowolé, a youth of Zairean origin, at the hands of Paris police. Kassovitz evokes the event in the film, recasting it as the violent arrest and beating of Abdel (Abdel Ahmed Ghili), a friend of the three protagonists (Abdel ultimately dies). Kassovitz also shot much of the film in the Cité des Muguets, a rent-controlled housing project outside of Paris, and invited many of the residents of the banlieue to appear in the film. Apart from the setting and the issues of violence and marginalization, *La Haine* is typical of banlieue films in its focus on a so-called *blanc-black-beur* trio (although it is more correct to say it is a Jewish-black-beur trio) and the direct representation of the urban periphery, as well as the exploration of violence and particularly police violence (Reader 1995; Tarr 1997; Vincendeau 2000). Unlike other banlieue films, however, it does not focus on the experience of the beur character. Tarr also suggests that *La Haine* downplays racism to a greater degree than most banlieue films, showing Vinz's experiences as much the same light as those of Saïd and Hubert and privileging Vinz over either of the others (2005, 70).

What most distinguishes *La Haine* from other banlieue films, however, is its cinematography. As noted, Kassovitz intended from the beginning to film the *banlieue* in black and white and to create more an aesthetically polished urban portrait than a typical of realist drama. Clearly, the use of black and white was essential to this project because although he was forced to film in color to guarantee funding for the film, Kassovitz later printed *La Haine* in black and white, ensuring the integrity of his original vision (Vincendeau 2005, 14). The use of black and white not only provides the film with what Vincendeau calls a certain "stylistic distanciation" (2005, 23) but it also marks the film *as a film* and links it to a tradition of urban or banlieue filmmaking in France, a tradition inaugurated by Feuillade in the silent era, and continued by the filmmakers associated with both poetic realism and the New Wave, all of whom filmed in black and white. *La Haine*'s stylized camerawork, therefore, and its use of black-and-white cinematography function to counter assumptions about the presumed incompatibility of France's current banlieue inhabitants by drawing attention to the fact that France has long had marginalized populations in its urban centers, that the place of these populations in the broader culture has long been contested, and, more particularly, that both the banlieue and its relationship to French identity have long been the subject of cinema.[13]

It is not only the cinematography of *La Haine* that points to a hidden heritage connection in contemporary banlieue cinema, it is also the substance of the film itself. *La Haine*'s narrative, for example, focuses on the three protagonists as they move out of the space of the banlieue and into the center of Paris. As noted, there is probably no greater heritage space in France than that of the capital. What is more, the capital is not only a cultural heritage center, it also is a center of film heritage since French cinema almost from its origins has centered on Paris and has presented movement within the city as central feature of French experience. For that reason, it is worth noting the degree to which Vinz, Hubert, and Saïd are *unable* to move in Paris. *La Haine* emphasizes the three protagonists' lack of mobility, both through their incapacity to accurately read or understand "high" culture, as in a scene in an art gallery, and through their inability to successfully utilize various forms of transportation. In one crucial scene of immobility, Vinz, Hubert, and Saïd attempt and fail to steal a car. They then miss the last train out of Paris and find themselves stranded, and it is these two failures that ultimately lead to the violent confrontation that ends the film.

The inability to navigate the city suggests that the trio is cut off from heritage itself, unable to connect with France's past, and, therefore, unable to function in the present. This suggestion is reinforced both by the images that compose the film and by other episodes in the narrative. In the *Cité des Muguets*, for example, Vinz, Hubert, and Saïd are literally surrounded, hemmed in by the enormous images of heritage figures such as Victor Hugo and Charles Baudelaire (both of whom were renowned for their representations of the Parisian lower classes). However, the three protagonists do not seem to recognize or acknowledge the presence of these figures; they are completely disconnected from them. The only function these figures have in the film is to form a type of cultural wall that encloses the inhabitants of the *cité* in their peripheral space. Ginette Vincendeau reads these images of Baudelaire and Hugo as images of a type of social breakdown that has produced the marginalization of the banlieue and its inhabitants (2000; 2005). These images do, indeed, point to a kind of social breakdown, which is specifically the failure to transmit the past to a certain population in France. But they also point to the problematic role heritage currently plays in France because they suggest that heritage is at one and the same time a pathway to cultural acceptance and a barrier that France's ethnic minorities are unable to cross.

If the film depicted Vinz, Hubert, and Saïd as cut off only from high culture or the dominant culture's *patrimoine*, it might be read as reinforcing the idea that France's ethnic minorities are incompatible with the nation precisely because of their lack of connection to a specific cultural past. However, the film depicts the trio as cut off from all heritage, from all access to the past, and this suggests that their marginalization is imposed rather than innate. For example, it has been suggested that the film ignores the origins of the three protagonists, particularly Saïd and Hubert, and that this functions to downplay issues of racism and exclusion (Tarr 2005, 68). While this is one possible reading, it is also true that *La Haine*'s failure to explore or emphasize the personal histories or family histories of the three protagonists draws attention to the absence of these histories and suggests that the three are as disconnected from their familial heritage as they are from the French cultural heritage. If, therefore, *La Haine* suggests that urban youth are cutoff from the national *patrimoine*, it also refuses the idea that it is because they are attached to some other heritage. This, in turn, undercuts the idea that the isolation from French cultural heritage is the result of fundamental cultural incompatibility. The film also functions, as does Jeunet's *Amélie*, to suggest that immigration and colonialism are absent from official narratives about the French past or at least that they were at the time the film was made. Vinz, Hubert, and Saïd, therefore, officially have no family histories to recount.

Quite apart from the refusal to explore or represent the particular histories or heritage that each of the three protagonists represents, *La Haine* points to the protagonists' alienation both from French history and from their own personal histories. In a famous scene from the film, the three encounter an old Jewish man (Tadek Lokcinski) in a public bathroom. The man tells them the story of how his friend Grunwalski missed a train and died as a result. Vincendeau describes that the story is one of deportation to Siberia but that it also evokes the Holocaust (2005, 107). The story in many ways also suggests France's history of violence and oppression of marginalized groups, and it functions as an indirect commentary on the trio's own situation, particularly since they will also miss their train and, as a result, at least one of them will end up dead. However, the bathroom episode also points to a certain alienation from history, both on the part of the protagonists and on the part of the culture as a whole. Vinz, Hubert, and Saïd's inability to comprehend the old man's story and its connection to their lives suggests an inability to connect with the past. This disconnection from the past translates into a fatal inability to read the present. What is interesting, however, is that the spectator is as unable as the three protagonists to properly decode the story and its meaning. We may surmise that the story is about Siberia because the man talks about snow. We might also conclude that the man is speaking about deportation to concentration camps during World War II, because those deportations often took place by rail. It is also possible that the man is referring to something else entirely. It is impossible to know, however, because neither he nor the film ever makes the real historical context clear. *La Haine* ultimately suggests that the spectator is as alienated from the man's history as Vinz, Hubert, and Saïd, and this alienation may be read as the dominant culture's failure to inscribe the history of immigrants into heritage, particularly since, whatever the man is talking about, it involves characters whose names do not sound "French," and it retells the experiences of some marginalized population. Although the story does not seem to refer to colonialism or to the oppression of post-colonial minorities, it does point to forgotten spaces of history that include both of these.

La Haine, then, proposes that the "permanent exile" in which France's ethnic minorities are sometimes presumed to find themselves derives neither from an inability to connect to the dominant culture nor from an attachment to a foreign culture of origin. Rather, it derives from the failure of the dominant culture to transmit either space of history and memory to those descended from immigration. Through its refusal to engage the particular histories of any of the protagonists, the film also draws attention to the failure to transmit certain spaces of dominant-culture history or memory to the population at large. It is, according to the film, this double absence of memory that perpetuates the marginalization of France's minority populations and that prevents those populations from fully functioning within the space of the nation.

Road to Nowhere: Dridi's *Bye Bye*

Although somewhat overshadowed by Kassovitz's *La Haine*, which was released the same year, Karim Dridi's *Bye Bye* (1995) was another prominent banlieue film that explored the relationship among history, memory, and contemporary racism. *Bye Bye* drew only approximately 120,000 spectators, whereas *La Haine* drew more than 2,000,000. Nevertheless, *Bye Bye* fared respectably well from a critical point of view, winning the *Palme d'or* at Cannes, for example. Like *La Haine*, *Bye Bye* was the second feature-length film by a young director who had already achieved reasonable success. Dridi's first film, *Pigalle* (1994), is set against a backdrop of crime and drugs, and it is the story of the tangled romantic relationship between a transsexual and a thief. Like

Pigalle, *Bye Bye* centers on characters who are marginal in or marginalized by society. Like *La Haine*, it focuses on the experiences of France's ethnic minorities, the so-called second generation.

Bye Bye, like *La Haine*, frames contemporary racism in terms of a disconnect between past and present, between history and memory, suggesting through its narrative and its mise-en-scene that the perception of ethnic minorities as "outsiders" is at odds with the facts of France's national past. Despite this apparent similarity between the two films, however, there are a number of differences. *Bye Bye*, for example, is filmed in a more typically realist mode than *La Haine*. It also deals almost exclusively with the experience of Franco-Maghrebis, whereas *La Haine*'s principal characters represent diverse ethnic groups. *Bye Bye* is set in Marseille, and *La Haine* in Paris. What is more, *Bye Bye* is not, strictly speaking, actually set in the banlieue but rather in the working-class "Panier" area in the older part of Marseille. Nevertheless, as Will Higbee suggests, *Bye Bye* does include scenes shot at the urban periphery and that, along with its thematic concerns, have placed it, like *La Haine*, under the rubric of the *cinéma de banlieue* ("Hybridity, Space, and the Right to Belong," 2001, 52). The differences between the two films notwithstanding, both *Bye Bye* and *La Haine*, seem to suggest that France's ethnic minorities often find themselves locked out of the country into which they were born, and both films read this marginalization as the effect of a certain degree of alienation from the past on the part of the larger culture and on the part of ethnic minorities themselves.

Bye Bye is the story of two brothers, Ismaël (Sami Bouajila) and Mouloud (Ouassini Embarek), who journey from Paris to Marseille en route to Tunisia. The brothers have left Paris, where they lived, to rejoin their parents, who have gone to Tunisia ahead of them. The brothers stop in Marseille, with the family of an uncle (Benhaïssa Ahouari). Ismaël gets a job working with his uncle on a construction site, while Mouloud spends time with his cousin Rhida (Sofiane Mammeri) and Rhida's drug-dealer acquaintance, Renard (Moussa Maaskri). Ismaël experiences periodic racism on the job site but manages to make one friend, Jacky (Frédéric Andrau), one of his majority-culture co-workers. Ultimately, Ismaël betrays Jacky, who then retaliates by showing the same racism towards Ismaël as those around him. Mouloud, during this time, becomes increasingly attracted to the life of crime led by Renard. He begins to see crime as a weapon against racism and a means of resisting his parents' efforts to bring him to Tunisia. In the end, Ismaël rescues Mouloud and agrees not to send him to Tunisia, and the film ends with the brothers as they attempt to leave Marseille.

Bye Bye begins and ends with a road trip, and it has, therefore, sometimes been regarded as a road movie. Road movies tend to emphasize movement and mobility (Laderman 2002), and in so doing, they draw from the bildungsroman, using a physical journey to suggest the development of characters into or away from society (Gemünden 1998, 155). European road movies typically emphasize movement across borders, thereby suggesting that dynamic and hybrid identities are progressively supplanting the fixed or stable identities once presumed to define Europe (Mazierska and Rascaroli 2006, 4). Such road trips, as Christian Bosseno argues, are also common in films made by or about Franco-Maghrebis (1992, 53). Films ranging from Rachid Bouchareb's *Cheb* (1991) to Kechiche's *La Faute à Voltaire* (2001) are centered on a physical journey undertaken by beur or Maghrebi protagonists. The same type of journey also structures various beur novels, including Sebbar's *Shérazade*. These literary or filmic journeys are nearly always incomplete, and they are almost inevitably experienced as a trauma. This has led Bosseno to conclude that they express the Beurs' isolation both from their culture of origin and their culture of residence. This suggests a lack of development or an inability to develop into society, rather than the assimilation into the social mainstream typically associated with the bildungsroman.

If beur films such as *Bye Bye* can be classified as road movies, they would have to be seen as incomplete or arrested road movies that record the isolation or exclusion of Franco-Maghrebis from society. Through their appropriation of the metaphor of the journey as social development, these films, nevertheless, imply the possibility of future integration. Dridi's *Bye Bye* functions in precisely this way. As the film begins, the brothers are in a car on the road, and the car breaks down as they arrive in Marseille. The film, therefore, suggests movement in the opening scene, but this movement is quickly stopped, and much of the rest of the film is characterized by stasis. Moreover, because the brothers, for various reasons, ultimately renounce their plan to continue to Tunisia, the movement across France and across international borders that is suggested in the film never actually occurs. What is, perhaps, unique or unusual about *Bye Bye*, however, is that Dridi frames this absence of movement as both chosen and imposed. This would seem to suggest that if French society is blocking the type of dynamic or multicultural identity that the brothers' movement might imply, the brothers themselves are also blocking it. The blocking mechanism is a failure, both on the part of French society and on the part of ethnic minorities, to come to terms with the past.

Dridi, who is Franco-Tunisian, had originally planned to shoot *Bye Bye* in Paris, in the Belleville neighborhood where he himself grew up. He later decided to shoot the film in Marseille, because, in his words, "it is a city rich in hybridity, in color" (Higbee, "Hybridity, Space, and the Right to Belong," 2001, 53). This hybridity is not only the result of relatively recent (im)migration. Rather, it has characterized Marseille throughout its long history. The city was founded by the Phocean Greeks and later conquered by the Romans. It was an important port from the fifteenth through the twentieth century, and it was one of the central launching points first for the Crusades and then later for France's colonial conquest of North Africa. The city was also of particular importance in managing trade between metropolitan France and colonial Algeria, as well as in managing the "guest" workers recruited from North Africa by the French government during the so-called Thirty Glorious Years following World War II.

Marseille, therefore, is a city that has long been shaped by the same processes of conquest and migration that have more recently shaped France as a whole. *Bye Bye* visually foregrounds the city's history in a number of ways. First of all, the film is set in Le Panier, an area of Marseille long associated with immigrants. The numerous shots of recent immigrants against the backdrop of this historically immigrant neighborhood, therefore, function as a visual reminder of the historic role immigrants have played and continue to play in the city's development (Higbee, "Hybridity, Space, and the Right to Belong," 2001, 54). Marseille's maritime past also figures prominently in *Bye Bye*. There are numerous shots of the sea and the port, and Dridi at one point even zooms in on the rusted anchor from an old ship that is being removed from a construction site.[14] These visual emblems of the city's past serve as a backdrop against which to explore contemporary racism. This racism is presented directly, in the form of insults shouted by Ismaël's co-workers, and visually, through the through the oblique angles and partially blocked shots that create a sense of isolation and marginalization in the film. It is also presented through the interior shots of the family's small, claustrophobic apartment, a space that points to the economic and social effects of a racism that confines immigrants to lower-paying jobs and inadequate housing.

In juxtaposing present-day racism and the numerous visual markers of Marseille's history, *Bye Bye* seems to suggest that the problems faced by ethnic minorities in France derive from both continuity with and rupture from the past. The repeated assertions that France is being "invaded" and that those of minority origin should merely "go home," for example, are a direct reappropriation of ideas of fundamental cultural difference inherited from the colonial era, ideas that suggest a degree of continuity with the past. However, these assertions also ignore the fact that ethnic minorities have long been in Marseille and that they were, for the most part, invited there by the French. For that reason, these assertions may also be read as expressing a disconnect from the past. In many ways, therefore, *Bye Bye* visually stages the effects of what has been termed the "colonial fracture," or the fundamental inability of France to reconcile the colonial past with the multicultural present.

Over the course of *Bye Bye*, this sense of rupture between past and present is reinforced. First of all, the film highlights the "ordinariness" of Aziz's family, thereby suggesting that they have been "integrated," which is to say shaped by the same cultural and historical forces and processes as their majority-culture counterparts. The film is filled with scenes of the family cooking and eating, of the children doing their homework while the mother looks on or helps. Ismaël and his uncle Aziz both work on a construction site alongside French co-workers. The family is also subject to the same pressures that affect many modern families. There is conflict between parents and children, particularly Rhida, the family's teenage son. Rhida's battles with his father about when he can go out, where he can go, and how late he can stay out are typical of the battles teenagers in industrialized societies have with their parents. The mother, as in many families, functions as a mediating figure who calmly orchestrates compromise between the father and the son. These depictions undercut the idea that the racism the family experiences is prompted by some fundamental difference between them and the dominant culture. Rather, racism is presented as detached from them and from the present-day reality. It is, the film suggests, rather like the rusty anchor featured in close-up, a relic from the past.

The fracture between past and present is also presented in very personal terms. Ismaël, for example, is haunted by the memory of another younger brother Nouredine. This memory is partially repressed, but it gradually resurfaces over the course of the film, and this incident may be seen as a structuring device for the entire film. It is progressively revealed that Nouredine died in an accidental fire, a fire for which Ismaël feels responsible. *Bye Bye* begins with a scene featuring Ismaël and Nouredine, and it is from there that it cuts to Ismaël and Mouloud in the car on the road to Marseille. This use of montage suggests that these two events are related, a suggestion that is reinforced later in the film, when it is directly stated that it is as a result of Nouredine's death that Mouloud is being sent to Tunisia. Nouredine's death represents a repressed prehistory to Ismaël and Mouloud's journey, a prehistory that influences actions in the present even though it remains largely unseen.

Nouredine's death also poses a paradox for Ismaël and the spectator. It is clear that Ismaël feels responsible for the death and that, therefore, he cannot bear to remember what happened. However, he is also haunted by it, unable to forget it. The film reflects this state of conflict by allowing the spectator to see bits of the events surrounding the death as they reemerge in spontaneous flashbacks, but it does not, until the end, completely reconstruct these events. Instead, the film presents Nouredine's death as a repressed memory that influences Ismaël's behavior in the present in ways that are not entirely clear. The repressed guilt may, for example, account for some of the impulsive behavior Ismaël exhibits, including his sexual encounter with his friend Jacky's girlfriend, Yasmine (Nozha Khouadra), the encounter that ends their friendship.

Ismaël's repression of Nouredine's death functions as a type of symbolic parallel within *Bye Bye* for the mechanisms by which France's repressed colonial past influences actions and attitudes in the present. Like Donadey and others, who argue for the existence of an "Algeria syndrome," *Bye Bye* suggests that present-day racism is the result of France's inability to come to terms with its colonial past. It is possible, for example, to see in Ismaël's grief over his dead brother a parallel for national grief over the loss of the colonies. However, *Bye Bye* does not frame the matter entirely in this way. Rather, what the film seems to argue is that France, like Ismaël, is unable to integrate past and present and unable, therefore, to reconcile them.

As noted, the presence of immigrants in Marseille and in France in general is the direct result of France's colonial history. However, this history has, until very recently, been suppressed from the national memory, such that (post-) colonial minorities in France are seen as invaders, uninvited guests whose presence cannot be accounted for by history (Donadey 1996, 2001; Rosello, *Postcolonial Hospitality*, 2001). This suggests that part of the problem in "integrating" these minorities is an inability, on the part of the nation itself, to remember the past. At the same time, however, the racism experienced by these minorities is, as noted, a result of continuity between the colonial past and the present, and it suggests an inability on the part of the dominant culture *to forget* or overlook ethnic origins. Contemporary racism is, according to this reading, the result of an inability to remember *and* an inability to forget the past. The result is a situation much like the one in which Ismaël finds himself, in which the repressed past causes actions and reactions whose real cause remains hidden from view. The only "cure" for this type of problem the film suggests is a reconnection with the past, a reconnection that allows for the past to finally be left behind.

This disjuncture between past and present is also expressed in Ismaël and Mouloud's journey, which involves movement away from the site of the brothers' personal past—Paris—and toward the site of their ancestral past—Tunisia. This is actually the reverse of the type of journey undertaken in a conventional bildungsroman, because it implies a development away from society—at least the society into which the brothers were born—and a movement back to the culture of origin of their parents. However, it is also a journey the brothers never complete. Mouloud, for example, does not wish to leave France and repeatedly refuses to go to Tunisia, a country he claims he does not know. The brothers, therefore, are stuck in Marseille, which functions as a liminal space between two different histories or pasts—the brothers' personal history and that of their parents. Similarly, if Paris signifies French national history (as it so often does) and Tunisia signifies another national or regional history, then the film leaves Ismaël and Mouloud caught in the space that binds these two sets of history—the edge of the water that connects them. It is, therefore, Marseille itself that links the story of these two brothers to the broader colonial past, and the film's abrupt ending, with the brothers again on the road but unable to move, suggests that any forward movement is predicated on resolving this breach between past and present, origin and destination. It is only in finding a way to reconcile their own personal origins with those of their parents that the brothers can actually determine in which direction to move. Similarly, it is only in resolving the disjuncture between colonial history and a present-day multicultural population that France can create for the brothers a space in which to move.

For that reason, the film draws a clear distinction between Ismaël and Mouloud, who represent the so-called second generation of immigration, and their parents, who represent the first. For the parents, a "return" to Tunisia is possible because it is literally the place from which they came. This "return" is also part of the film's past tense, because it precedes the action of the main narrative. The parents themselves are also part of the film's past tense because they never appear onscreen and their only intervention in the narrative comes in the form of a telephone call, which marks them as distant or removed. Ismaël and Mouloud, therefore, are literally cut off from all aspects of the past. They are physically removed from their parents, and they are cut off from any point of origin—either their parents' or their own.

Marseille, like the brothers, is also located between various spaces of the past. However, it is also a mediating space in which various elements of diverse pasts overlap and converge and in which the present and the past may be reconciled. The film renders this visually, through shots of Ismaël pondering the Mediterranean and suggests, specifically through shots of a trans-Mediterranean ferry that operates between the two shores of the Mediterranean, a way of reconciling the spaces of France and Tunisia and the specific past each represents. Moreover, because the ferry is always shown arriving in France, never departing, it suggests that this connection between the two spaces already exists and that it exists in France. It is a connection that simply has to be recognized and embraced.

This connection to the past is also presented through Ismaël's grandmother who lives in France with Aziz and his family. Dridi has said of the grandmother that she functions as the family's memory and that her silence is illustrative of "the social function which the elderly perform in Arab families." Her age, her dress, and her commanding presence all function to make her an icon of the family's culture of origin. Freedman and Tarr note that the grandmother silently forms the center of the family (2000, 181–82).[15] The grandmother, then, functions as a mediating figure, one who recognizes and accepts that Ismaël and Mouloud are from France but who equally binds them to the culture of origin of the family. She is an expression of the idea that these two identities or pasts can coexist in the same space. The grandmother's centrality to the process of reconciliation is demonstrated when Ismaël, who ultimately decides he will honor Mouloud's wishes and that the two will not go to Tunisia, seeks not his father's approval of the decision but that of his grandmother.

Through the family, therefore, *Bye Bye* asserts that Ismaël and Mouloud are tied to both France and the Maghreb. The film also asserts, however, that France and the Maghreb are both tied to one another. As noted, the ferry entering the Bay of Marseille implies such a connection, as does the city of Marseille itself. Other subtle reminders of these connections are embedded throughout the film. In Rhida's bedroom, for example, are posters that refer to the Marseillais musical group Massilia Sound System, a group that fuses reggae and ragga—both brought to France through immigration—with more traditional Occitan musical forms. Rhida also wears a T-shirt in one scene that bears the name of the musical group IAM. IAM, who are one of the better known hip-hop groups in France, has famously asserted Marseille's hybrid, Mediterranean identity both in their lyrics and their musical composition. *Bye Bye*, therefore, includes musical clues that suggest that Marseille's specificity is precisely its hybridity, a suggestion that is reinforced in scenes showing Africans, North Africans, and French of European descent all living, working, and socializing together.

However, the film does not place the full burden of reconciling past and present on society. Ismaël faces a crucial choice in *Bye Bye*, to stay in France or to "return" to Tunisia. This choice could be read as a choice about self-identification, an either/or choice about whether to claim French or Tunisian identity. Mouloud faces the same choice, and while he repeatedly asserts that he is French and does not belong in Tunisia, he also openly questions his relationship to French society. As a result of Mouloud's frustration with the racism and humiliation he associates with being French and Arab, he becomes attracted to the world of drugs and violence. Through Renard, who drives an expensive car and has expensive jewelry, Mouloud begins to see crime as means of feeling empowered despite racism, a way of claiming an identity that is free from any ties to the past. Renard himself expresses this sense of power and liberation by telling Mouloud that no one will ever call him a dirty Arab if he is carrying a gun.

Bye Bye presents Renard and the world of crime he inhabits as one way of reconciling past and present and of resolving colonialism's legacy of racism and inequality. Renard represents a break with the past, a renunciation of personal and familial origins and the embracing of a new, modern identity constructed and glorified through contemporary mass culture. Renard's identity is derived by imitating the gangsters he has seen in Hollywood films and in music videos. However, *Bye Bye* presents Renard as a vicious and selfish opportunist who preys on everyone around him and justifies his behavior by attributing it to French racism. Renard lures Mouloud into his circle, not to empower him but to get him to sell drugs. He also prostitutes a young friend of Rhida's, who is of European origin. Renard is an antiracist, an egalitarian because he exploits everyone equally, be they Arab or Caucasian, male or female.

Ismaël and Mouloud, however, ultimately reject this type of equality, just as they reject the essentialized identities that are imposed upon them by their parents and the majority culture. Real equality, the film suggests, must benefit all sides, and it cannot come with a break from the past, only through reconciliation. The brothers take to the road again, presumably in search of another space where they can construct a coherent identity for themselves. On their way out of Marseille, Mouloud paints the word "Bye" on the back of the car, signaling the rejection of the past as represented in the racism and violence in the relationship between the French of European origin and the French of Maghrebi origin. Moreover, this "Bye" is also a refusal of the complete submission to and acceptance of racial prejudice and discrimination, as exemplified by Aziz, or the turn to crime and violence, as exemplified by Renard—the two roles currently offered post-colonial minorities in France.

There is a second "Bye" in the title of the film, however, and this "Bye" comes when Ismaël and Mouloud abandon the car altogether and with it the prospect of resolving their identity crisis in some other space. This crisis must be resolved, *Bye Bye* suggests, at the point where immigration and colonialism, racism and multiculturalism converge. The brothers must find a way to forge a new identity that is not, as Tarr suggests, bound up either in the past of their parents or in France's colonial legacy (1999, 176). But they must also find a way to forge an identity that is not completely disconnected from these pasts, either. The film leaves the brothers without having accomplished this precisely because the broader culture has not yet found a way to accomplish it. Nevertheless, it is clear that the film affirms the possibility of a successful resolution because the final scene shows the two brothers walking away from the sea back toward the center of France, their journey incomplete but nevertheless underway.

Marivaux in the *Cité*: Chetif's *L'Esquive*

La Haine and *Bye Bye* are not unique in pointing to memory and heritage as tied in problematic ways to the plight of France's (sub)urban populations. Numerous banlieue films, ranging from Rachid Bouchareb's *Cheb* (1991) to

Malik Chibane's *Hexagone* (1994), depict France's ethnic minorities as cut off both from the past of their parents and the dominant culture *patrimoine*. As noted, such films often represent France's ethnic minorities as unable to successfully navigate contemporary culture, and this inability is frequently rendered in spatial terms, where movement implies successful navigation. Kechiche's film *L'Esquive* (2004) also explores the relationship of heritage and multiculturalism in the space of the banlieue, and it, like both *Bye Bye* and *La Haine*, figures insertion into the dominant culture in terms of movement or the ability to move. However, Kechiche also engages heritage in a very different way than either Kassovitz or Dridi, suggesting that the problem for France's minority populations lies not in a disjuncture between past and present but in the problematic way that heritage in France is typically used and understood.

L'Esquive was Kechiche's second feature-length film, and it followed the fairly successful *La Faute à Voltaire* (2000), a film that dealt with the experiences of a recent immigrant in Paris. *L'Esquive*, in contrast, focuses on the French-born inhabitants of a Parisian housing estate and so is a banlieue film in every sense of the word. The film had moderate success at the box office attracting approximately five hundred thousand spectators, and it was widely acclaimed, winning four Césars, including one for best film (Tarr 2005, 30).[16]

Set in the housing project of Franc-Moisin in the Parisian banlieue, *L'Esquive* is the story of a group of youth who stage a performance of Marivaux's eighteenth-century play *Le Jeu de l'amour et du hasard* [The game of love and chance].[17] Marivaux's play stands for heritage both because of its iconic status in the culture and because, as Vinay Swamy states, it is also connected to classically heritage conceptions of the French language since "the language of [Marivaux] has come to be considered particularly emblematic of the qualities of French language, and incarnates all that is supposedly classically French" (2007, 60). The play is closely associated with the eighteenth century and the Enlightenment, both privileged moments in the national past. It is an embodiment of France's most idealized traditions, among them the traditions of democracy and equality (Blatt 2008).

Tarr comments that *L'Esquive* is an internally conflicted film that suggests the possibility of successful integration of banlieue adolescents and, at the same time, realistically depicts the "continuing divisions and inequalities which have a particularly negative impact on *banlieue* males" (2007, 140). It is true the film offers a conflicted view of the potential for the insertion of immigrants and their children, but I offer that this reflects an attempt to depict the conflicted relationship France has to its own democratic heritage, rather than a reflection of any ambivalence on the part of the film itself. Competing interpretations of Marivaux's play are offered within the film, and these function as competing interpretations of the Enlightenment and of French heritage. Essentially, the film asks whether the heritage embodied by the play is one of democracy and equality, as is often asserted, or whether it is one of oppression and inequality. In this way, *L'Esquive*, much like *Le Pacte des loups* (2001), meditates on the real legacy of the Enlightenment, on its relationship to the present, and therefore on the entire construction of the idea of integration.

Like Kassovitz's *La Haine*, *L'Esquive* features a multiethnic group of teenagers, and like *La Haine*, the film declines to represent or explore the origins or histories of any of its central characters.[18] The result is that the only history or heritage explored in the film is that of the dominant culture, embodied by the Marivaux play. Through the refusal to engage with the particular pasts of the film's characters, Lydia (Sara Forestier), Krimo (Osman Elkharraz), Rachid (Rachid Hami), Fahti (Hafet Ben-Ahmed), and Frida (Sabrina Ouazani), *L'Esquive* indirectly suggests that they all share a common heritage, a heritage that is defined both by their shared milieu—the banlieue—and by the dominant culture—the *patrimoine*. This dual heritage, that of place and culture, are both represented in the film through language use. The banlieue is represented through the slang that all of the teenagers use and the dominant-culture *patrimoine* through the language of Marivaux. It is worth noting that most of the teenagers are able to manipulate both types of language with relative ease, which indicates their legitimate right to define their identity through both.

The principal characters in the film, therefore, are geographically, rather than ethnically, determined. Their identity is shaped by their common presence in the banlieue, not by their ancestry. This is a borrowing from French heritage in that it reappropriates the logic of regionalism, which has become a central component of mainstream heritage, as suggested. As in more typical heritage works, the cultural identity of the characters is asserted through their presence on the land, but that the particular space of land to which they are linked is modern and urban undermines any attempt to read this connection as ancestral. Moreover, because the space to which the characters are identified is a marginal one, *L'Esquive* asks us to consider whether France has been as willing to recognize the particular identities linked to the banlieue as it has those identities linked to its rural provinces, a question reinforced by the film's (atypical) failure to depict the Parisian center (Swamy 2007, 61).

The film's refusal to engage with ancestral origins is not, however, an attempt to disguise that several of the characters are or appear to be of immigrant origin. On the contrary, it is quite evident, both by their names and their appearances that Krimo, Frida, Rachid, Fatih, and other characters in the film are of Maghrebi origin, and Magali speaks Portuguese to her mother. If the film acknowledges that diversity of origins is typical of the banlieue, it does not privilege the idea of origins or ancestry, and in some cases, most notably that of Lydia, it leaves the question of origins completely open. One way in which the film both acknowledges and downplays ancestry as constitutive of identity is, as noted, through the use of language. All of the teenagers use *verlan* mixed with Arabic words and expressions, and all of the characters say "*Inch' Allah*," although we have no reason to believe they are all Muslim. On the one hand, this affirms the multicultural nature of France, at least in certain *milieux*. On the other, it suggests that heritage may be less a question of ancestry than of social class and place. Saying "*Inch' Allah*" and using other Arabic words is equivalent to using *verlan*. It does not indicate at all what someone's ethnic identity is, but it says a great deal about the background from which they come, about their experience, and about their milieu.

The exploration of the relationship of *milieu* and social class to heritage is central in the film, and it is a question that is raised directly by the play itself. The subject of Marivaux's play is love, but it is also social class because masters and servants swap roles in the play, impersonating one another with greater or lesser degrees of success. In this way, the play explores questions of class mobility, by investigating whether it is possible for a person of one social class to pass for a person of another social class. In one important scene, *L'Esquive* draws attention to the role that class ascension, or social mobility, plays in *Le Jeu de l'amour et du hasard*. In so doing, the film invites the spectator to ponder whether it is any more possible in twenty-first-century France for a person to move within social classes than it was in the ancien régime. Moreover, the film asks us to consider what role heritage, or more particularly, the dominant-culture's definition of heritage, plays in determining the answer to that question.

In the scene in question, Lydia, Rachid, and Frida are performing a scene from act 2 of *Le Jeu de l'amour et du hasard* in front of their high-school classmates. Lydia plays Lisette, the maid, who is, in turn, pretending to be Sylvia, her mistress. Frida plays Sylvia, who is pretending to be to Lisette, and Rachid, who plays Arlequin, the valet, is pretending to be his master, Dorante. Lydia, unhappy with Frida's performance as Sylvia playing the maid, complains to their teacher that Frida is acting too much like a lady and not enough like a maid. She asks the teacher whether Frida should not act more like the maid, since that is the role her character is supposed to be playing.

That this scene takes place inside of a school is not insignificant. The school is one of the central transmitters of cultural memory or heritage. Moreover, as Tarr relates, the French school is also purportedly the site of republican universalist values (2007, 136), those values that are understood as the legacy of the Enlightenment and the Revolution. Marivaux's play, when performed in the school, then, becomes the embodiment of French revolutionary heritage, the official cultural memory of the values the Revolution produced. When Lydia asks the teacher to evaluate Frida's performance, she is, therefore, asking for the official-culture verdict on whether or not equality and the social mobility that it implies are part of France's Enlightenment heritage. When the teacher answers, she states directly that Lydia's question is central to any understanding of the play. But in her answer, the teacher contradicts Lydia's own understanding of the play, stating that Marivaux is arguing *against* rather than for equality and mobility, because, according to the teacher, Marivaux's play suggests that ladies cannot successfully pretend to be maids, and maids cannot successfully pretend to be ladies. One's destiny, according to Marivaux, is determined by one's milieu.

It is arguable whether this is the only possible reading of the play. Lydia's question implies the opposite reading. What is significant, however, is that this reading is, according to the film, the *official* reading of the play. This, in turn, suggests that the official version of France's Enlightenment heritage is not a democratic heritage, which regards all people as equal but, rather, an aristocratic heritage that regards all people as the product of their social class. What *L'Esquive* asks us to consider is whether we are to accept this reading of the play. *L'Esquive* functions, like Lydia's question, to undermine this particular reading of *Le Jeu de l'amour et du hasard* and with it assumptions about the assimilability of France's minority populations. The film, for example, repeatedly points to the dominant-culture's frequent refusal to accept the possibility that those from France's suburban spaces are capable of social mobility, even as it suggests both the desire and the capacity for such mobility on the part of (sub)urban youth.

This idea is reinforced visually by the way *L'Esquive* presents the banlieue. It is worth noting that it is not represented as a violent space as is typical of banlieue films. It is, however, presented as a *closed* space, a space of confinement. In most of the scenes in which we see the principle characters, they are filmed in medium or long shots, with the buildings of the *cité* both surrounding and towering over them like a wall. This suggests the near impossibility of movement beyond that space, and it is consistent with the trope of stasis that characterizes most banlieue films. Moreover, *L'Esquive* includes one scene that suggests quite directly that the dominant culture is openly hostile to such mobility.

In that scene, Lydia, Frida, Krimo, and Fahti sit in a car to talk about Krimo's romantic interest in Lydia. The car itself suggests movement and, specifically, the potential for movement out of the *cité*, even if the car does not physically leave the space of the banlieue. Moreover, the car is filmed in such a way that it is not surrounded by the buildings of the banlieue. Many of the longer shots featuring the car show it against a background of open space and open sky, which reinforces the capacity for movement already suggested. Quite suddenly and unexpectedly, toward the end of the scene, however, the police arrive and begin questioning and harassing the youth, despite that there is little evidence they have done much of anything wrong. The scene ends with all of the youth being arrested and, presumably, taken off to jail. It is difficult not to read the police in this scene, like the teacher, as an arm of the state, and in that regard, their intrusion suggests official, which is to say, dominant-culture hostility and overt resistance to any attempt on the part of the youth to move beyond the space of the banlieue.

The framing of the *cité* in the arrest scene parallels, in some ways, the framing of the classroom scenes in which the play is performed. In those scenes, the students are shot surrounded by three walls of the classroom, but often visible in the frame, on the fourth wall, is a large window. Through the window, the *cité* is visible, but since the classroom is on an upper floor, a great deal of open space is also visible above and beyond the buildings of the banlieue. The window, like the car, suggests an entry or the possibility of movement beyond the banlieue, but it also suggests an inability to move. It is true that the students and the spectator can see beyond the *cité* through the window, but it is also true that the window remains closed in all of the scenes. In this way, the window functions like a transparent wall through which it is possible to see the world beyond the *cité* but through which no movement is possible. This is reinforced by the teacher's indirect assertion that the banlieue residents will never moved beyond the *cité* because their backgrounds and their milieu will prevent them from doing so.

While it is fairly clear that *L'Esquive* suggests that French society refuses to allow the inhabitants of the banlieue to move beyond that space, it is not clear that the film, as a whole, suggests that movement or mobility is impossible. Other scenes in the film, specifically, scenes in which Marivaux's play is performed, directly contrast those of the performance in the classroom. In these outdoor scenes, the students are rehearsing the play outside of school in an outdoor amphitheater or park (see fig. 5). The characters are often filmed in long shot, and on one side, the buildings of the *cité* are clearly visible, as they are in many of the other exterior shots in the film. However, on the other side is open space and open sky, much as there is in the scene with the arrest. This again suggests that it is possible for the protagonists to move out of the banlieue, and this mobility, interestingly, is tied directly to the performance of the play.

These rehearsal scenes point, I think, to an alternative reading of the play within the film and, ultimately, to an alternative reading of heritage and its relationship to social mobility. They suggest that movement out of the ban-

Fig. 5. Frida (Sabrina Ouazani), Lydia (Sara Forestier), and Rachid (Rachid Hami) rehearsing Marivaux in *L'Esquive* (2004).

lieue is possible and that such movement is directly tied to an engagement with the very cultural *patrimoine* that seems to suggest the impossibility of such movement. Specifically, it is by assimilating heritage, by learning to play roles—by adopting speech patterns, class markers, and dominant-culture competence—that the characters of *L'Esquive* can move beyond the banlieue. This idea of mobility is reinforced by Lydia's own reading of the play. When Lydia criticizes Frida for acting too much like a lady and not enough like a maid, she refuses the logic that says that a person's identity is dictated by their origins. What is more, she draws attention back to Frida's own milieu and origins, to the fact that she is *not* a lady, that she is from a social class much closer to that of a maid. Frida's inability to accurately act like a maid, therefore, is itself a performance that directly suggests the ability to transcend one's origins, and it contradicts the teacher's assertions about the meaning of Marivaux's play.

Other indicators in *L'Esquive* reinforce this reading. Lydia's decision to dress in costume even when she is only rehearsing the play suggests a strong desire on her part to move beyond her milieu as well as an ability to identify with the privileged sites and periods of the dominant-culture *patrimoine*. It is this ability that marks Lydia and Frida and Rachid, who also all successfully perform their roles, as capable of moving beyond the banlieue. This suggestion of mobility is reinforced by the film's final shot, in which Lydia walks through the *cité*, away from the camera, as though she is on her way.

Lydia's probable mobility contrasts with that of Krimo. Although he, too, dreams of escape, as evidenced by the pictures of sailboats he draws, nothing in the film suggests he will succeed. Indeed, although Krimo has a role in the play (he takes over Rachid's role as Arlequin), he is never able to successfully perform that role. Moreover, although he attends the outdoor rehearsals, he is never successfully able to perform his role outdoors, and his indoor performances are repeatedly interrupted by the teacher. Ultimately, Krimo gives the role back to Rachid, and in the final performance, he watches through a closed window as the play is staged. This suggests he is cut off from the social mobility that participation in the play suggests. In the last shot in which he appears, Krimo is enclosed in his apartment, which suggests he is unlikely to move on in the way that Lydia, Frida, and Rachid probably will.

Some critics have seen the contrast between Lydia's probable mobility and Krimo's lack of mobility as a suggestion that "gender as well as ethnicity may be a determining influence in social mobility" (Tarr 2007, 139). However, such a reading is complicated by Rachid participating, rather successfully, in the performance of the play. Rachid is, therefore, marked for mobility where Krimo is not. The difference between the two of them—what determines their mobility or their lack of mobility—is less their gender (or their ethnicity for that matter) than their willingness and ability to successfully perform roles, which is, in turn, predicated upon their willingness or ability to identify with the Marivaux play and the cultural heritage it represents.

Krimo's exclusion from the social mobility that seems open to Lydia and the others also functions as a critique of the dominant culture and particularly the state and the way both use heritage to block access to resources and opportunities. It is clear from Krimo's desire to perform the role of Arlequin and from his efforts to watch the play when he is (presumably) replaced in that role that he also desires this mobility. However, unlike the other characters in the film, he is not able, on his own, to achieve it. It might be imagined that the school—a privileged site of transmission of cultural heritage and the much-vaunted center of the process of integration—would teach Krimo how to successfully perform his role and, therefore, how to attain the social mobility he desires. However, the school's function in the film is to reinforce hierarchies, not break them, and no such teaching occurs.

In an interview with Richard Porton that appeared in the journal *Cinéaste*, Kechiche raised directly the question of cultural heritage and pointed it to it as means through which inhabitants of the banlieue could gain access to the wider culture. Speaking about the difficulties he encountered in making *L'Esquive*, Kechiche remarked that there is in France a certain "milieu that owns cultural property and [that] doesn't want to loosen its grip on this sort of ownership" (Porton 2005, 47). While Kechiche was speaking about the film industry and not specifically about *L'Esquive*, his observations can quite easily be transferred to the content of the film. The interpretation of the Marivaux play that is offered by the teacher reflects the type of privilege and cultural ownership of which Kechiche speaks. It is, according to *L'Esquive*, by imposing such a meaning on cultural heritage, by suggesting from the outset that access to heritage and the social classes who control it is denied to those who live in the banlieue that elites in France impose a lack of social and cultural mobility on France's post-colonial minorities.

However, as *L'Esquive* suggests, Marivaux's play does not necessarily mean that cultural access is determined by birth. Rather, this is only one possible reading of the play within the film and therefore only one possible understanding of heritage. As Kechiche observes in the same interview, banlieue residents, in some ways, demonstrate a greater range of cultural knowledge than the cultural elites who would exclude them. This is suggested in *L'Esquive* through the ability of the teenagers in the banlieue to successfully engage both with the language of their own milieu—the *verlan* and Arabic-punctuated French they speak—and with the language of the dominant culture— the language of Marivaux—whereas the elites in question (the teacher, for example) are able to master only the latter. Moreover, the inclusion of the teenagers' own, now marginal, form of French in the film points to the fact that Marivaux's own French—now considered the embodiment of French linguistic heritage—was itself once considered marginal (Swamy 2007, 60). France's real heritage, therefore, at least according to the film, is not any particular mode of expression or any specific set of texts. It is, rather, a certain dynamism and movement, an ability to adapt that is embodied by the banlieue residents and the hybrid language they speak, a language that may itself one day be considered a central part of the cultural *patrimoine*.

L'Esquive, then, offers a different standard by which to measure cultural prestige than that typically associated with heritage or official culture. Social mobility, the film suggests, depends not upon the protection and perpetuation of the class and milieu inherited at birth but upon the ability to transcend both of these. Moreover, according to the film, those who are of mixed heritage are at a distinct advantage in cultivating this skill because they already have the ability to function within their own milieu and to engage with the dominant culture *patrimoine*. *L'Esquive*, therefore, asserts that the "failure" of banlieue residents to "integrate" into the broader society is not their own. It is, rather, the failure of society to accept such integration. This reading of the situation of ethnic minorities in France is fairly close to Azouz Begag's reading, with which this chapter begins. Kechiche, however, goes further than Begag in that he insists that despite such blockages, ethnic minorities and other marginalized group must continue to press for mobility, a mobility they will ultimately achieve. This returns us to the title of the film, *L'Esquive*, which refers to victory in a combat sport, a victory achieved through superior dexterity. France's minorities will succeed, Kechiche's title seems to promise, precisely because their cultural hybridity makes them more dexterous culturally than their majority-culture counterparts.

This call to continue to battle is the final message of the film, a message articulated, once again, through a performance. For Marivaux's play is not the only text to be performed in *L'Esquive*. Prior to the final performance of that play in the film, the younger children of the banlieue stage a play of their own, an allegorical play about a community of birds that is trying to migrate. This play is based on the fable *La Conference des oiseaux* by the twelfth-century Persian poet Farid ad-din Attar (Nettlebeck 2007, 317). It tells the story of a community of birds that undertakes a long journey only to wake up and find they have not moved at all. Rather than give up, the birds continue to fly, confident they will eventually arrive at their destination. The migration of the birds is a clear reference to the migration or immigration that has formed France's urban peripheries, and the dream of movement suggests the desire for social mobility and "integration" on the part of the populations who inhabit them. Ultimately, *L'Esquive* suggests, these populations will realize their dream. However, the film also emphasizes that the dominant culture will continue to try to prevent that dream from being realized. The key to mobility, according to the film, is an engagement with the very culture that seeks to prevent this movement, an engagement embodied in the interaction between Marivaux's classical French comedy and Atta's mystical Sufi fable.

Heritage has often been understood as the privileged space through which the dominant culture works to exclude and permanently marginalize its minority populations. Heritage narratives, such as those found in some recent histories and in heritage films, are presumed to collectively propose a vision of Frenchness based on ancestry and shared culture, a vision that inscribes those of immigrant origin as permanent foreigners, whatever their citizenship or country of birth.

Heritage, however, is essentially only a vision of the nation that defines identity through shared spaces of culture and memory. What heritage means and how it is used depend very much on what those shared spaces of culture and memory are determined to be. Those who propose a multicultural understanding of Frenchness have not, in general, rejected heritage as a means of defining the national group. Rather, they have worked to draw attention to the quasi-ancestral construction of heritage, to its emphasis on homogeneity, and, most of all, to the incompatibility of this particular construction of the national past and the reality of France's history and diversity.

By simultaneously appropriating and contesting the logic of heritage, multicultural writers and filmmakers are able to draw attention to the problematic construction of heritage in contemporary France, a construction that obscures or denies the colonial past and, therefore, denies the shared historical and cultural spaces that bind France's post-colonial minorities to the majority culture. Moreover, they draw attention to the selective use of this quasi-amnesia to exclude populations within the nation who should rightfully be included. In so doing, these writers and filmmakers point to alternative spaces within the collective memory and alternative readings of heritage that refigure Frenchness to include those who have previously been excluded, and they permanently undermine the notion that the marginalization of ethnic minorities in France is self-imposed. Moreover, by expressing belonging in terms of movement, where conventional heritage expresses it in terms of stasis, these narratives are able to suggest that the conventional model of heritage is outmoded, something preventing rather than guaranteeing progress, something that must ultimately be left behind.

5

Recovered Memories: Diversity, History, and the Expanding Space of the Past

*I*n their song *"J'y suis, j'y reste"* from the 2002 album *Utopie d'occase*, the French rock/rap/ska group Zebda sing about the multicultural reality of the banlieue in Toulouse, where they grew up. Zebda's portrait of the Toulousain banlieue highlights aspects of the city's regional identity—the *bourrasque* wind, the Occitan tradition, and the Basque country—as well as Toulouse's hybridity, the product of (post-)colonial immigration—the beat of the *djembés*, the residents from Senegal, Malta, and Jerusalem. In the logic of the song, these diverse elements blend and coexist to form an identity unique to Toulouse, an identity reinforced by the song's musical composition, which combines *la chanson française*, salsa, African rhythms, reggae, ska, raï, and hip-hop. If the lyrics of the song record the social marginalization and discrimination to which France's ethnic minorities are often subject, the combination of music and lyrics affirms the relatively seamless coexistence of a regional French identity and a clearly multicultural identity at the same time as it references the historical processes that have created this blend.

This exploration of the articulation of a (post-)colonial heritage in France begins with a song from a multiethnic pop group from Toulouse because of the place Zebda has occupied in recent French cultural memory, because of the way the group embodies strategies and practices used in arguing for the recognition of France's multicultural or (post)colonial heritage and because of the particular role popular music has played in shaping perceptions of identity and national identity in France.[1] Zebda was one of the most popular rock groups of the late 1990s and early 2000s, and they were honored with numerous awards at France's *Victoires de la musique*, most notably for their 1998 album *Essence ordinaire*. Danielle Marx-Scouras has said of Zebda that their trajectory "mirrored that of France in the 1980s and 1990s, a period marked by debates about immigration and national identity" (2005, 23). And it is clear to anyone familiar with the group that the essence of their music and ultimately their success were the articulation of a multicultural French identity.

In addition to emphasizing the diversity that characterizes contemporary France, particularly its urban centers, Zebda's songs have also inscribed the history and experience of immigration into the space of collective memory. Perhaps the most famous example of this was their song "Le Bruit et l'odeur," from the album of the same name. The song was a response to an inflammatory speech about immigrants given in 1991 by President Jacques Chirac. In "Le Bruit et l'odeur," Zebda took Chirac's words, which referred to cultural difference (the "noise and smell" of African and North African immigrants), and sampled them into the song to ensure they remained part of the cultural memory. Zebda turned the sense of those words on their head transforming them into a hymn to the role the formerly colonized played in defending and liberating France during the two world wars and to rebuilding France after World War II.[2]

Zebda blends their exploration of "alternative" sites of memory with references to more traditional spaces of memory. For example, "Le Bruit et l'odeur" opens with the lines

> Je suis tombé par terre
> C'est pas la faute à Voltaire
> Le nez dans le ruisseau.
> [I fell to the ground
> It's not Voltaire's fault
> with my nose in the gutter.]

These lines are a reworking of a quote from chapter 15 of Victor Hugo's *Les Misérables*, in which the character Gavroche sings,

> Je suis tombé par terre
> C'est la faute à Voltaire
> Le nez dans le ruisseau.
> [I fell to the ground
> It's Voltaire's fault
> with my nose in the gutter.]

The reference to Hugo, who, in turn, references the heritage of the Enlightenment and the Revolution, presents the discrimination and exclusion suffered by France's ethnic minorities as a continuation of historical processes of oppression and exclusion that date to the Revolution and before. Gavroche is a marginalized character, a poor orphan who lives on the street, and the lines Zebda quote come just prior to his death. Gavroche attributes his marginalization to a failure of the Revolution and the Enlightenment that produced it. In reworking, Zebda link the racism and marginalization experienced by ethnic minorities to that suffered by Gavroche, but at the same time, they suggest there is also something unique about the situation of France's postcolonial minorities. This blending of quotes from Chirac and Hugo, along with references to immigration and racism, creates a new space of heritage, one that borrows from more conventional forms of heritage but emphasizes urban rather than rural experiences and opens the space of collective memory to colonialism and its aftermath. This is reinforced by the musical composition, which blends musical styles to create complex new forms that encode the process of blending produced by colonization and immigration by leaving distinct elements of each musical component intact.[3]

Zebda is not the only musical group to reference the post-colonial heritage in their music. Numerous French musical groups, including IAM and Massilia Sound System, both based in Marseilles, Les Fabulous Trobadours, an Occitan rap group, Alliance Ethnic, a rap group based in the Parisian banlieue of Creil, and Manau, a Breton hip-hop ensemble, have fused the already hybrid musical forms of hip-hop, reggae, ragga, or ska and, more specifically, regional elements that derive from the groups' particular cities or regions of origin. Jean-Marie Jacono, for example, suggests that the rap group IAM uses rhythm as a means of metaphorically rendering the spatial dynamics of Marseille (2002, 26). Moreover, IAM, like Zebda, have closely identified themselves with their city of origin, a reference that is clear even in the group's name, which has alternately been read as meaning "I am" (a challenge to Paris's status as the cultural capital of France), Imperial Asiatic Man (affirming Africa as the cradle of humanity and linking Marseille via the Mediterranean to Africa), *Invasion Arrivant de Mars* (invasion arriving from Mars, where Mars is a truncated version of the city's name), and *Indépendentistes Autonomes Marseillais* (autonomous Marseillais separatists, affirming the independence of the city). Whatever the real meaning of the group's name, Chris Warne asserts that its very multivalence "conveys dynamic, not static notions of identity" (1997, 148). And this dynamic identity is rooted in the hybrid identities of the city itself.

Similarly, the group Manau, whose name is Celtic for the Isle of Man, fuse regional and multicultural identities in their music and lyrics. The songs on their first album, *Panique Celtique* (1998), blended Celtic music with hip-hop, celebrating the mix of a strongly recognizable regional identity and a more contemporary, multicultural one. One of the songs from the album, "Mais qui est la belette?" turned a well-known French folk song, "Le Loup, le renard, et la belette" into a hip-hop hit. Later albums, most notably *Fest Noz de paname* (2000), became progressively more hybrid, as the group mixed elements of jazz, funk, and other diverse musical forms into the hip-hop/Celtic mix. The eponymous title track from *Fest Noz de paname* also mixes traditional regional identities with post-colonial identities, since the song recounts the migration from France's rural provinces and elsewhere that formed contemporary Paris. The title of the song reflects this fusion, since "Fest noz" is Breton for a party, and "Paname" is a popular (slang) name for Paris, often used by rappers. These function as reminders that French identity has long been formed by (im)migration, whether from inside or outside the nation's borders.

Popular music is far from the only space in contemporary culture in which heritage is being reworked to create what might be termed a post-colonial *patrimoine*. A number of films, beginning in the 1990s, also similarly posit the existence of a common heritage linking France's ethnic minorities and its majority-culture citizens. Unlike the "beur" or banlieue films discussed in the previous chapter, these films represent the past more directly. In so doing, they seem to work to fill in omitted spaces in the collective *patrimoine* and to counteract the historical amnesia that has surrounded France's colonial past and its history of immigration. These films, like Zebda's songs, argue that many of those immigrants whose children and grandchildren are now seen as "inassimilable" were the same colonial subjects who helped sustain and rebuild France in earlier eras and who were once schooled in French culture as a part of the *mission civilisatrice*.

Recovered Histories: Immigration, Intégration, and Benguigui's *Mémoires d'immigrés*

Perhaps the single most important filmmaker to participate in the creation of a post-colonial heritage is Yamina Benguigui. Her film *Mémoires d'immigrés, l'héritage maghrébin* (1997) is widely considered to be the definitive cinematic text on North African immigration into France. *Mémoires d'immigrés* is a three-part documentary that seeks to tell the story of Maghrebi immigration into France and of the legacy of this immigration. The nearly three-hour film was originally made for television by Canal Plus, the privately owned French television channel, but it received such acclaim and attention after its broadcast in May and then June of 1997 that it was released in theaters in January of the following year. Although a documentary and, therefore, radically different from the nostalgia and melodrama characteristic of mainstream French-heritage cinema, Benguigui's film is dominated by the question of memory. The film seeks to open up the closed space of French national memory so as to inscribe in it the experiences and memories of the French of Maghrebi descent. Benguigui describes the film as an effort to "reconstruct the thread of memory of Maghrebi immigration in France" in order to permit the children of that immigration "to truly feel that they are citizens [who are] integrated into French society" (2000). The film has been regarded as a document of French history and memory that represents "the difficult history of immigrants that is omnipresent in their memories but whose role in forming French society has been eclipsed."[4]

Yamina Benguigui was born in Lille to an Algerian family who immigrated to France during the Algerian War. *Mémoires d'immigrés* is her second film, following the documentary *Femmes d'Islam* (1994), which was also released to critical acclaim. It was followed by a third, narrative film, *Inch' Allah Dimanche* (2001), which similarly explored the relationship of colonialism and immigration but through realist melodrama rather than through documentary. Sylvie Durmelat argues that Benguigui, through her filmmaking, has "begun to accumulate symbolic, cultural and economic capital, which accredits her as a legitimate representative and agent of the transmission of memories about the history of Maghrebi immigration" (2000, 173). In the context of *Mémoires d'immigrés*, Durmelat sees Benguigui's basic task as constructing "a place for the collective memory of Maghrebi immigration in France, a memory that has hitherto been marked by national amnesia . . . the silence of the parents, and the ignorance, or rather, the indifference of French society" (2000, 171). Through the presentation of interviews with immigrants, their children, and grandchildren and with central figures from the French government, Benguigui explores the way in which Maghrebi immigration has formed contemporary France and demonstrates the degree to which this immigration has been left out of official memory.

Benguigui's film accepts memory as the site of collective or national identity. In this respect, the film works to include those of Maghrebi origin in the national space through an acceptance of traditional models of identity rather than through a challenge to them. Instead of questioning the legitimacy of a model that makes identity in the present contingent upon experiences of the past, Benguigui attempts to broaden the catalog of memories and experiences that constitute the national past. Memory and history structure *Mémoires d'immigrés* at every level. First and foremost, the film is composed of testimonies from immigrants and their children, who discuss the legacy of immigration in their own lives. This use of the oral form when combined with a division of experience by generation emphasizes transmission from one generation to another and continuity across generations. As a result, the film is more closely linked to memory than to history, and it borrows from dominant-culture conceptions of heritage the idea that memory is the defining characteristic of identity as well as the idea that memory may be transmitted across generations.

What is more, Benguigui emphasizes a certain period of immigration, that of the colonial-era. Despite that there has been a fairly long-standing migratory flow between France and the Maghreb, she focuses on the generation who "stayed," those who came during the "Thirty Glorious Years" following World War II.[5] This generation occupies a privileged space in post-colonial history because this is the generation who ultimately settled in France and subsequently brought their families to join them. Moreover, this generation came to France at a time when the colonial empire was still largely intact. Therefore, their presence in the *metropole* points to the double sites of colonialism and immigration, as well as to the colonial rhetoric that inscribed the colonized both inside and outside the space of the nation.

These immigrants and their labor, as *Mémoires d'immigrés* points out, played a central role in the industrial revolution that reshaped postwar France. Thus, Benguigui's film, like Zebda's "Le Bruit et l'odeur," points to the double right of those descended from immigration to claim France as their home, a right promised by colonial rhetoric and earned through efforts in rebuilding the republic. The film foregrounds these efforts as well as the service of colonial regiments during World War I and World War II. In this way, Benguigui, like Zebda, suggests that the very existence of the current republic is due in some measure to the presence of post-colonial minorities in France.

Like mainstream heritage films, Benguigui's film is more about memory than about history. This is evident in its lack of engagement with the historical facts of colonialism and, specifically, the colonization of French Algeria. Although the question of immigration is dealt with in historical terms, very little is done to present the history of colonialism (Durmelat 2000, 184). If, however, the film largely omits the *history* of colonialism, it is not true that it omits the *memory* of colonialism. Various reminders of the colonial past are throughout the film, from references to the participation of colonial regiments in both world wars to discussions of colonial-era recruitment of immigrant labor.

One of the most poignant examples of the way in which Benguigui records the memory of colonialism without representing its history appears in the first segment, which deals with the experiences of the "fathers," or the immigrant laborers brought to France to work in factories and mines. One of the fathers, Mohammed Toukal, describes how his wife miscarried during one of the roundups of Algerians that occurred in France during the Algerian War. Toukal begins his story by talking about his father, who had been a soldier in

World War II and who had been captured by the Germans and then interred in a German concentration camp. Mohammed then goes on to tell the story about his wife, juxtaposing, without commentary, two different experiences of discrimination and oppression.

The juxtaposition of these two stories serves multiple functions. First of all, the reference to World War II evokes a space of collective memory shared by Toukal and his majority-culture counterparts in France. Secondly, the first story locates the second in historical time. Because of his age and the age of his father and the reference to World War II, it is apparent that the roundup of which Toukal speaks occurred in the 1950s or 1960s, although he himself never says when it occurred. Therefore, despite his refusal to historicize the event, it is clear that Toukal is speaking of the roundups that occurred during the Algerian War and very probably the roundup and massacre that occurred in Paris on October 17, 1961. Toukal's reluctance to name the events or the context in which they took place suggests that he is referencing events that are forbidden, forgotten. Where the historical context of the story about his father is clear and refers to a shared space of memory, the context of the second is hidden. It, like World War II, is a shared space of memory because it concerns events in France and more recent events at that. Thus, precisely because he recounts his own experience without historicizing it, Mohammed Toukal points to a history that binds him to the dominant culture *and* to the erasure of that history from memory.

This erasure also points to another. If it is remembered that French soldiers fought in World War II, it is not, or was not until recently, remembered that colonial troops fought alongside the French. Toukal's testimony, therefore, evokes a double absence. His subtle recovery of both spaces of memory, which is echoed and repeated by others in the film, suggests that post-colonial minorities are, in the words of columnist Philippe Bernard in the February 22, 2005, *Le Monde*, "indigenous people of the Republic," citizens who have earned the right to be counted as such because of their shared history. Moreover, Toukal points very quietly to the irony of the fact that France celebrates its participation in a war that was fought to end oppression, while it forgets the fact that it went on to fight a war to perpetuate it.

Toukal's testimony reveals Benguigui's principal strategy in structuring *Mémoires d'immigrés*. Typically, it is argued that a series of differences separates the French of Maghrebi origin from the "French of French roots." Benguigui takes a different view. She argues, through her film, that "problems" of integration and acceptance stem, instead, from a *lack* of difference. First of all, she suggests, there are a number of shared spaces of history and memory, not the least of which is a shared history of French colonization and decolonization, but these spaces have been repressed or forgotten. Secondly, as Toukal's anecdote about his father reveals, shared spaces of memory are not necessarily identical. Various historical experiences and memories may be shared by minority and majority members, but this does not necessarily mean that they are shared in the same way.

In addition to emphasizing similarities of experience, *Mémoires d'immigrés* also highlights the degree to which the French government and French society as a whole have rendered immigrants and immigration invisible. Many of the men talk of working in mines, a place where they literally remained unseen. Others discuss their work on assembly lines in French automobile factories, a space where they often became equated with the machinery. In speaking about their experiences, the men reveal themselves and roles they played in (re)building France, they recover for the spectator a memory that had been buried.

In filming the men, Benguigui borrows from the cinematography of the heritage film. She alternates close-ups of the men speaking and long shots that frame them against the abandoned mines and desolate factories where they once worked. This shot structure is similar to the way in which characters is heritage films are shot in close-up and then in long shot against the rural landscape or the village. In appropriating this structure, Benguigui reworks the nostalgia for the rural that characterizes the heritage film and transforms that nostalgia. Rather than glorifying a disappearing rural past, she uncovers a disappearing industrial present, connecting the immigrants to the prosperity of the Thirty Glorious Years and at the same time recording France's subsequent economic decline.

I have suggested that Benguigui works with the concept of sameness in two ways, at once emphasizing commonality and foregrounding difference. Perhaps the best example, in the first segment, of the way in which she achieves this is her technique of punctuating the interviews with the immigrants with comments from former French government officials. Among those officials interviewed in the first segment are Joël Dahoui, a former "labor selector" for the Office of International Migration, Stéphane Hessel, a former ambassador to Algeria, and Philippe Moreau Desfarges, a former advisor to the Secretary of State for Immigrant Workers. The juxtaposition of the immigrants speaking and the bureaucrats speaking suggests a certain tension between history and memory, both because the testimony from the officials often contradicts the testimony of the immigrants and because all of the bureaucrats are shot from behind desks, as if to emphasize their official function. It also suggests, however, that the same historical moment or event may be shared in common but experienced differently.

Benguigui, in this section, also works to undermine "the myth of return," one of the most powerful myths surrounding immigration. This myth holds that immigrants intend always to return to their country of origin and that their primary loyalty, therefore, is to that country. It suggests that immigrants do not want to integrate, and it marks them as permanently different from their native-born counterparts. The bureaucrats raise the question of return in discussing the French government's largely unsuccessful efforts to "return" immigrants to their countries of origin. Their testimony is countered by the various and repeated assertions by the immigrants themselves that they cannot return to the countries from which they came. More important, the men repeatedly insist, their children cannot "return" because France is their home. By pointing to the fiction of this myth, even in the first generation, Benguigui's film "seeks to produce a social space in its own right for the new generations (rather than a problematic space in between two cultures)" (Durmelat 2000, 176).

The emphasis on sameness is repeated in the second segment of *Mémoires d'immigrés*, which deals with the experiences of the mothers. Unlike the fathers, who worked out in society, the mothers were confined to the space of the home, either their own or someone else's. They had, in general, less contact with the majority culture and are presumed, therefore, to be even more "different" than the fathers. The woman featured in the film contradict this presumption by emphasizing the points at which their experiences overlap with those of "French" women—marriage, childbirth, motherhood. Benguigui shot all of the interviews in the women's homes, foregrounding the similarities that characterize the domestic space, regardless of the culture of origin of the inhabitants. One woman named Khira Allam, for example, is filmed in her living room surrounded by pictures of her family, silk flowers, and a collection of clocks. Two sisters named Rabéra Flissi and Zohra Flissi are filmed in their Paris apartment, with their television figuring prominently behind them. Their interview is introduced by shots of the Seine and the Eiffel Tower, iconic images that reinforce the familiarity of their surroundings.

Commonalty is presented in this second segment through the use of music, as well as through the use of setting. Benguigui opens with a song from Dalida, a Franco-Italian-Egyptian singer, who was enormously popular in France during the 1960s. Khira Allam's segment ends with a song by Enrico Macias, a pied-noir singer also popular in France during the 1960s. Khira introduces Macias by saying that his music most expresses her own feelings about Algeria. The subject of the particular Macias song that is included in the film, a song entitled "Non, je n'ai pas oublié [I have not forgotten]," is memory, and particularly the memory of Algeria. Macias recounts in the song his longing for a country and a moment that are lost, spaces that, as the song affirms, must be remembered. Macias, however, is not Maghrebi. He is a North African Jew whose music has enormous appeal in metropolitan France. Given that Algeria is his birthplace and the subject of many of his songs, the inclusion of the Macias song in Benguigui's film again suggests commonality and particularly the idea that Algeria is a site of memory not merely for the Maghrebis but for France as a whole.[6]

What is perhaps more significant with regard to the logic of the film is its failure to deal with questions of religion. Neither the men nor the women openly discuss religion, and nothing in the film points to religion either as a space of memory or difference. Since officially religion lies outside of the space of the republic and, therefore, presumably outside the spaces of republican identity and collective memory, Benguigui's decision not to reference religion at all may point to her suggestion that religion should, indeed, remain a non-site of memory, at least with respect to the national community. Moreover, given the heated debates surrounding Islam in France, the decision not to address religion may have stemmed from more practical considerations of not wanting to alienate the ethnic majority spectator. In any case, it may be read as an assertion of a fundamental *lack* of difference between the French of Maghrebi origin and their majority culture counterparts rather than an affirmation of such difference.

It is interesting given the relative absence of the issue in the film as a whole that Benguigui deals, at least, indirectly, with the question of the *hijab* (headscarf), arguably the most powerful symbol of Islam in contemporary France.[7] At the visual level, Benguigui separates associations of Islam with veiled women by filming predominantly women whose heads are not covered. Veiling is also treated overtly, however. Interestingly, it is not the women Benguigui interviews who embody the refusal to wear the veil. It is, rather, a young French-Algerian woman interviewed in 1966 as part of a television documentary on Algerians in Paris made by François Hibadeau and Guy Nimoy. This young woman openly denounces the veil. She also repeatedly states that she is French, that she only knows France, and that she cannot, therefore, live the way women in Algeria live. Benguigui places this comment, made by a woman of approximately the same generation as those she interviews, in between her own interviews. Given that the absence of the *hijab* constitutes, for many in France, the mark of successful "intégration," Benguigui seems to be visually allaying French fears about the failure of Maghrebis to integrate, while suggesting, through the archival footage, that this "intégration" was already occurring in the first generation.

Where differences in experience are shown to exist—as in cases of arranged marriage—Benguigui attempts to show that France has acted as a force of change, that "intégration" has done its work, as emphasized by the refusal of the mothers to replicate their experiences in their daughters' lives. The women in the film, however, do speak out about French racism, as do the men in the first segment. A woman named Yamina Baba Aïsa directly criticizes France's policy of bringing men from the Maghreb to rebuild France and then ignoring the needs of them and their families. Rabéra Flissi and Zohra Flissi speak of their outrage that their father fought for France during World War II, and yet they, who feel themselves to be so French, are not allowed to naturalize. Like the men, the women by insisting that their children are French, born and raised in France, also criticize the dominant culture's characterization of their children as foreigners.

The film's third and final segment features the second and third generations of Maghrebi immigration, those who were born in France or who came as children. This segment is perhaps the most complex of the three, as it attempts to bridge the memories of the parents with the experiences of the children and to merge the commonalties and differences of experience between the immigrants and the majority population by presenting the children as the products of both. Perhaps the most complex aspect of this segment is, in the words of columnist Olivier Mauraisin in the December 23, 1998, *Le Monde*, Benguigui's attempt to justify the demands for equality made by this generation and at the same time to delink ethnic minorities and the violence and crime commonly associated with the banlieue.

Benguigui accomplishes this double task by focusing on those who have "succeeded" in French society. She features Azouz Begag, for example, as well as Mounsi, another well-known writer and musician. She also interviews women, such as Soraya Guezlane, a magistrate in the French judicial system. The interview with Mounsi best demonstrates the balancing act that Benguigui accomplishes in this segment. Mounsi, who is filmed in the dormitory where as a child he lived with his father, talks about how he became a juvenile delinquent and then overcame his criminal behavior through writing and his music. He talks of the material lack and emotional lack endured by his father, who worked six days a week, and that he turned to crime because he realized that if he replicated his father's quiet acquiescence to this life, then the same life would await him.

Mounsi's sentiments are echoed by a man named Ahmed Djamaï, who is filmed on the site of the *cité de transit*, or immigrant labor camp, where he spent his childhood. Djamaï says that his family was promised a stay of only two years in the *cité de transit* but that they stayed eighteen because of quotas on public housing for Maghrebi immigrants. Djamaï says that as a child, he often saw television footage of children in the Third World and came to believe that he lived in the Third World because the conditions in which he lived were identical to those he saw on the television. He also criticizes, with some bitterness, that he and his family were not French enough to qualify for decent housing, and, yet, he was French enough to be called to do his obligatory military service at the age of eighteen.

In this section, as well, Benguigui borrows from and reworks the iconography of the heritage film. The *cités de transit* and the bidonvilles or, in many cases, the spaces they once occupied are filmed in a way that is reminiscent of the village in the heritage film. Benguigui shoots her characters, her protagonists, against the backdrop of these spaces. She draws attention to the fact that like the village or the farm in *Le Retour de Martin Guerre* or *Jean de Florette*, these spaces were formative with respect to identity. They had a specific character and have produced a specific type of experience. Moreover, like village life as depicted in heritage films, these spaces have, for the most part, disappeared from the real landscape and they are, therefore, literally sites of memory. In pointing to them, Benguigui quietly calls for their re-membering.

Benguigui also points to the silence surrounding the history of immigration not only in the larger culture but also in the lives the immigrants and their children. Nearly all of those interviewed in this segment, for example, speak of their own ignorance of their parents' past. Magistrate Guezlane says that she lived in the shadow of the myth of "return" to a culture about which her parents never taught her. Begag says that myth is the only thing his parent's generation transmitted. Begag's comment, however, also points to the parents' refusal to criticize a country that often exploited them. He says that silence is a form of acquiescence that his and subsequent generations cannot and will not accept, and he points to the 1983 march against racism as evidence that the French of North African origin expect and demand equality, even if their parents and grandparents did not.[8] Benguigui's film is similarly a refusal of this silence and a demand for equality. Rather than taking to the streets, however, Benguigui works, through the film, to create a space in collective memory for the experiences of North African immigrants and for the experiences of their French children.

Benguigui's film, ultimately, does a great deal to present North African immigration as a legitimate but forgotten element of France's national past. In doing so, the film asserts connections between the Maghrebi community and the majority culture, but it also downplays significant differences of experience between the Maghrebi community and the wider society as well as differences that exist within the Franco-Maghrebi community itself. Although Benguigui does acknowledge differences between the experiences of the French-Maghrebis and those of the majority population, she often paints these differences either as insignificant or as the product of economic of governmental, rather than cultural forces. For example, the film points to the fact that the existence of bidonvilles was, in large measure, the result of the failure of the French government to provide adequate housing for immigrants and their families. Thus, her film suggests, it is racism and discrimination, not cultural difference, that account for many of the perceived "differences" between the Maghrebi community and the majority population. Those forced to live without indoor plumbing, running water, electricity, roads, or sanitation services undoubtedly have different experiences than those who have access to them. These differences, however, have nothing to do with race, religion, or culture of origin beyond that these differences were imposed upon immigrants and their families through a racial quota system that limited the number of ethnic minorities who could be placed in public housing.

Space, not culture, is determinative of identity, at least according to the logic of Benguigui's film. It is the difference between the space of the bidonville and the space of a middle-class house that accounts for many of the differences between Franco-Maghrebis and their majority-culture counterparts. Similarly, it is the difference between the space of the Maghreb and that of France that accounts for the differences between immigrants and their children or the difference between the space of the factory and the space of the home that accounts for the differences of experience between the men who immigrated to France and the wives who followed them.

Space also becomes the structuring element of memory in Benguigui's film. Her version of heritage is organized around space—common spaces and uncommon spaces—rather than time. The fathers in her film are connected to France through the experience and memory of mines and factories. These are spaces they have in common with other workers in France, even if their memories of these spaces may be different. It is through the memory of the home space that the mothers are connected to majority-culture mothers, and it is through the space of the school, the university, the workplace, that the children and grandchildren are connected to other children and grandchildren. Moreover, it is movement within and among these spaces that connects father to mother and generation to generation rather than the transmission of a single set of memories across time. It is this restructuring or reorganization of memory that allows Benguigui to break with the implicitly ancestral characteristics of heritage and to assert that collective identity derives from the possession in common of the *memory of certain spaces*, rather than the possession in common of *certain spaces of memory* that inscribes immigrants and their children in the collective space of the nation.

Toward a Multicultural Heritage: Begag's *Le Gone du Chaâba*, Ruggia's *Le Gone du Chaâba*, Gerdjou's *Vivre au paradis*

Like Yamina Benguigui, in whose film he appears, Azouz Begag has worked to inscribe the experiences of the French of Maghrebi origin into the space of collective memory. Begag was born in Lyon in 1957 to Algerian parents. He is widely seen as a success story for integration. He has written a number of novels detailing the experiences of immigrants and their children, including *Le Gone du Chaâba* (1986), *Béni or le Paradis privé* (1989), and *Zenzela* (1999), as well as numerous essays on the subjects of immigration and integration. Begag has also served as a researcher at the Centre National de Recherche Scientifique (National Center for Scientific Research) (CNRS) and as France's first Minister of Equal Opportunities, appointed under President Chirac.

The best-known of Begag's many novels is undoubtedly the semiautobiographical text *Le Gone du Chaâba*. Set in a bidonville outside of Lyon, the Chaâba of the title, the novel tells the story of one young boy's search for an identity that can accommodate his experiences as an immigrant, the culture of origin of his Algerian parents, his life in the bidonville and later the banlieue, and the France in which Azouz, the narrator, was born and in which he lives.[9] Ultimately, the novel finds this identity through memory, and it is through memory, both personal and collective, that Azouz is able to forge a link between two seemingly divided cultures.

In many respects, *Le Gone du Chaâba* tells the story of a community through the story of one central protagonist (Mehrez 1993, 36). In that respect, the novel is similar to more traditional heritage works, which also seek to create a collective sense of remembering through one individual's experience or subjectivity. This merging of collective and individual experience is evident in the title, which points to the experience of a single individual who is part of a larger community—the little boy or *"gone"* from the bidonville or Chaâba (Mehrez 1993, 36). Moreover, the title also points to the narrator/protagonist's bicultural identity by combining the word "gone," a French word, with the word "Chaâba," an Arabic word, an act that "situates Azouz . . . at the junction of rival cultural systems between which the novel shows him to be torn" (Hargreaves 1995, 39). However, just as the title manages to represent both cultural systems in a single space, so, too, does the novel chronicle Azouz's seemingly successful attempt to negotiate an identity that combines these two typically opposed terms. Moreover, as the title suggests and as the novel makes clear, the ability to blend these two distinct heritages derives from unexpected convergences of the two.

Le Gone du Chaâba shares a number of features with heritage works. It is, for example, characterized by a certain nostalgia that presents the past as a simpler, less-complicated era when identities were more stable. Kathryn Lay-Chenchabi comments, for example, that novel represents and romanticizes the now-lost space of the bidonville, a space remembered as one of family and community (2001, 2). This representation parallels the representation of the village in conventional heritage, which is similarly regarded as a now-disappeared space of idealized familial and community values. Moreover, like conventional heritage works, *Le Gone du Chaâba* conceives of identity in specifically regional rather than distinctly national terms. The word "gone" in the title, for example, is a specifically regional word, unique to Lyon and the area around it (Hargreaves 1995). However, the regional space in this case is also distinctly multicultural, it consists of Chaâba, a North African community that exists at the margins of the region in which it is found.

Beyond the valorization of both the past and community, *Le Gone du Chaâba* also resembles more traditional heritage texts in its emphasis on filiation. One of the central figures in the novel is Azouz's father, Bouzid. In addition to his role as father of the family, Bouzid is the founder of Chaâba, and his dual role reflects that of kings or patriarchs in more typical heritage works. He is, in that respect, both the father and king of traditional patriarchy, and his personal history overlaps with the history of a community that has a specifically regional character. The result is that the Chaâba becomes figured as a type of village, in much the same way as Provençal villages in the works of Marcel Pagnol, with the difference being that it is a new communal space created by immigration, rather than an ancient one.

Alec G. Hargreaves argues that Begag's novel is written for the majority French public, not for those of immigrant parentage (1995, 89). As evidence of this, he points to Begag's explaining only those cultural references that are specific to Maghrebi immigrants, never those that are common to French culture in general. However, I suggest that the text implies both a majority culture audience *and* a minority culture audience. Various markers in the text suggest this duality. It is evident, as noted, in the novel's title, which blends French and Arabic colloquialisms. It is also reflected in the character of Azouz. Since the novel is a retrospective, a flashback, Azouz is actually a dual character, the older, university-educated French man and the child of immigrant parents. Embodied in this duality is the North African heritage of his parents and the French cultural heritage he learns in school, the institution considered to be the center of French cultural transmission since the nineteenth century.

The use of a divided consciousness often functions ironically in the text to place into question the assumptions of the dominant culture about itself and about the situation of immigrants within that culture. However, it also functions in a manner that replicates that of the cinematic flashback, allowing the reader to be in two places at once and, therefore, to merge his or her own memories with those of the character/narrator, expanding the space of collective memory outward beyond the text. This is true not only because it is clear that the narrator speaks from a position of cultural awareness that is familiar to the implied reader but also because the novel reproduces spaces of memory that belong to the dominant culture, spaces such as the school. This, in turn, allows a majority culture reader to participate indirectly in unfamiliar space of the Chaâba and at the same time binding that space of memory to other, more familiar memorial sites. This creates an overlap between the wider space of collective memory and the space of memory embodied by the text.

One other significant function of the overlapping spaces of heritage in the novel is to question the perception that these two heritages are incompatible, a function performed, in general, by the representation of Azouz's experience at school. In the novel, the school often functions as a site of misrecognition of difference, and it serves to point out the spaces of misrecognition that exist in the broader culture. I use the word "misrecognition" to refer to those moments of perceived cultural difference that are actually the result of socioeconomic difference. Numerous examples of this type of misrecognition are in the text. One example occurs in a scene in which the teacher asks all of the children to remove their shoes so that he can inspect their socks because clean socks are evidence, at least in the teacher's mind, of Frenchness. One of the children, a boy named Moussaoui, refuses to remove his socks because he is embarrassed that they are not clean, because he, like the other children from the Chaâba, live in muddy conditions and because their parents are presumably too poor to afford a pair of socks for each day of the week.

Absent the intervention of the narrator's dual consciousness, this episode might be read as a moment of cultural difference of the type that leads some in France to point to the refusal of those of North African origin to conform to dominant culture values. The text undercuts this reading and points to class as the origin of the problem, a reading that suggests that even the poor among the majority population might not be able to conform to this standard of Frenchness. Moreover, the text ironizes the entire episode, because it is revealed that Azouz, who had the good fortune to be wearing clean socks on the day in question, passes the sock test and is, therefore, regarded as a model student, whereas Moussaoui is seen as a rebellious troublemaker. The teacher's opposing characterizations of the two boys, who are, in many ways, identical, thus, undercuts his judgment and the context in which it was made. Moreover, this reading shows that an action whose aim is ostensibly to bridge cultural differences actually functions to widen class differences, which, in turn, undercuts the need for such attention to cultural difference at all.

Another example that suggests that economic and not cultural differences account for what is often termed the "inassimilability" of those of North African origin is the scene in which Azouz and his classmates are asked to write a composition about a vacation in the countryside. As with the clean socks, this is something that neither Azouz nor his neighbors have ever experienced for reasons that are clearly economic. Whereas Moussaoui writes nothing because he has nothing to write, Azouz simply plays as though he has had such an experience, making something up based on what he has read or heard in school. That Azouz has had no such experience is an indictment of an entrenched class system that leaves those of Maghrebi origin in a marginalized position because they cannot conform to the cultural expectations of the society in which they live. However, Azouz's ability to successfully imagine undermines again the reading of class difference as cultural difference. However, it does something more. In writing his composition, Azouz assumes a false memory, that is to say, one that is not his own. His ability to assume this memory derives both from his exposure to textual representations or personal narratives of similar experiences and also to his familiarity with the cultural context in which such narratives are produced. Azouz, therefore, can imagine his summer holiday in the country not only because he hears or reads about those of others but also because he experiences a summer holiday from school and because he knows what the countryside around him looks like. In that respect, Begag points back to the function of his own novel, which similarly invites those of the majority population to assume and imagine the experiences of the minority population, an assumption that is contingent upon fundamental similarities between the two.

The school in Begag's novel functions very differently than it does in many texts and films by and about France's ethnic minorities. It is not presented as a space where the official culture or the state limits or oppresses minorities, as in Kechiche's *L'Esquive*. Rather, it tends to function as a site of negotiation, a double space of commonality and difference. In part, this is because the school is itself a *lieu de mémoire* in French culture.[10] Representations of the French school abound in literature and film, and scenes of humiliation in the classroom, such as those experienced by Moussaoui, have figured centrally in such literary classics as Gustave Flaubert's *Madame Bovary* and in such film classics as François Truffaut's *Les 400 coups* (1959). The representation of the school experience in Begag's novel, therefore, is one that resonates both with those of North African origin and those of the majority culture. For that reason, the very scenes that seem to foreground cultural difference might also be read as foregrounding cultural commonality. Moussaoui's persecution may be read as less the product of his refusal to integrate than a product of a school system that often thrives on ridiculing its students, and his inability to conform to educational expectations makes him one in a long line of literary and cinematic figures in French culture who are, similarly, failures from the point of view of the teacher.

Apart from its function as a space of cultural exchange, the school also functions as a space of shared heritage, particularly because it is through the school that history is transmitted. Begag uses the school and particularly a teacher named Monsieur Loubon to draw attention to the shared history of colonialism as well as to the suppression of that history. Monsieur Loubon, a Pied-Noir, develops a special bond with Azouz, a bond rooted in a shared connection to Algeria because both Azouz's family and Monsieur Loubon's family consider Algeria as their home. Like the character of Julien Desrosiers in Leïla Sebbar's *Shérazade*, Monsieur Loubon, the "European," has more knowledge about Algeria than Azouz, the "Algerian." Moreover, as in Sebbar's novel, Mr. Loubon and Azouz spend a great deal of time connecting through the transmission of this heritage, whether through the use of Arabic or a discussion of colonial history. Samia Mehrez comments that this encounter with Monsieur Loubon enables Azouz to reconcile the problem of identity that has plagued him because he discovers in Algeria "a third space that he had been experiencing in absentia, through the recreations and representations of his parents" (1993, 39). I suggest that what Azouz finds in this encounter is a third space of French history that allows him to understand that his two conflicting heritages do not conflict in the way he presumed they did.

In 1998, *Le Gone du Chaâba* was adapted for the screen by director Christophe Ruggia. *Le Gone du Chaâba* was Ruggia's first feature-length film. It performed respectably at the box office and was well received in critical circles, garnering a nomination for a César Award for best first film. Ruggia's film is focused on remembrance, and it, too, seeks to inscribe the experience of Maghrebi immigrants and their children into the space of the national memory. The film is closely tied to dominant-culture conceptions of heritage, both because it is an adaptation of a literary text, a characteristic of heritage cinema, and because Ruggia privileges certain parts of the novels that emphasize both memory and nostalgia. Like more "classical" heritage films, *Le Gone du Chaâba* explores and romanticizes a space from the past that is encoded, from the beginning as disappeared. Specifically, the film omits the space of the banlieue, to which the family moves in the second part of Begag's novel, and represents only the space of the Chaâba. Since the banlieue still exists, it may function as a site of memory but not one of nostalgia. The Chaâba, however, long since razed by the French government, is a space that *only* exists in memory. The film also shares with heritage films its emphasis on outdoor scenery, as well as a tendency to frame individuals against a landscape, be it the Chaâba, the school, or the surrounding city. Finally, like heritage films, *Le Gone du Chaâba* tends to represent the experiences of the protagonist, named Omar (Bouzid Negnoug) in the film, as emblematic of the experiences of a wider community and as pivotal in the development of history and collective memory.

Le Gone du Chaâba, however, also shares a number of characteristics with works that are typically classified as "Beur" narratives. For example, it emphasizes the commonalties that exist between Beurs and the majority French population but also highlights the differences in experience so as to record those differences within the space of history. Through the unfamiliar presentation of well-known places, including the city and the school, and through its emphasis on highly recognizable and familiar experiences, the film, like the novel, foregrounds spaces of experience and memory shared by the majority French and the minority Franco-Maghrebi populations. In the novel, as noted, this function is accomplished by Azouz, the narrator. In the film, it is accomplished by the removal of the narrator. The spectator of Ruggia's film, unlike the reader of Begag's novel, witnesses and experiences events directly instead of having the events recounted and interpreted. In this respect, *Le Gone du Chaâba* replicates the function of heritage films, which tend to function as vicarious memories through which even those unfamiliar with the experiences presented may assume a type of collective memory. In effect, Ruggia's film re-creates a lost space of French history in order to replace it with a site of memory.

To further enable identification between the majority French population and the Franco-Maghrebi population, Ruggia's film emphasizes those aspects of Begag's novel that represent experiences typical of both the Franco-Maghrebi population and the majority population. The film, for example, devotes far more space to the school than to the Chaâba, something that the novel does not do, and in that regard, the film inscribes itself into a tradition of French films about youth and education including Jean Vigo's *Zéro de conduit: Jeunes diables au col* (1933) and Truffaut's *Les 400 coups*. Moreover, playing off this topos of education, Ruggia frames the film as a coming-of-age story, devoting a great deal of time and attention to the interaction between Omar, the central character, and his friends. In this way, the viewer is able to connect with the experience of childhood, both as it has been experienced directly and as it has been represented in other films.

Another particularly important element of Ruggia's film, as Hargreaves describes, is its inclusion of the novel's three subject positions: that of the protagonist, or the "Beur"; that of the (presumed) majority ethnic spectator; and that of the parents, which equates to immigrants themselves (2001, 345). The use of this three-dimensional consciousness permits the transmission of two different spaces of memory to the spectator, that of the immigrant and that of the child of immigrants. This is particularly true because Omar brings to the spectator the experience of his own understanding, love, and admiration for his parents. This, in turn, functions not only to inscribe the experience of immigrants in the space of collective memory but also to do so in a uniquely positive way. The end result is that *Le Gone du Chaâba* undermines assumptions of unbridgeable differences between those of Maghrebi origin and those of the majority population. Through the use of Omar's mediating gaze, unfamiliar experiences, such as that of living in a shantytown or that of having foreign parents, become familiar and at the same time, familiar experiences, such as taking dictation in a classroom, become common spaces of memory through which identification is made.

Another film that recreates the space of the bidonville is Bourlem Guerdjou's *Vivre au paradis* (1998). The story of Lakhdar (Roschdy Zem), an Algerian (Bedouin) immigrant worker in France who brings his family to join him, *Vivre au paradis* also presents a view of life in the bidonville and foregrounds the desire for integration. In the context of Guerdjou's film, however, it is the father, not the son, who dreams of integrating, as much of the narrative focuses on Lakhdar's efforts to move his family into an apartment. Like *Le Gone du Chaâba*, *Vivre au paradis* is an adaptation of an autobiographical Beur novel, *Vivre au paradis: d'une oasis à un* bidonville (1992), written by Brahim Benaïcha. Moreover, like Ruggia's film, Guerdjou's re-creates the lost space of the bidonville, in this case located in Nanterre, on the outskirts of Paris.

Although both films are adaptations of novels by second-generation French of Maghrebi origin and although both deal with life in the bidonville, they are very different from one another. Guerdjou's film has nothing of the nostalgia of Ruggia's film, made evident by the much more somber lighting and the documentary style in which it was made. Moreover, Guerdjou's film focuses on the experiences of the first generation, the parents, whereas Ruggia's film focuses on the experiences of the second generation, or the children. Nonetheless, *Vivre au paradis* works to inscribe forgotten spaces of history and memory into the broader heritage, even if those spaces are different than those recreated by Ruggia's film.

Carrie Tarr observes that Guerdjou's adaptation of Benaïcha's novel is characterized by a "displacement of the voice and point of view of the novel's Beur protagonist and in its handling of time" (2005, 130). Specifically, Guerdjou's film reorients the narrative so that events are depicted from the point of view of the parents, most particularly Lakhdar, rather than from the point of view of the son. Whereas *Le Gone du Chaâba* effects an identification between the French of Maghrebi origin and the dominant-culture through an identification between Omar and the spectator, *Vivre au paradis* effects an identification between immigrants and the dominant culture through the identification between Lakhdar and his wife, Nora, and the spectator. The result is that *Le Gone du Chaâba* inscribes integration into the collective memory, whereas *Vivre au paradis* inscribes immigration and the colonial history that produced it.

This emphasis on immigration and colonial history is also evident in the film's colonial, rather than post-colonial, setting. Guerdjou's film takes place between 1960 and 1962, whereas Ruggia's is set in 1965. This focus on the period between 1960 and 1962 constitutes a departure from the source text, which begins earlier and ends much later, and it suggests that much of Guerdjou's interest in making the film was to inscribe that particular period of history into French collective memory. Tarr observes that Guerdjou directly stated that one of his primary goals in making the film was to commemorate the events of October 17, 1961, events that are (a forgotten) part of French history but not of Algerian history (2005, 130). This effort to inscribe colonial history into the space of French history is also evident in the film's use of space. Unlike Benaïcha's text, the film does not begin in Algeria; rather, it begins and ends in France. Algeria is represented in the film but only briefly in a match-action sequence detailing the trajectory of a letter from Lakhdar to Nora. Therefore, although colonial Algeria is a point of reference in the film, it is not emphasized as a point of origin, particularly for Lakhdar, who is only shown in France. Moreover, any presentation of Algeria in the film is filtered through the context of events in France. The history of Algeria, in this way, becomes a space in the larger history of France.

This reframing of the colonial past in *Vivre au paradis* works to expand French collective memory to incorporate sites and spaces from the colonial past that have, typically, been omitted. The film defamiliarizes spaces and events within France in order to force the spectator to see them from a different point of view. In the film's opening sequence, for example, a space that is in the heart of France is presented as though it lay outside of France, as if it were foreign. The camera shows Arabic-speaking men living in crowded, dark, poorly constructed rooms, like those Europeans might typically associate with the developing world. It is only after a few moments that captioning reveals that these men live in Nanterre and that the space they occupy is therefore in France. This restaging of hidden spaces in the national center points to other spaces that lay hidden, in both geographical and historical terms. The sudden recognition that these Arabic-speaking men are in France, for example, raises the question of how they got there, which, in turn, points to the absent history of immigration in France. If this is the most extreme example of defamiliarization and/or misrecognition that occurs in the film, it is not the only one. Lakhdar and his workmates are often shown against the emerging skyscrapers of contemporary Paris, as if to remind the spectator of how those skyscrapers came to be there and, thus, to point to the role immigrants played building contemporary France.

The representation of the bidonville in the film also points to similar processes of misrecognition that have occurred in collective memory. The bidonville looks to the spectator to be a "foreign" space because the material conditions of that space are completely at odds with dominant conceptions of France at the time and because both the bidonvilles and their memory have been erased. This process of erasure is encoded by the film, even during the time period that is presented. Apart from the sense of the invisibility of those who live in the bidonvilles to the wider society, the film includes a scene of police demolishing a home in the bidonville, which, in turn, suggests state efforts to deny or demolish that space. Tarr comments that the bidonville is presented in the film as "an imagined community cut off from the rest of the world" (2005, 133). But the question Guerdjou raises is, who has imagined the community in that way? In the logic of the film, it is not the inhabitants of the bidonville, because we see numerous shots of the men crossing back and forth into the outside world and because Lakhdar, whose experiences structure our perception of events, is so intent on integrating into French society himself. Rather, the film suggests that is the outside world that has shut out the bidonville and its inhabitants, an idea reinforced by the numerous shots of fences, barbed wire, railroad tracks, and other boundaries that surround the bidonville. However, the film also suggests that despite this partitioning, hidden connections exist between bidonville and the city outside it, a suggestion reinforced by scenes in which Lakhdar and others cross in and out of the bidonville. This suggests a willingness and capacity of the part of the immigrants to engage with the majority culture, but it also suggests that this willingness is not reciprocal.

The same is true of the film's treatment of colonial history. As noted, the French-Algerian war, the activities of the Front de Libération (National Liberation Front) (FLN), and the eventual independence of Algeria are figured in the film both through context and narrative. Nora is actively involved in the efforts of the FLN as she gives both money and shelter to FLN activists. The events of October 17, 1961, are also linked to the activities of the FLN, because the demonstration that begins those events was organized by the FLN in order to protest a curfew imposed on Algerian immigrants living in France. However, the activities of the FLN as depicted in the film all take place in France, and the reactions to those activities, such as the late-night roundups and the eventual massacre, also take place in France. In that way, the film emphasizes that the history of colonialism and resistance is not part of a foreign history, it is also part of the history of France, a history whose memory, like the bidonville itself, has been partitioned or erased.

This process of erasure is also suggested in the film through Lakhdar's dream of obtaining an apartment, a dream that might be seen as the equivalent of a desire to move outward into society, to become like everyone else in France. If Lakhdar is largely unsuccessful, it is not because he lacks the willingness to integrate. It is rather because the government refuses to allow him to do so. In this way, the film seems to say that the culture or the state works consciously to keep immigrants invisible. If the family ultimately moves out of the bidonville, ten years after requesting that move, this is only to allow another act of erasure, that of the bidonville itself.

This double process of insertion and erasure also characterizes the events of October 17, 1961. As the film suggests, Algerians in France appropriated a model of peaceful demonstration approved by the wider culture and used it to attempt to make their presence in Paris seen and felt. In so doing, they wished also to register their discontent with a curfew that also worked to keep them invisible. The state reaction was to suppress the demonstration and to make it seem as though the demonstration had not happened. When that effort did not fully succeed, the state engineered another, more complete erasure. Coverage or discussion of the event and the brutal reaction to it was censored, and over time it became as though October 17, 1961, never occurred.

Ultimately, *Vivre au paradis* is a commemorative film that marks the experiences of the first generation of immigrants (Tarr 2005, 134). However, it also situates the collective memory of those immigrants within the broader framework of French history and memory. The film takes place almost entirely in France, and the events and circumstances that shape the lives of the film's characters are events that have their origins in France and that, for the most part, take place in France. Even though during the celebrations of Algerian independence, many residents of the bidonville speak of a return to Algeria, this never occurs in the film.

Guerdjou, Ruggia, and Begag, all create narratives that detail the uneasy processes of immigration and integration. All three inscribe both processes inside the space of French history and memory, and all three imagine memory in terms that are more spatial than temporal. For Begag and Ruggia, collective memory is imagined as a series of overlapping spaces, some of which are held in common and some not. Because of the spatial orientation, however, even the unfamiliar becomes familiar due to its connection or proximity to that which is known and shared. For Guerdjou, memory is imagined as a series of nested spaces, in which opening one reveals another that was hidden. In this model, the unfamiliar is presented as that which was known but unrecognized or even that which was known and suppressed.

War and Remembrance in Bouchareb's *Indigènes*

One of the most significant contributions in recent times to the development of a post-colonial heritage, both in terms of content and reception, is Rachid Bouchareb's 2006 film, *Indigènes*. *Indigènes* is the story of four North African recruits into the French colonial army or the French African Army during World War II.[11] The four, Saïd (Jamel Debbouze), Yassir (Sami Naceri), Messaoud (Roschdy Zem), and Abdelkader (Sami Bouajila), enter the colonial army as members of the so-called *tirailleurs* (riflemen or infantrymen) and go to fight in Italy and then France in an effort to liberate France from the Nazi occupation. Despite valiant service, they, like their other African comrades, suffer near-constant discrimination in the army and, ultimately, three of the four, Saïd, Yassir, and Messaoud, give their lives for France, while Abdelkader lives to suffer a final indignity, the freezing of his war pension, along with those of all other members of the colonial army, by the French government in 1959.

Indigènes is one of the most acclaimed and most recognized of all films made by a French director of North African origin. It won awards at Cannes for its ensemble cast, won a César for best screenplay, and was nominated for numerous other awards, including an Oscar for Best Foreign Language Film. Although Bouchareb classified *Indigènes* as an Algerian film for the Oscar committee, the project was an international collaboration. It received subsidies from the French government, a number of regional, local governments in France, and the governments of Algeria and Morocco. It is largely set in France but was filmed in both France and Morocco. *Indigènes* inserts itself directly into contemporary issues of immigration, *intégration*, and heritage, and it engages both with French heritage cinema, with beur and banlieue cinema, and with non-Western post-colonial cinemas. Bouchareb states, however, that it was in many ways targeted to a French audience. In a 2006 interview with *Time* magazine, for example, he asserts that the film addresses French society's need to "understand its history," and he directly links the gaps in French history to the riots in France's banlieues the preceding year, suggesting that the riots were due, in part, to a certain degree of alienation from history on the part of French society and on the part of ethnic minorities (Bouchareb 2006).

Before exploring the film's connections to multicultural cinema, it must be recognized that *Indigènes* differs from beur and banlieue cinema in a number of ways. It is set, for the most part, in the past, not the present. It represents, at least briefly, the Maghreb and, most particularly, colonial Algeria, as the point of origin of most of the characters. *Indigènes* was shot in both French and Arabic, which is also a divergence from beur and banlieue films, which typically feature only French. Finally, the film features a number of sequences in which the characters are praying, and this is also atypical of beur and banlieue films, which are marked by a reluctance to openly represent Islam.

Despite its differences from beur and banlieue films, *Indigènes*, nonetheless, shares many of the characteristics of those films. Director Bouchareb is one of the more important directors of films grouped under one of the two rubrics. Secondly, three of the four lead actors, Naceri, Zem, and Bouajila, have connections to beur or banlieue cinema, Naceri having appeared in Thomas Gilou's *Raï* (1995) and Rachida Krim's *Sous les pieds des femmes* (1997), Zem having appeared in Guerdjou's *Vivre au paradis* (1998) and Merzak Allouache's *Chouchou* (2003), and Bouajila having appeared in Karim

Dridi's *Bye Bye* (1995), Abdellatif Kechiche's *La Faute à Voltaire* (2001), and Jean-Pierre Sinapi's adaption of Jack-Alain Leger's (Paul Smaïl's) *Vivre me tue* (2002). While Debbouze has not appeared in beur or banlieue films, he is a well-known comedian whose Moroccan origins figure prominently in his stand-up routine. In addition, *Indigènes*, like beur and banlieue films, references immigration without directly representing it, particularly since the trajectory the soldiers take, from Algeria into France, mirrors the journey taken by immigrants and since the period after World War II marked the most significant period of immigration from North Africa into France (Noiriel 1988; Hargreaves 1995).[12] Finally, like beur and banlieue films, *Indigènes* explores questions of racism and discrimination, and although it does so in the context of the past, it clearly points to the persistence of these problems in the present.

In addition to its connection to beur and banlieue films, *Indigènes* also shares a number of characteristics with the heritage film. It is a relatively high-budget film, set in the past, using "authentic" settings and costumes. Also, like heritage films (and popular French films in general), it was co-produced by one or more French television channels, in this case, France 2, France 3, and Canal Plus (Molia 2007). It features and is filmed in a number of regions with recognizable identities, including Provence and Alsace, and even received partial funding from those regional governments. It is also very closely tied, as are heritage films, to issues of national identity, as evidenced by the numerous shots of the tricolor, the singing of *La Marseillaise,* men in berets, and the rural landscape in general. What separates *Indigènes* from the more typical heritage film, however, is the absence of nostalgia in its representation of the past; the landscapes featured in the film are not always pristine—they are quite often either barren or bombed out and destroyed. More important, *Indigènes* constructs memory not through individual subjectivity but rather through the space of cinema itself. The result is not a linear, monolithic construction of the past and of memory but rather a prismatic construction, where a single space or site of memory may be viewed in any number of ways.

Despite the publicity surrounding *Indigènes*, it is not the first film nor even the first French film to reference to service of colonial troops to France, even if it is the first major feature film to deal with the question directly. Rather, that subject has been dealt with, at least indirectly, in a number of heritage films and banlieue films. On the heritage side, colonial troops are depicted in Bertrand Tavernier's *La Vie et rien d'autre* (1989) and Pierre Javaux's *Les Enfants du pays* (2006). On the banlieue or multicultural side, the issues of service and of the freezing of war pensions were also dealt with in a rather prominent way in Senegalese director Ousmane Sembene's *Camp de Thiaroye* (1987) and more overtly in Benguigui's *Mémoires d'immigres* (1997). There are, as noted, also references to the participation of colonial soldiers in popular music and literature. Therefore, rather than uncovering a completely forgotten space of French history and collective memory, *Indigènes* gave prominence to an active, if latent, space of memory that exists in both traditional and multicultural conceptions of heritage. *Indigènes*, then, seems to be less about *whether* this particular historical reality is remembered than about *the way* it is remembered. It is less, therefore, about the content of memory than its structure.

Much of the publicity surrounding *Indigènes* has centered on the film's reminder that France has failed to honor a commitment it made to those from the colonies who served in the army, a failure manifested in the freezing of the pensions of those soldiers in 1959.[13] The film drew so much attention to the issue that following its release that Chirac finally made good on a 2002 promise to restore those pensions.[14] It is a mistake, however, to believe that the entire focus of the film is the injustice of the frozen war pensions. Rather, I argue that the film uses the issue of war pensions to explore the greater questions of the memory or absence of memory of the role the colonial soldiers played in the history of France and more broadly to explore the relationship between cinema and memory.

This exploration of cinema's connection to memory is evident from the opening credits of *Indigènes*. The film opens with a collage of black-and-white film clips of North Africa during the colonial period. The presence of these clips draws attention to the fact that cinema, since the time of the Lumière brothers, has presented exotic images of the (former) colonies for the consumption of French spectators, which has, in turn, created an exotic "memory" or image of Africa and North Africa in the collective imagination. However, because these clips fade from black and white to color, they also suggest the movement from silent-era cinema to contemporary cinema. This raises the question of how the space of the colony has, or has not, been represented in cinema over time, and it foregrounds the cinema's capacity to both construct and suppress memory. This tension between re-presentation and suppression is reinforced by the fact that the black-and-white film clips point to a colonial past that is evoked but never fully represented in the space of *Indigènes* itself.

The film later revisits the question of cinema's construction of the past. In a scene near the end of *Indigènes*, a scene that takes place after the final battle scene in Alsace, a French military cameraman is shown filming the victory in order to record it and transmit it to the wider French public. In that scene, the cameraman is creating the official memory of what occurred in the village (see fig. 6). However, he deliberately excludes the colonial troops from the scene, replacing them with white, French soldiers, who actually arrived after the battle. By inserting recently arrived white, French troops into the frame, this cameraman is overwriting the real history of the victory, which involves the liberation of the village by colonial troops, and replacing it with a constructed version in which continental French troops are the liberators. This will, in turn, create a false memory of the liberation for those who see the film and create a false version of the past for posterity.

This scene has a number of functions, beyond suggesting cinema's capacity to write or re-write history and memory. First, it points back to the black-and-white films at the opening, also shot by French (Western) filmmakers, and it, therefore, prompts a meditation on the ways in which they, too, have rewritten or reconstructed the past. Second, and as a result, it renders Bouchareb's film a double space of memory, one that evokes both the liberation of France from the Germans and France's colonial past. Finally, it points to Bouchareb's own film and draws attention to its attempt to re-present the past, to recover this double, problematic space of memory (colonialism and occupation/liberation).

I have said that *Indigènes* constitutes a double site of memory, but it is a multivalent site of memory that implies yet others. The presence of this French film camera filming the liberation of France recalls the relative absence of French films on that particular moment of French history. If French cinema has been increasingly willing to deal with the once-suppressed memory of the German Occupation, it has been less willing to depict the liberation of France, which has more often been featured in Hollywood films such as Ken Annakin, Andrew Marton, and Bernhard Wicki's *The Longest Day* (1962) or Steven Spielberg's *Saving Private Ryan* (1998). Bouchareb overtly references such war films in *Indigènes*, along with others (Hargreaves, "Indigènes," 2007, 245).

Fig. 6. A cameraman filming the liberation of a French village but omitting the liberating forces from the shot in *Indigènes* (2006).

The double recovery of the colonial past and the period of occupation and liberation through other war films reshapes the entire idea of collective heritage. First of all, it suggests a certain similarity between the two periods, both of which have been problematic spaces in the French national memory (Rousso 1990; Donadey 2001). Secondly, and perhaps more important, it allows for the recovery of both spaces through the reappropriation of existing cinematic images. For example, by appropriating and not substantially altering the conventions of the typical (Hollywood) war film, Bouchareb takes a familiar screen memory—the liberation of France—and ever so slightly rewrites it so that French troops and colonial troops are shown liberating France, rather than the invading American armies typically depicted in such films. He, therefore, reclaims the memory of this particular moment for France. At the same time, however, he points to the way in which the colonial past shaped the national past and, therefore, to the overlap of colonial and national memory. Moreover, by evoking other World War II films, particularly Hollywood films, Bouchareb renders the liberation of France a prismatic space of memory that is uniquely cinematic and that includes the experiences of North Africans, French, and Americans.

As Henry Rousso argues, the memory of French collaboration during World War II was shortly thereafter suppressed in the broader culture, and references to both occupation and liberation were figured through the mythological memory of widespread French resistance (1990, 2001). This is the phenomenon Rousso refers to as "Vichy Syndrome." This suppression of memory was reflected in French cinema, which, from the 1950s onward, dealt very infrequently with World War II.[15] From the 1990s onward, however, the memory of World War II has increasingly resurfaced. In cinema, this led to films such as Claude Chabrol's *L'Oeil de Vichy* (1993), Jacques Audiard's *Un héros très discret* (1996), and Bertrand Tavernier's *Laissez-passer* (2002). What these films have in common, apart from their re-presentation of Vichy France, is their exploration of cinema's role in the Nazi Occupation and the French collaboration. *Indigènes*, although not focused on questions of collaboration or resistance, directly references both, albeit obliquely. In one scene, for example, a civilian official orders a colonel to severely punish colonial troops in order to keep them in their place. The colonel responds by asking the official what post he held in the Vichy government before switching sides. Through this scene, Bouchareb calls into question the official understanding of the liberation as the moment France and Europe were freed from fascism and racism. The reference to side switching suggests that the racism of the Vichy regime continued past liberation, a suggestion reinforced by the obvious racism in the official's orders. Through this scene, therefore, *Indigènes* links the history of Vichy to colonial history and suggests that any reevaluation of the history and memory of World War II depends upon a reappropriation and reevaluation of the history and memory of colonialism.

This interweaving of memory and cinema involves not only World War II but also, through references to Edward Zwick's *Glory* (1989), the American Civil War. These references then link France and World War II to slavery in the United States and the participation of black soldiers in the war that would ultimately free them. This, in turn, points back to the images of the colonies present in the opening credits and history of colonialism that forms the backdrop of the narrative and ties the story of the colonial troops in World War II to the histories of all of those oppressed by racism. Moreover, it may also point to the war in Algeria, which occurs in the interstices of *Indigènes* temporal frame, as it was another war in which the oppressed may be seen to have liberated themselves.

Bouchareb's version of the liberation, then, restores the French to the story and reaffirms that the French played a significant role in the liberation of their country. However, it does so by posing the question of what it means to be French. By showing the degree to which colonial regiments contributed to the liberation and, therefore, to the creation of the present-day republic, *Indigènes* suggests that those colonial troops and those like them earned the right to consider themselves French, a right to live in France, and a right to count themselves as French. The film affirms this through repeated scenes of bloodshed and sacrifice, but it also does so more directly through the words of the characters themselves. Saïd, for example, speaking to the pied-noir Sergeant Martinez after their victory in the campaign in Italy, directly states that France is his country as much as Algeria is his country, and he further states that his service has earned him the right to stay there. Similarly, Messaoud openly considers remaining in France and marrying a French woman, even though he does not live to do so. Abdelkader repeatedly and often states that as a result of their service, the colonial troops are entitled to equal treatment, and he, the lone survivor, is shown in France more than fifty years later. Moreover, the colonel of the regiment promises Abdelkader that if the troops successfully defend the village in Alsace, their bravery will be remembered, and it will win them the equality that Abdelkader repeatedly demands.

That Abdelkader is the only one of the four main characters to survive and that we see him in France at the end of the film beg the question of whether France has kept the promise it made to those colonial troops, whether implicitly or explicitly. As noted, this promise is figured as more than the simple promise to fairly compensate them for their service. It is encoded in the film as a promise to them that they can consider themselves French. This promise is made through the words of the colonel and through the unspoken promise of recompense for their service, but it is also made through the colonial *mission civilisatrice*, which *Indigènes* also directly references. The recruitment scenes set in Algeria that open the film feature reference the *mission civilisatrice*. In those scenes, a man walks through an Algerian medina, calling upon Algerians to go and fights for France, the motherland. In the September 26, 2006, *Le Monde*, historian Benjamin Stora criticizes Bouchareb for depicting the recruitment of colonial troops as entirely voluntary, when it was often forced. However, by depicting such recruitment as entirely voluntary, Bouchareb suggests the internalization of a discourse generated by France itself, one that told colonial subjects that they were French and should consider themselves such. The suggestion made in this opening scene is reinforced later in the film when colonial troops sing the French African Army anthem "C'est nous, les Africains" and the French national anthem "La Marseillaise." While the singing of the Marseillaise reflects the internalization of French colonial doctrine, "C'est nous, les Africains [We, the Africans]" points directly to French colonial policy's promise of ultimate citizenship. The words of "C'est nous, les Africains" refer to Africans "coming from the colonies / To save the fatherland" and the desire to "carry high and proud / The beautiful flag of greater France." Such references point to a conception of the colonies as part of France that was part of colonial-era propaganda but that has since been forgotten. They also draw attention back to the fact that the republic that contemporary immigrants are currently imagined to threaten is the one that those immigrants and their parents and grandparents gave their lives to help create.

The film also directly emphasizes commonality at various points, most notably, in the opening shots of the Algeria, Italy, and Provence segments, each of which opens with a black-and-white shot of a rock landscape. The similarity of the landscapes in each of these opening shots undermines the idea of irreconcilable difference, by pointing to the fundamental similarities in the landscapes of these three places, which, in turn, suggests an underlying similarity in the people who inhabit them. Bouchareb also heightened this sense of similarity by filming the sequences that are set in the Vosges mountains in the Atlas mountains of Morocco, which again suggests an inability to distinguish one landscape from the other. What is more, the ability of the four protagonists to move seamlessly from Arabic into French and back again suggests there is no incompatibility between the two languages, and by extension, no fundamental incompatibility that separates these colonial subjects from the population of metropolitan France. Even the prayer scenes, very often omitted in French films featuring characters of African or North African origin, function more as markers of similarity than of difference, since the prayer scenes occur in the context of war and battle, in places where the spectator would expect them—in burying the dead, for example, or in praying for victory. In that respect, the Muslim prayers in *Indigènes* function as indicators of a common humanity, which again reaffirms the idea of similarity rather than difference.

In effect, despite the inclusion of characters speaking Arabic and characters engaging in Muslim worship, *Indigènes* works, like many beur and banlieue films, to downplay cultural difference and to suggest that the majority French population and the French of African origin are more similar than they are different. This is reinforced by the film's repeated portrayal of the desire and willingness of at least three of the four main protagonists to serve France and to remain in France, which, in turn, contradicts ideas that those of African origin in France cling to identities of origin or that they wish to supplant French identity with another one. For that reason, although *Indigènes* only references the contemporary situation indirectly, it, nonetheless, invites a reading of the current situation of France's (post-)colonial minorities through forgotten spaces of the past. In so doing, it makes a case for the inclusion of France's post-colonial minorities, by suggesting that the republic, as it is presently understood, would literally not exist without them.

The past, then, as it is constructed in *Indigènes* is not the homogenous space of the conventional heritage film. It is a multifaceted, multivalent space that functions through both temporal and experiential connections, through national and transnational connections, and, ultimately, through the space of cinema itself. It is a construction of the past that foregrounds the limits of conventional heritage and that challenges the unified nature of such visions of the past. *Indigènes* seems to present itself as a corrective re-presentation of problematic spaces of the past, a means of re-creating and re-membering those moments from history that have been problematic or whose interconnections have been overlooked.

Indigènes also disrupts the relationship of past to present and problematizes the strictly linear conception promoted by heritage films and the cinema in general. It does so in its "return" to a filmic and historical present that is suppressed until the end of the narrative. Typically, films that include two different periods separated by a sizeable temporal gap are structured through flashback, where the film begins in the narrative present, moves back into the past, and then back into the present. This structure implies not only continuity between past and present but also causality. The past that is shown is the past of the present (as in *Saving Private Ryan*). *Indigènes*, however, disrupts this continuity by withholding the filmic present from the spectator until the end of the film. This disruption breaks the implied causal link between past and present and causes the spectator to meditate on the relation between the two. Contrary to mainstream heritage films, *Indigènes* does not reformulate the present through the past. Rather, it calls for a reformulation of the relationship between past and present.

Hamid Naficy argues that cinemas of diaspora and immigration are characterized by an opposition between place as an expression of identity and social belonging and place as displacement or a sense of exile (2001). Conventional readings of French cinema tend to concur with this reading, asserting that French heritage films reinforce a deep sense of identity and belonging through place, whereas beur and banlieue films reflect an absence of this. Such a reading assumes that immigrants and their descendants have no historical or memorial connection to the places in which they reside. It also assumes that however long they reside in a given country or territory, they remain permanently detached from it, anchored instead to some other point of origin.

While this assumption may hold true for certain populations of immigrants, it does not seem to hold true for France's (post-)colonial immigrants, for their children or their grandchildren. Rather, France's post-colonial minorities share with their majority culture counterparts the history of colonialism and empire, the history of a process of immigration that was central in shaping modern France, and the memory of numerous encounters and spaces that this shared history has created. Far from signifying the perpetual exclusion of France's minorities, therefore, a heritage conception of collective identity implies their *inclusion*. For if one defines Frenchness as the product of shared history and memory, it is almost impossible to argue for the fundamental incompatibility of people whose histories have overlapped with that of France for more than a century and whose cultures of origin have been permanently altered by that span of shared history.

The problem, therefore, has not been that heritage excludes France's postcolonial minorities. The problem has been, rather, that heritage has been constructed in such a way as to omit or ignore the history and memory that binds France's ethnic minorities to the majority population. This problem cannot be resolved merely by reinserting colonial history into French history, primarily because history's structure—which imagines history as events that unfold and repeat across time in a single space—prevents such reinsertion. What is needed, therefore, is a new model of history and/or of memory, one that imagines both in nonlinear terms.

All of those involved in decolonizing history and collective memory have understood this temporal structure to be at the root of the problem. Writers and filmmakers like Benguigui, Begag, Ruggia, and Guerdjou have attempted to resolve this problem by rooting both history and memory in lived physical spaces. Bouchareb, however, regards cinema as the space through which to restructure the past, perhaps because of cinema's role in creating and sustaining the current problematic structure. Bouchareb, therefore, has more in common perhaps with Christophe Gans or Jean-Pierre Jeunet than with Benguigui, Begag, Ruggia, or Guerdjou. This latter group of filmmakers understand the problem to be one of representation and not of memory, and they all, therefore, work to restructure the images society has created of the past, rather than to restructure the past itself.

Conclusion: The Fall of Time and the Rise of Space from the Post-Colonial to the Posthistorical

*M*any contemporary analyses of heritage presume that there is something fundamentally new about defining individual or collective identity in the present through a connection to the past. Nothing could be further from the truth. The past, in the form of ancestors, names, and histories, has long been the basis of individual and cultural identity, whether in precolonial Africa or in postindustrial Europe. The modern nation, however, did reformulate the connection to the past in significant ways. It asserted fundamental connections among individuals who were not bound by blood, and in doing so it metaphorically re-rendered blood and ancestral ties into historical ones, tying collective identity to a common past and a common destiny.

The cinema was central to the nation's historical reformation. In France and elsewhere, the cinema took up history's mission of asserting continuity and progress, generating narratives that shored up the sense of collective destiny, thereby reinforcing the idea of a collective, national identity. In the 1980s, however, the cinema and history seem to have parted ways and this despite the "return" of the historical film. Perhaps the most evident example of this great divorce was the much-publicized dispute between historian Natalie Zemon Davis and director Daniel Vigne over the retelling of the story of Martin Guerre. Davis objected to a retelling of the past that was not, in her view, consistent with the facts. Vigne, for his part, was less interested in the historical record than in the dramatic potential of the story. Davis's view was that of the historian—that the past is knowable and quantifiable and that the present depends on its accurate transmission. Vigne's view is that of the filmmaker—that the past is a fictionalized re-presentation composed of omissions, inventions, and absences. The past, in this view, is neither knowable nor transmissible. It is understandable to the present only in terms of metaphor and analogy. When critics of heritage films lament the heritage film's substitution of "heritage space" for "narrative space," are they not bemoaning the substitution of contemporary fantasies about the past for any serious attempt at historical transmission?

The split between history and heritage, therefore, may be less a result of a nostalgic desire to return some halcyon period of more stable identities than a rejection of history's "civilizing mission" and an accusation against history that it, too, is a fantasy, a modern reinvention that also distorts and omits. It is not, however, a rejection of the past or its centrality in shaping the present. It is merely a reformulation of the relationship between past and present, one that conceives of that relationship not in linear, temporal terms but in spatial ones. It regards the relationship not in terms of continuity but in terms of parallels—between a given space in the past and the present—and in terms of proximity—between a given space and a neighboring space, between a person and the space he or she occupies. Heritage films encode this reformulation in their emphasis on spaces and places and in their exploration of the way in which individuals come to reside in certain locations and how that fact of residence affects them and those around them.

This reformulation, however, has transcended the heritage film. Those who are either immigrants themselves, who are the descendants of immigrants, or who are merely interested in the status of immigrants in France have long recognized that the most-compelling argument for the inclusion of immigrants in the national community lay not in contesting the idea that collective identity derives from shared heritage but in affirming that idea. However, they have also recognized that the dominant construction of both history and collective heritage is problematic. They, too, have worked to uncover, recover, and foreground spaces of shared history and memory that official history has consciously or unconsciously omitted and denied. And they, too, have frequently reframed the past in spatial rather than temporal terms.

What we may be witnessing in France and elsewhere, then, is not so much the articulation of post-colonial identities as posthistorical ones. Certainly, the one depends upon the other, for it is only in the fragmentation of the colonial era's conception of time as an ascending line of progress that the formulation of such spatial identities is possible. However, it is also more than a reformulation of identity and belonging in light of the end of empire. It is a reformulation of human experience that understands connections in multidirectional, multivalent ways, that conceives of space in geographic terms certainly, as the relationship to a specific geographic space, but also in the way in which Pierre Nora envisions it, in terms of mental spaces, cultural spaces—equivalences and parallels. It is certainly a result of the push and pull between the empowered and the powerless—a struggle over access to space in the most literal sense, but it is also the result of a shifting presentation of space in technological terms—the rise of cyberspace, for example, or the transmission of cinematic space.

This privileging of space over time has not negated the importance of the past in interpreting the present, a fact made evident by the struggles over history embodied in the February 2006 law on the teaching of French colonial history. Rather, it has deemphasized the importance of hierarchies and chronologies in understanding or framing the past and foregrounded the importance of historical spaces and the spaces in which and from which history may be articulated.

As the February 2006 law demonstrates, understanding whether the current reformulation of the past that is ongoing in France is truly post-colonial or whether it is, as some fear, merely a domestication of the colonial past and a (re)colonization of post-colonial minorities at the heart of the *metropole* depends on a reading not on the content of the past but of its structure. Articulating the past in linear terms constitutes, in many ways, a reaffirmation of colonial-era narratives of progress, narratives that de facto deny the right of ethnic minorities to count themselves as legitimate residents of France. Does it, therefore, follow that articulating the past in spatial terms constitutes a refusal of that narrative? And if so, how?

One answer to that lies in the films treated in this study. Progressively, through a spatial rather than a temporal engagement with the past, these films, from *Le Retour de Martin Guerre* to *Les Glaneurs et la glaneuse* to *Indigènes*, have articulated a conception of collective identity that regards any inhabitant of a specific space as, in some measure, a "legitimate" occupant. These films, on the whole, have not regarded what might broadly be termed failures of inclusion—whether the inclusion of Martin Guerre or the inclusion of the grocer Lucien—as originating with the individuals in question but rather as failures of the narratives that define inclusion. They see history (or heritage) not as a unified narrative that links past and present in terms of cause and effect but more as a unifying narrative that creates links among inhabitants, that views the past in terms of parallels and connections. And in this process of reformulation, the cinema becomes a mediating space, one in which those parallels and connections can be asserted, represented, experienced.

In many ways, this tendency to reframe the past in spatial and experiential rather than temporal terms has moved beyond history. This is evident in *Les Lieux de mémoire*, which abandons the usual, linear, causal narrative of history and replaces it with a series of spaces, spaces to which various connections are possible. It is also evident in the creation of the Cité nationale de l'histoire de l'immigration in 2007. Beyond an official opening of a space for immigration in the history and *patrimoine* of France, the museum is literally a space, rather than a narrative, and one that opens onto or references other spaces. The building in which the museum is housed, for example, Le Palais de la Porte Dorée, was created for the Colonial Exposition in 1931 and was later used as the Musée de la France d'Outre-mer and the Musée national des Arts d'Afrique et d'Océanie. If the present museum does not directly reference these previous uses of the space it now occupies, it is not necessarily because the past has been domesticated. Rather, it is because the new museum functions in spatial, relational terms in which a single image, object, or building evokes others, both past and present, near and far.

The museum also offers some clues as to how the national space, the nation itself, acts within or upon this apparent reformulation. Although it is clear that the museum is an official space, an arm of the state, it was a response to forces exercised in spaces beyond the state's immediate control—contested spaces like the banlieue or the liminal spaces in which immigration occurs. Moreover, like the heritage film, which was also the product of state funding, the museum has meanings beyond those the state can control. Its location, for example, points to the same processes of historical omission and suppression that are at the center of the heritage film, which, in turn, points to a constant need for reevaluation and reframing that is more consistent with the view of history articulated by *Le Pacte des loups* or *Indigènes*, for example, than that of a traditional historical narrative. Moreover, the museum points to the evolving status of the nation itself. Just as the films in question reference films, texts, and histories that cannot be confined to a single national history, the museum suggests parallels among the experiences of immigrants in all societies and foregrounds the formation of France by people from diverse societies. This does not suggest the death of the nation, as it was popular to suggest several years ago, but it does reflect a broader rethinking of the function of the nation in the contemporary era. Not only migration but also the rise of mass culture and mass communication have meant that whatever control the state once exerted over narratives about the past, that is, whatever power it had to shape collective identity, now exists side by side with influences ranging from popular music to advertising. Identity cannot, in this context, be imagined in unitary terms but rather as a series of relations, a shifting kaleidoscope of images, memories, and allegiances. The nation still has resonance in this kaleidoscopic model, but it is merely one facet, important as much for its connections to other facets as for the color or shape it embodies. This is not to say that the state has no power over the individual. The state still controls access to education, to housing, to employment, to the nation itself. It is rather to say that the state's influence, like everything else, is evolving. It, too, is being felt more than ever in specifically spatial terms.

Filmography

Notes

Bibliography

Index

Filmography

Aghion, Gabriel. 2000. *Le Libertin*.

Andréani, Henri. 1911. *Le Siège de Calais*.

Angelo, Yves. 1994. *Le Colonel Chabert*.

Annakin, Ken, Andrew Marton, and Bernhard Wicki. 1962. *The Longest Day*.

Annaud, Jean-Jacques. 1986. *The Name of the Rose*.

Arnaud, Étienne, and Louis Feuillade. 1911. *André Chenier*.

Audiard, Jacques. 1996. *Un héros très discret*.

Autant-Lara, Claude. 1937. *L'Affaire du courrier de Lyon*.

Barratier, Christophe. 2004. *Les Choristes*.

Becker, Jacques. 1953. *Touchez pas au grisbi*.

Benguigui, Yamina. 1997. *Mémoires d'immigrés, l'héritage maghrébin*.

Bernard, Raymond. 1923. *Miracle des loups*.

———. 1934. *Les Misérables*.

Berri, Claude. 1983. *Tchao Pantin*.

———. 1986. *Jean de Florette*.

———. 1986. *Manon des sources [Manon of the springs]*.

———. 1993. *Germinal*.

Billon, Pierre. 1948. *Ruy Blas*.

Blain, Gérard. 1987. *Pierre et Djemila*.

Bouchareb, Rachid. 1985. *Baton Rouge*.

———. 1991. *Cheb*.

———. 2006. *Indigènes*.

Bourgeois, Gérard. 1911. *Richelieu*.

Broca, Philippe de. 1997. *Le Bossu*.

Calmettes, André, and Henri Pouctal. 1911. *Le Colonel Chabert*.

———. 1912. *Camille Desmoulins*.

Cantet, Laurent. 2008. *Entre les murs*.

Capellani, Albert. 1909. *La Mort du Duc d'Enghien*.

———. 1909. *La Vie de Jeanne d'Arc*.

Carné, Marcel. 1938. *Hôtel du Nord*.

———. 1945. *Les Enfants du paradis*.

———. 1950. *La Marie du port*.

Chabrol, Claude. 1991. *Madame Bovary*.

———. 1993. *L'Oeil de Vichy*.

Charef, Mehdi. 1985. *Le Thé au harem d'Archimède*.

Chéreau, Patrice. 1994. *La Reine Margot*.

Chibane, Malik. 1994. *Hexagone*.

———. 1995. *Douce France*.

Christian-Jacque. 1937. *Les Perles de la couronne*.

———. 1954. *Madame Du Barry*.

Clair, René. 1930. *Sous les toits de Paris*.

Cohl, Émile. 1909. *La Bataille d'Austerlitz*.

Corneau, Alain. 1991. *Tous les matins du monde*.

Dahan, Olivier. 2007. *La Môme*.

Dayan, Josée. 1998. *Le Comte de Monte Cristo*.

Decoin, Henri. 1951. *La Vérité sur Bébé Dongé*.

———. 1955. *L'Affaire des poisons*.

Delannoy, Jean. 1944. *Le Bossu*.

———. 1958. *Maigret tend un piège*.

Denis, Claire. 1988. *Chocolat*.

———. 1999. *Beau Travail*.

Denola, Georges. 1909. *Charlotte Corday*.

Desfontaines, Henri. 1914. *La Reine Margot*.

Desfontaines, Henri, and Louis Mercanton. 1911. *L'Assassinat d'Henri III*.

Dormann, Jacques. 2001. *Vercingétorix*.

Dréville, Jean. 1954. *La Reine Margot*.

Dridi, Karim. 1994. *Pigalle*.

———. 1995. *Bye Bye*.

Durand, Jean. 1909. *Cyrano de Bergerac*.

Feuillade, Louis. 1910. *Roland à Roncéveaux*.

———. 1912. *Napoléon*.

———. 1913–14. *Fantômas*.

———. 1915. *Les Vampires*.

Fontaine, Anne. 1993. *Les Histoires d'amour finissent mal en general*.

Gance, Abel. 1927. *Napoléon*.

———. 1930. *J'accuse*.

Gans, Christophe. 2001. *Le Pacte des loups*.

Gilou, Thomas. 1995. *Raï*.

Guerdjou, Bourlem. 1998. *Vivre au paradis*.

Guitry, Sacha. 1936. *Le Roman d'un tricheur*.

———. 1942. *Le Destin fabuleux de Désirée Clary*.

———. 1954. *Si Versailles m'était conté*.

———. 1956. *Si Paris nous était conté*.

Hatot, Georges. 1897. *Mort de Marat*.

———. 1897. *Mort de Robespierre*.

Heuzé, André. 1914. *Le Bossu*.

Hudson, Hugh. 1981. *Chariots of Fire*.

Hunébelle, André. 1959. *Le Bossu*.

Ivory, James. 1992. *Howard's End*.

Jacquot, Benoît. 2000. *Sade*.

Javaux, Pierre. 2006. *Les Enfants du pays*.

Jeunet, Jean-Pierre. 2001. *Le Fabuleux destin d'Amélie Poulain*.

Jordan, Neil. 1984. *The Company of Wolves*.

Kassovitz, Mathieu. 1993. *Métisse*.

———. 1995. *La Haine*.

Kechiche, Abdellatif. 2000. *La Faute à Voltaire*.

———. 2004. *L'Esquive*.

Kemm, Jean. 1922. *L'Enfant roi*.

———. 1925. *Le Bossu*.

Lamorisse, Albert. 1956. *Le Ballon rouge*.

Lean, David. 1984. *A Passage to India*.

Leconte, Patrice. 1996. *Ridicule*.

Lee, Ang. 2000. *Crouching Tiger, Hidden Dragon*.

Le Henaff, René. 1943. *Le Colonel Chabert*.

Lumière, Auguste, and Louis Lumière. 1897. *Mort de Marat*.

———. 1897. *Mort de Robespierre*.

Luitz-Morat. 1926. *Jean Chouan*.

Malle, Louis. 1974. *Lacombe Lucien*.

———. 1987. *Au revoir les enfants*.

Melville, Jean-Pierre. 1955. *Bob le flambeur*.

Morlhon, Camille de. 1910. *La Reine Margot*.

Morlhon, Camille de, and Ferdinand Zecca. 1910. *1812*.

Nuytten, Bruno. 1988. *Camille Claudel*.

Ophüls, Marcel. 1969. *Le Chagrin et la pitié*.

Pagnol, Marcel. 1953. *Manon des sources* [*Manon of the springs*].

Pouctal, Henri. 1913. *Danton*.

Rappeneau, Jean-Paul. 1990. *Cyrano de Bergerac*.

———. 1995. *Le Hussard sur le toit*.

Renoir, Jean. 1926. *Nana*.

———. 1936. *Une Partie de campagne*.

———. 1938. *La Bête humaine*.

———. 1938. *La Marseillaise*.

Resnais, Alain. 1961. *L'Année dernière à Marienbad*.

———. 1963. *Muriel*.

Rivers, Fernand. 1945. *Cyrano de Bergerac*.

Robert, Yves. 1990. *La Gloire de mon père*.

Rodriguez, Robert. 1996. *Dusk till Dawn*.

Rohmer, Eric. 2001. *L'Anglaise et le duc*.

Roüan, Brigitte. 1990. *Outremer*.

Roubaud, André. 1932. *Danton*.

Ruggia, Christophe. 1998. *Le Gone du Chaâba*.

Ruiz, Raoul. 1999. *Le Temps retrouvé*.

Schlondörff, Volker. 1984. *Un amour de Swann*.

Schoendoerffer, Pierre. 1992. *Dien Bien Phu*.

Scola, Ettore. 1982. *La Nuit de Varennes*.

Sembene, Ousmane. 1987. *Camp de Thiaroye*.

Spielberg, Steven. 1998. *Saving Private Ryan*.

Sti, René. 1934. *Le Bossu*.

Tavernier, Bertrand. 1984. *Un dimanche à la campagne*.

———. 1989. *La Vie et rien d'autre*.

———. 1992. *L.627*.

———. 2002. *Laissez-passer*.

Tirard, Laurent. 2007. *Molière*.

Tourjansky, Victor. 1931. *L'Aiglon.*
Truffaut, François. 1959. *Les 400 coups.*
———. 1962. *Jules et Jim.*
Varda, Agnès. 2000. *Les Glaneurs et la glaneuse.*
———. 2002. *Deux ans après.*
Vigne, Daniel. 1982. *Le Retour de Martin Guerre.*
Wachowski, Andy, and Larry Wachowski. 1999. *The Matrix.*
Wajda, Andrzej. 1983. *Danton.*
Wargnier, Régis. 1992. *Indochine.*
Zemmouri, Mahmoud. 1997. *100% Arabica.*
Zwick, Edward. 1989. *Glory.*
Zwoboda, André. 1945. *François Villon.*

Notes

Introduction

1. Examples of the diverse range of activities associated with that year are the exhibition honoring the work of Claude Monet held at the Grand Palais from February to May of 1980; one honoring the architect Viollet-le-duc, also held at the Grand Palais; restoration projects and museum projects including the restoration of the nineteenth-century commercial sailing ship the *Belem* (which is now used for historical cruises celebrating France's maritime history) and the establishment of a museum to commemorate rural life in the Villefagnan in the Charente, for which funds for both were dedicated in 1980. I give this brief sampling only to convey an idea of what is included under the rubric of heritage. For more on the activities associated with *L'Année du patrimoine*, see Lebovics (2004).

2. I am borrowing Stuart Hall's distinction between heritage as the general tendency to frame identity through the past and The Heritage or sometimes just Heritage to refer to the officially sanctioned version of the national past and its relationship to the nation at any given moment (2005, 23–24).

3. There is no direct equivalent of the term "heritage" in French. I have used the term "*patrimoine*" here because it is the closest term available in French. The word "heritage" and the word "*patrimoine*" have both had similar trajectories of development. Both originally referred to a property inheritance left from one family member to another (Lebovics 2004, 84; Lowenthal 1998, 4). In the late twentieth century, both words became applied to the developing notion of a shared cultural heritage. The French word *patrimoine*, however, has developed a specifically national-cultural connotation that the English word does not quite have. This derives in part from the application of the term to national art and architectural treasures, a use common as early as the 1970s (Vadelorge 2003, 11).

4. French cinema has not been globally dominant since before the First World War, at which time it was the foremost cinema in the world both in terms of production and market share (Abel 1998). If French cinema has not dominated the marketplace for more than a century, it has nonetheless had periods of great cultural and artistic prestige, most notably during the 1930s, often considered French cinema's golden age, and during the 1960s, when it was strongly associated with the avant garde. French cinema's prestige and market share were both seen to decline following the end of the New Wave in the 1970s, and it was this that prompted Mitterrand to seek a "restoration" of sorts.

5. The system of *avance sur recettes* was created in 1960 and is administered through the *Centre National de la Cinématographie* (CNC). It provides various funding mechanisms, among them a system of loans that allows filmmakers to borrow up to 5 percent of a film's total production costs against future box-office returns. Although this type of loan was theoretically intended to support independent-film production and to permit the creation of feature-length films by unknown writers and directors, it tends to favor

high-budget, high-profile films by well-known directors, which might explain why the heritage film has disproportionately benefited from this type of funding.

6. These are only a partial list of films that could be classified as heritage films.

7. For more on the evolution of the term, see Lowenthal (1998), Lebovics (2004), and especially Desvallée (1998).

8. History's role in constructing the national past is explored in greater detail in chapter 1. For more on the notion of French exceptionalism, see Godin and Chafer (2005).

9. Chapter 1 discusses the evolution of history and historiography. However, I point out at this juncture that the historical film, from the beginning, incarnated Ernest Renan's vision of national identity in that it functioned as a concrete and transmissible memory of "the great things we have done" (1882).

10. The endurance of heritage can be partly explained by the creation of a number of governmental agencies charged with it. Among these are the Directions Régionales des Affaires Culturelles (DRAC), created in 1977 and charged with safeguarding and transmitting regional heritage, Le Conseil du patrimoine ethnologique, created in 1980 and charged with overseeing and funding ethnological research in France, Le Conseil supérieur de la recherche archeologique, created in 1985, and La Commission nationale de l'inventaire général et des richesses artistiques de la France, also created in 1985. For more on these institutions and their respective roles as well as an inventory of what has been included in the national *patrimoine,* see Sire (1996).

11. Hall writes specifically about the rise of heritage in Britain, but he does apply his observations more generally, and they do reflect the thinking of scholars like Herman Lebovics who have studied the issue in France.

12. The term "immigration" is in quotes here, because, as I discuss, immigration was a virtual nonissue at the moment it irrupted into the public sphere. These debates are really about Frenchness and what it means to be French.

13. Stuart Hall uses the term "the National Heritage" to mean the officially sanctioned version of heritage at any given moment (2005, 23). I am borrowing his use of the term.

14. See Ross (1996). She convincingly argues that this emphasis on technology and "progress" was heightened in the 1960s as a means for reordering national identity in the face of the loss of the colonial empire that had previously defined it. Although the nineteenth century emphasized progress, the past was central to the vision of the move to the idealized future. Ross suggests that in the 1960s, only the present and future were emphasized, and the past was completely suppressed. It is also possible that the retreat from the past Ross identifies was a means of overwriting and suppressing France's surrender to and collaboration with Nazi Germany during the war, as has been suggested by Rousso (1990). The relationship among collective national identity, the past, and colonialism are examined in chapter 1.

15. In 1975, when it became clear that France was experiencing a severe and prolonged economic downturn, the government introduced measures designed to significantly slow or stop all new immigration. This was a reversal of a long-held policy of active immigrant labor recruitment, which had created much of the immigration up to 1975. The policy of active recruitment had been, in effect, relatively unchanged from 1945 until 1975. Moreover, there had been a steady and increasing immigration into France at least as far back as 1851. For more on immigration patterns, see Hargreaves (1995) and (2007, *Multi-ethnic France*) and Noiriel (1983) and (2005).

16. My assertion that the colonial past is and has been an absence refers to the failure of the grand narrative of French history to integrate the colonial past into the national

past. This has been referred to as the "colonial fracture." It is not an assertion that there is no memory of the colonial past, nor is it an assertion that there are no references to the colonial past anywhere in French history. Moreover, it must be noted that both the colonial past and immigration are, to varying degrees, increasingly present in both French history and Heritage. France passed a law on February 23, 2005, for example, mandating the teaching of colonial history as part of national history. In October 2007, the Cité Nationale de l'histoire de l'immigration opened at the Palais de la porte dorée, former site of the Musée national des Arts d'Afrique et d'Océanie. Both of these events suggest a broadening of the space of history and heritage, potentially as a result of the forces explored in the present work. However, both have also led to charges that France, like other former colonial powers, is domesticating counterheritage and the histories of immigrants and the formerly colonized in order to subjugate immigrants and minorities once again. As evidence of this, many point to the fact that the February 2005 law mandated that only the positive aspects of colonization be taught. As further evidence, many also cite the fact that the Cité nationale de l'histoire de l'immigration sits in a pavilion constructed for the 1931 Exposition coloniale, although neither the history of that exposition nor the broader history of colonialism is addressed in the museum.

17. For in-depth studies of integration and integration politics in France, see Derderian (2004), Favell (2001), Hargreaves (*Multi-ethnic France*, 2007), Kastoryano (2001), and Silverstein (2004).

18. "Colonial fracture" is the term given for the omission of colonial history from French history, an omission that results not only in a fracturing of the historical past but of the (post)-colonial present, which cannot be accounted for without the colonial past. For more on the concept, see Blanchard, Bancel, and Lemaire (2005).

19. See Sayad (2004) on the issue of naturalization.

1. Constructing Memory: The History of Heritage in France

1. For more on the *mission civilisatrice* and its relationship to national identity, see Conklin (1997), Lebovics (1992, 2004), Shepard (2006), and Wilder (2005).

2. For an alternate reading of Montesquieu, see Sala-Molins (*Le Code Noir ou le calvaire de Canaan*, 2002).

3. Montesquieu deals with the question of slavery in book 15 of the text. He appears to argue for slavery, but the dominant interpretation is that he was arguing disingenuously, constructing a straw man argument. As with later abolitionists, it is fairly clear that if Montesquieu is opposed to slavery, he, nonetheless, supports the generally racist view that black Africans are inferior to Europeans. This is evident in his use of climate theory, in book 15 of the text, and throughout the entire book.

4. Climate theory holds that all individuals had been created equal but that differences in climates had produced functional differences among civilizations. Civilizations that had developed in colder, northern climates are believed to be superior to those produced by warmer climates. Climate theory also asserts that climate, political action, and historical evolution are the principal factors in determining the status of a particular culture. Climate theory is, in many ways, a reworking of the theological distinctions among the races inherited from the Renaissance, but it also reflected the growing influence of science in eighteenth-century France, since climate theory replaced theologically grounded theories of race with theories that were considered more scientific and biological in nature. The numerous references to the theory in domains ranging from art criticism to medicine over the course of the century show that it also overlapped fairly extensively

with the humanist thinking of the period. Montesquieu's *Lettres persanes* (1721), for example, has references to climate theory. For an analysis of Montesquieu's reading of this subject, see Miller (2008).

5. For a discussion of Volney and a more general reading of the carryover of racial thinking from the eighteenth to the nineteenth century, see Staum (2003). For a general study of climate theory and the general theory of cultural distinction during the eighteenth century, see Vyverberg (1989), and Sala-Molins (*Le Code Noir ou le calvaire de Canaan*, 2002).

6. Climate theory may have also introduced one of the fundamental paradoxes that would come to characterize republican thought, the paradox that Gary Wilder terms the concept of the "imperial Republic." Its overlap with humanism produced a discourse that held that egalitarianism, democracy, and colonialism could coexist. Climate theory, for example, accepted that all men had been created equal. It was, therefore, consistent with the increasingly egalitarian current of the Enlightenment. However, it also suggested that because of culture, nations were fundamentally unequal. Most important, because climate theory assumed that culture was mutable and could therefore be made to evolve, it provided a justification for the domination of "southern" cultures by "northern" ones, which, in turn, provided a legitimizing discourse for colonialism. This type of thinking was less an evolution of the logic of the Code Noir than an expansion of it.

7. Michelet makes this argument in both the introduction to *L'Histoire universelle* (1834) and *Le Peuple* (1840).

8. This is actually a more circular than linear conception of history since repetition implies more of a circle than a line. Ceri Crossley argues that Michelet's work shows the distinct influence of Giambattista Vico's *Scienza Nuova* (1993, 195). Vico conceived of history as a circle that traveled through three distinct stages, the divine, the heroic, and the human. The circular aspects of Michelet's own conception of history may have come from Vico.

9. These assumptions are still current in contemporary thought concerning "development." The terms "developed" and "underdeveloped," for example, assume that development is uniform across nations, an assumption that dates to the colonial era. For more on the implications of this type of thinking, see Lazarus (2004).

10. The logic of present absence is evident in the treatment of colonial conquest by nineteenth-century historians. Certain events and incidents related to French colonization made it into history books as early as the nineteenth century. The resistance to the French colonization of Algeria by Abdelkader and his army, for example, is included in some French historical texts and certain literary texts, most notably Eugène *Une Année dans le Sahel* (1858). However, the resistance is characterized as an illegitimate rebellion against the French. Therefore, the event is included, but only its impact on France and the French is recorded. The event is present in French historiography, but its significance to Algerians is absent.

11. Michelet's overall work tends to suggest that the progression away from rural feudalism and toward modernity is equivalent to the progress toward the nation and away from "ethnic" identities. However, he argues, most notably in *Le Peuple*, that the city dweller is alienated in a way that the rural peasantry is not, and he locates France's democratic roots at particular places in a rural, pastoral past. Finally, he reads his own age, which is modern, as fallen, so there is a definite tendency to valorize the rural and the pastoral in his work, despite his repeated assertions in *L'Histoire de France* and elsewhere that the concept of race is "powerfully influenced by land" and that man had to "unroot himself

from the land" and move from an identity grounded in the rural village to one grounded in the larger notion of *patrie* (1869, 2:192).

12. The February 2005 law should demonstrate that there has been fairly dramatic movement in official narratives of the national past. The tipping point seems to have come in 1993 with the opening of the Memorial des guerres d'Indochine in Fréjus, in southern France. Since that time, France's colonial past has been increasingly visible, if contested.

13. It was the Greek historian Herodotus who first reported that the pyramids were built with slave labor. This was and is widely accepted as true, although it has been rejected by modern archaeologists, particularly after the 2002 excavation of Egyptian workers' quarters.

14. Both Steven Englund (1992) and Hue-Tam Ho Tai (2001) assert that *Les Lieux de mémoire* shows the direct influence of nineteenth-century French historiography. Nora went on to write an entire volume on Michelet, entitled *Michelet, Historien de la France* (1999), which suggests that Michelet's influence on him was indeed profound.

15. See, for example, Gillette and Sayad (1976), Noiriel (1983), and Hargreaves (1995).

16. This anxiety about presenting staged action as reality is evident even from the Lumière Brothers' films, especially the film of workers leaving the Lumière factory, which was staged and then marketed as the depiction of the actual event.

2. Family Pictures: Ancestry, Nostalgia, and the French Heritage Film

1. To distinguish French films from the British films under the same label, some critics of French cinema, including Van Dijk and Esposito, have preferred to use the term "*films de patrimoine*" or "*cinéma de patrimoine*" or, alternatively, "*film de terroirs.*"

2. For more on David, see Bordes (2007) and Roberts (1992).

3. For a comprehensive study of the development of the silent cinema, see Abel (1998).

4. For a complete discussion of how and why Hollywood supplanted France, see Abel (1998).

5. This rethinking of narrative cinema occurred at the same time as a rethinking of historiography and historicity that played out in the rivalry between structuralism and the Annales School. The simultaneity of the two shifts further suggests the interconnection of film and historiography. For more on the New Wave, see Higgins (1998) and Monaco (1977). For more on the Annales school, see Burke (1990) and Hunt and Revel (2006).

6. Resnais is often regarded as a New Wave director but is sometimes more closely associated with the *Groupe de la Rive Gauche*, an appellation coined by American film critic Richard Roud to refer to Resnais, Georges Franju, Chris Marker, and Agnès Varda (Alter 2006, 14). I have here identified Resnais as a member of the New Wave because I am citing Higgins, who analyzes his work in this context. For more on the New Wave and the Rive Gauche, see Neupert (2007).

7. The star system and the practice of crediting actors are the legacy of the French film studio Studio Film d'Art, which sought to elevate cinema to an art form by casting in films well-known stage actors. Studio Film d'Art specialized in literary/historical scenes. For more on the studio and its influence on French cinema, see Abel (1998).

8. It is ironic that Natalie Zemon Davis, the consulting historian on the film, was so unhappy with what she perceived as inaccuracies in the film, particularly as relates to the depiction of Bertrande, that she eventually wrote a book recounting her version of the story. For more, see Davis (1983, 1988, and 2003).

9. Guy Austin cites *Martin Guerre* as an early example of the heritage film, along with *Danton* and *La Nuit de Varennes*, both from the same year as *Martin Guerre*. Other

critics, including Greene, Esposito, and Powrie have focused on later films, particularly those of Claude Berri. However, they do not challenge the inclusion of these earlier films.

10. Carrière has written the screenplays for a number of major heritage works on both television and in cinema. These include (for the cinema) Volker Schlöndörff's *Un amour de Swann* (1984) and Jean-Paul Rappeneau's *Le Hussard sur le toit* (1995) and *Cyrano de Bergerac* (1990) and for television *Bérénice* (2000), *Madame de . . .* (2001), *Ruy Blas* (2002), *Le Père Goriot* (2004), and *Marie-Antoinette* (2006).

11. The theme of uncertain paternity is something of a topos in Pagnol's work, particularly his filmmaking. It is a central issue, for example, in his Marius trilogy, which were the first of the films he made and which are, arguably, much better known and much more beloved than *Manon des sources*. It is worth noting, however, that the ambiguities surrounding the issues of paternity and identity that are present in *Manon des sources* and *L'Eau des collines* are much less present in the Marius trilogy, which suggests that Berri's decision to remake these particular works was as much motivated by an interest in such questions as a desire to tap into nostalgia for Pagnol.

12. The term "jus soli" regards citizenship as a right that conveys to anyone born on the national territory. The term "jus sanguinis" considers citizenship as a right transmitted from a citizen to his or her children. France is seen has having a hybrid model of citizenship that recognizes both jus soli and jus sanguinis, although historically, one or the other has tended to be privileged at any particular moment. Since the 1980s, the French government has sought to restrict the role of jus soli through a number of revisions to citizenship laws. For more on jus sanguinis, jus soli, and the role of each in the history of French citizenship, see Brubaker (1996), Silverman (1992), and Weil (2005).

13. If the narrative contains characters who are all "insiders" from the point of view of national identity, the actors who play the "insiders" might be read as "outsiders," at least by right-wing standards of Frenchness. Montand, an icon of French cinema, was born Ivo Levi to Italian-Jewish parents, and Daniel Auteuil, who subsequently became a cinema icon, was born in Algeria. Berri was probably not unaware of the implications of this casting, since he was born Claude Langmann. The decision to cast foreign-born actors as "insiders" and a native-born actor, such as Depardieu, as the "outsider" may constitute yet another way of questioning the ancestral conceptions of identity explored in the film.

14. The law brought an immediate outcry from French historians, many of whom joined to form the group Liberté pour l'histoire. This group regards the law as one of several granting the state greater control over official history.

15. It was only a few years later that Algeria reemerged with force into the public discourse. Jean-Luc Einaudi's 1991 work on the so-called Battle of Paris in October 1961 was significant in opening the floodgates, particularly his testimony at the trial of Maurice Papon for his role in deporting Jews during the holocaust. Moreover, the publication of the memoires of General Paul Aussaresses (2001) also reopened debates about Algeria and the role of torture during the war.

16. I am not arguing that Etienne's mother was literally French, meaning that she had French citizenship. I am, rather, arguing that the cultural nation, which is often rendered metaphorically as a family, is embodied in Eliane. Camille, therefore, becomes through her adoption a member of that cultural family—her "national" identity is transmitted to her by her adoptive mother. Étienne, one presumes, "inherits" this identity from his birth mother but is also adopted by Eliane, making him doubly bound to the national family.

17. For more on republican citizenship and its blind spots, see Favell (2001), Hargreaves (2007, *Multi-ethnic France*), and Weil (2005).

3. Heritage and Its Discontents: Memory, History, and the Expanding Space of the Past

1. In addition to the books cited, a number of Web sites have information on the beast of Gévaudan. Most notable are the Cevennes tourism site at http://les.cevennes.free.fr/en/gevaudan.htm and a number of sites authored by Derek Brockis, who translated Abbé Pierre Pourcher's book into English, one of the sites being http://labete.7hunters.net/auvergne.htm.

2. *Le Pacte des loups* was the second-highest-grossing French film in the U.S. market in 2001, after Jean-Pierre Jeunet's *Le Fabuleux destin d'Amélie Poulain* [The fabulous destiny of Amélie Poulain] (2001), discussed later in this chapter.

3. Statues of the creature were erected in the 1950s, one located in Auvers and the other in Marvejols, The museum is much more recent and is located in the town of Sauges.

4. Gans is from Antibes, which is not in the region where the attacks occurred but is in southern France. This may explain his familiarity with the story because the story lives primarily in regional memory, although it is known elsewhere in France.

5. He offers different explanations for why he did this, but he does point out that the net result is that he manipulates the chronology of events in the film.

6. Nearly every review of the film discusses its generic hybridity, and so there are too many examples of this to cite, as are the numerous film references and allusions in *Le Pacte des loups*. *Le Pacte des loups* is in some ways a pastiche of earlier film images, in much the same way as Jean-Pierre Jeunet's *Amélie*, discussed further on.

7. This element of the film has received much criticism. Those who object to it reproach Gans for departing from the historical facts in which the film is ostensibly rooted. However, I note that if there is no specific evidence to support Gans's filmic conclusions, they are, nonetheless, rooted in certain historical facts. The Gévaudan was a hotbed of insurrection. It is in the part of France where the Cathars had their stronghold, and it was a site of political and religious discontent for long after. Moreover, there were fears of a full-scale revolt in that region during the period in which the film is set, and several of those who later wrote about the beast also theorized that the stories might have been exploited by revolutionary forces in the region. Gans's interpretation of these historical facts, therefore, is consistent with his overall treatment of the subject. He does not offer a complete fiction but, rather, a hypothetical alternative to history as it has been received.

8. Serge Kaganski went the furthest in his critique of *Amélie*, accusing the film of thinly veiled racism. Other French critics, including Serge Daney, did not go so far but did accuse the film of promoting a stereotyped Frenchness. Some international film critics echoed the criticisms directed against the film in France. Among these were Peter Bradshaw of *The Guardian* newspaper in the United Kingdom and J. Hoberman of the *Village Voice* in the United States.

9. As with *Le Pacte des loups*, *Amélie* was digitally enhanced to ensure that there was vivid and consistent use of color. Color is also particularly important in the film (its significance is discussed further on).

10. Dudley Andrew mentions *Le Ballon rouge* in his analysis of *Amélie*, but it is not clear whether or not he reads Jeunet as evoking the film deliberately.

11. Although, as Caitlin Killian observes, most women of North African origin in France give their children Arabic (or Berber) first names, there are those who give their children French or even "cosmopolitan" first names (names that work in various languages). The consequences of naming are not lost on these women. Killian notes that they often choose Arabic names despite their awareness that it may subject their children to

racism (2006, 221–22). Lucien's name, in and of itself, therefore, invites an entire meditation on the subject of naming and the identity politics associated with it.

12. Jeunet has told this story many times. It appears Watson was even learning French
to be able to play the role, but in the end, for what Jeunet calls "personal reasons," she
declined the part.

13. Many critics have read *Amélie* as Jeunet's homage to the French New Wave. However, Jeunet has repeatedly stated that he does not particularly like New Wave films and
that he finds the critical fascination with them baffling. He even went so far as to say
that the New Wave was a long time ago, and people should get over it. The inclusion of so
many references to Truffaut's films in *Amélie*, therefore, seems to be another reference to
the disconnect between the reality of Paris and the image of it to which so many cling.

14. Interestingly, many of these photographs have recently been "recovered" both in
historian Gérard Noiriel's photographic history of immigration in France entitled *Gens
d'ici venus d'ailleurs* (2004) and in the recently opened Cité Nationale de l'histoire de
l'immigration.

15. Christophe Gans, as noted, has made the same observation, comparing Jeunet's
specular image of Paris to his own specular image of eighteenth-century France.

16. *La Tour de la France par deux enfants* is a significant *lieu de mémoire* that figures
repeatedly in Nora's work. It is also an active site of memory, as suggested, since it has
repeatedly been reprinted, even though it is no longer used in schools.

17. As with nearly everyone in the film, Varda does not discuss the origins of either
man, but it is clear from Saloman's accent that he is from Africa, although the precise
country is not clear. Similarly, Charlie sounds as though he is from Vietnam, and at one
point in the sequel to *Les Glaneurs et la glaneuse, Deux ans après* (2002), Varda says he
has the face of Ho Chi Minh, which suggests he may have been from Vietnam.

18. In the sequel to *Les Glaneurs et la glaneuse, Deux ans après* (2002), Varda discovers that Charlie has died and that Saloman is not allowed to live in the house they once
shared. Instead, she finds him living in a van, working for what meager existence he can
eke out. His circumstances prevent him from gleaning, as he has nowhere to keep or cook
what he finds. Varda's update on Saloman in the sequel functions as a silent critique of
society because it raises the question of whether the society has given back what he gave
by excluding rather than including him.

4. Memory's Blind Spots: Immigration, Integration, and the Post-Colonial Heritage

1. Begag was France's first French Minister for Equal Opportunity. He was appointed
to the position by Dominique de Villepin but resigned in 2007 to support the candidacy
of François Bayrou for the presidency. In part, Begag's resignation may also stem from
his objection to remarks made in November 2005 by then Foreign Minister Nicholas
Sarkozy regarding the inhabitants of France's suburbs or *banlieues*. Sarkozy, at the time,
was also a candidate for the presidency.

2. Begag made these comments in a critique of the texts signed Paul Smaïl, which were
actually authored by Jack-Alain Leger.

3. "Beur," the term used by Begag, is reverse slang (*verlan*) for "Arab." The word is
formed by splitting and then reversing the syllables of "Arab" and describes, specifically,
the "second generation" of Maghrebi immigrants in France or the French of Maghrebi
descent. Initially, the term was coined by members of the group it defined and was popu-
larized through Radio Beur, a radio station that catered to that generation, but it has
passed into popular, political, and even academic discourse. In recent years, the term

has been highly contested, in part because it connotes the poverty and violence widely associated with the *banlieue*, in part because many of those it describes are of Berber and not of Arab descent, and in part because it is seen as a means of maintaining a barrier between the French of Maghrebi descent and the rest of the population of France. Other terms used to describe this population include "French of Maghrebi descent" and "the second generation." These terms are also contested. I have decided to use the word "multicultural" in this chapter for reasons of simplicity and also because, as noted, the narratives I am describing are authored by people of various backgrounds and generations. For a history of the word "Beur," see Durmelat (1998).

4. I have deliberately avoided the term "Beur" literature or film in this chapter because despite that many of the writers and filmmakers are "Beurs," the characteristics I have observed are evident in the works of writers and filmmakers of different backgrounds. For examples of the dominant reception of "Beur" writing, see Hargreaves (1995) and Mehrez (1993).

5. Although numbered among the Beur novelists, Sebbar is the daughter of a French mother and an Algerian father. She is also a generation older than most of those typically included in the Beur generation. She is just one example of why I find the term problematic and prefer to use the term "multicultural" in discussing these types of texts.

6. For more on the events of October 17, 1961, see Einaudi (1991).

7. Tassadit Imache's novels, including *Une fille sans histoire* (1989) and *Le Dromadaire de Bonaparte* (1995), similarly explore the space of history and memory. Grounded, like Sebbar's novels, in the reality of present-day, urban France, Imache's novels foreground the experience of the *banlieue*, the urban periphery around Paris and at the same time look back to the history of colonialism that ultimately led North Africans to emigrate to France. As Karima Laachir argues, Imache's novels attempt "a rereading of French colonial history in Algeria from a pluralistic point of view while stressing the violent manifestations of its colonial legacy in contemporary France" (2005, 449–50).

8. For more complete studies of these authors, see Donadey (2001) and Hargreaves (1995).

9. For a more complete study of these films, see Tarr (2005).

10. For more on the 2005 riots, see Hargreaves (2005), Kastoryano (2006), Roy (2005), Schneider (2008), and Silverstein and Tetreault (2006).

11. For more on Feuillade, see Callahan (2005) and Lacassin (1995).

12. A number of studies have been done of *La Haine*, including Higbee ("Screening the 'Other' Paris," 2001), Sedock (2004), and Schroeder (2001).

13. For a study of the evolution of the banlieue, see Bellanger (2008) and Prévost (1998).

14. The numerous shots of the sea may also function to recall Marcel Pagnol's *Trilogie Marseillaise*. The three films in the trilogy, *Marius* (1931), *Fanny* (1932), and *César* (1936), are probably three of the most famous French films set in Marseille, and the Mediterranean and the port figure prominently in them. If so, this reference may function as a marker of Marseille's unique identity. Other such references are in *Bye Bye*, most particularly references to the contemporary bands IAM and Massilia Sound System, both of which are closely associated Marseille and both of which are seen to express a strong and notably hybrid Marseillais identity. These bands are referenced prominently in shots showing Rhida's room and the clothes he is wearing. If the shots of the sea and port are filmic reference to Pagnol's trilogy, they reinforce the idea that the sea in general and colonial conquest in particular have been central to Marseille's development because Marius, in the Pagnol films, is drawn by the sea and leaves in search of access to exotic, foreign lands.

A reference to Pagnol, of course, would also be a means of suggesting that Marseille, for all of its uniqueness, has played a central role in forming the broader culture as well as a means of conveying legitimacy to Dridi's film in much the same way that such connections legitimize heritage films.

15. Carrie Tarr describes the character as a great aunt, but she is called "grandmother" by the characters in the film, and Dridi himself has referred to her as the grandmother.

16. As Tarr notes, the film had 283,578 spectators in its initial release and 188,468 upon rerelease, following its success at the Césars, the French national film awards.

17. The title comes from act 2, scene 5, when Arlequin, speaking to Lisette, says,

> Enfin, ma Reine
> je vous vois et je ne vous quitte plus
> car j'ai trop pitié d'avoir manqué de votre présence
> et j'ai cru que vous esquiviez la mienne.
> [Finally, my queen
> I see you and will no longer leave you
> for I greatly regret having been absent
> and I wrongly believed you were avoiding my own (presence)].

This scene figures prominently in the film.

18. Laurent Cantet's *Entre les murs* (2008) addresses similar themes, also in the context of a (sub)urban school.

5. Recovered Memories: Diversity, History, and the Expanding Space of the Past

1. For a complete history and study of Zebda, see Marx-Scouras (2005).

2. Zebda's influence on the treatment of (post-)colonial memory extends beyond their own music. Abdellatif Kechiche's exploration of immigration in the film *La Faute à Voltaire* (2001) may be read as containing a double reference, one to Zedba and one to Hugo, and therefore reappropriating the fusion of traditional heritage and the post-colonial offered in Zebda's "Le Bruit et l'odeur." It is also worth noting that Rachid Bouchareb's exploration of the contribution of the French African Army, discussed later in this chapter, may have been influenced by Zebda, since they pointed to the role of the colonial regiments and, specifically, to the campaign at Montecassino in Italy in "Le Bruit et l'odeur," which was released a full ten years before the film was made.

3. For a thorough discussion of Zebda's impact in contemporary France, see Marx-Scouras (2005).

4. Joël Tinazzi, "La Parole a une valeur thérapeutique," *Le Monde*, 6 March 1998.

5. For specific details on migration patterns between North Africa and France, see Sayad (2004) and Hargreaves (*Multi-ethnic France*, 2007).

6. Enrico Macias was born Gaston Ghrénassia in Constantine, Algeria, in 1938. He was introduced to Malouf music (a combination of Andalusian and Arabic music). He went to France in 1951, as a result of the growing unrest in Algeria, and began recording songs in 1962. He changed his name to Enrico Macias in 1964. Macias has had a successful career spanning several decades. He was, incidentally, one of the earliest popular musicians to blend Spanish and Arabic musical forms with that of *la chanson française*, and he may, therefore, have influenced contemporary musicians such as Zebda, although it is true that his music is much less hybrid than such contemporary musicians. For more on Macias, see Calmettes (2005).

7. For a complete study of the *hijab* and its connotations in France, see Bowen (2006), Keaton (2006), and Scott (2007).

8. For more on the march, see Hargreaves (*Multi-ethnic France*, 2007).

9. "Begag" here refers to the author of the novel and "Azouz" to the narrator of the novel.

10. In this regard, numerous entries on various aspects of school appear in *Les Lieux de mémoire*, entries that deal with everything from particular textbooks to the creation of the educational system.

11. For a complete history of the French African Army, see Echenberg (1990) and Lormier (2006).

12. Historian Benjamin Stora, in a September 27, 2006, interview in *Le Monde*, says that the film failed to adequately represent this aspect of the past. He terms the time members of the colonial army spent on French soil an "apprenticeship for immigration"; however, I believe the film renders this metaphorically rather than simply eliding it.

13. For an analysis of the financial significance of the freeze in contemporary terms, see "Pour la sortie d'*Indigènes*, Chirac harmonise les pensions des anciens combattans coloniaux," *Libération*, September 26, 2006.

14. *Le Monde*, September 26, 2006, and September 27 2006.

15. Some notable exceptions are Louis Malle's *Lacombe Lucien* (1974) and *Au revoir les enfants* (1987) and Marcel Ophüls's *Le Chagrin et la pitié* (1969). For more on these films and others belonging to the Mode Retro, see Morris (1992).

Bibliography

Abel, Richard. 1998. *The Cine Goes to Town: French Cinema 1906–1914*. Berkeley: University of California Press.

Ageron, Charles Robert. 1997. "L'Exposition coloniale de 1931." In Nora, 1997, 493–515.

Alter, Nora M. 2006. *Chris Marker*. Urbana: University of Illinois Press.

Anderson, Benedict. 1991. *Imagined Communities: Reflections on the Origin and Spread of Nationalism*. London: Verso.

Anderson, Perry. 2004. "Dégringolade." *London Review of Books* 26 (17): 3–9.

Andrew, Dudley. 2004. "*Amélie*, ou Le Fabuleux Destin du Cinéma Français." *Film Quarterly* 57 (3): 34–46.

Ashworth, G. J., Brian Graham, and J. E. Tunbridge. 2007. *Pluralising Pasts: Heritage, Identity and Place in Multicultural Societies*. London: Pluto.

Assman, Jan. 1995. "Collective Memory and Cultural Identity." *New German Critique* 65:125–33.

Aussaresses, Paul. 2001. *Services Speciaux: Algérie 1955–1957*. Paris: Perrin.

Austin, Guy. 1996. *Contemporary French Cinema: An Introduction*. Manchester, UK : Manchester University Press.

Balibar, Etienne. 1996. "The Nation Form: History and Ideology." In Balibar and Wallerstein, 1996, 86–106.

Balibar, Etienne, and Emmanuel Wallerstein. 1996. *Race, Nation, Class: Ambiguous Identities*. London: Verso.

Begag, Azouz. 1986. *Le Gone du chaâba*. Paris: Seuil, Collection Virgule.

———. 1989. *Beni, ou le paradis privé*. Paris: Seuil.

———. 1999. *Zenzela*. Paris: Seuil.

———. 2006. "Of Imposture and Incompetence: Paul Smail's *Vivre me tue*." *Research in African Literatures* 37 (1): 55–71.

Bell, David A. 1997. "Paris Blues: Realms of Memory: The Construction of the French Past." *New Republic*, 1 September, 32–37.

———. 2001. *The Cult of the Nation in France: Inventing Nationalism, 1680–1800*. Cambridge, MA: Harvard University Press.

Bellanger, Emmanuel. 2008. *Histoire de la banlieue rouge*. Paris: Atelier Ed De.

Benaïcha, Brahim. 1992. *Vivre au paradis*. Paris: Desclée de Brouwer.

Ben-Amos, Dan, and Liliane Weissberg, eds. 1999. *Cultural Memory and the Construction of Identity*. Detroit, MI: Wayne State University Press.

Benantar, Adenbennour. 1996. "Laissez parler les Algériens." In *La France en Question*, 1996, 181–96.

Benguigui, Yamina. 2000. Interview by Christine Menzhagi. *Idées en mouvement*, March. http://www.les-idees-en-mouvement.org/Dossier.77/ybenguigui.html.

Beriss, David. 2004. *Black Skins, French Voices: Caribbean Ethnicity and Activism in Urban France.* Boulder, CO: Westview.

———. 2004. "Culture-as-Race or Culture-as-Culture: Caribbean Ethnicity and the Ambiguity of Cultural Identity in French Society." In *Race in France: Interdiscliplinary Perspectives on the Politics of Difference,* by Herrick Chapman and Laura L. Frader, 111–40. Oxford, UK: Berghann.

Birnbaum, Pierre. 2001. *The Idea of France.* New York: Wang and Hill.

Blanchard, Pascal, Nicolas Bancel, and Sandrine Lemaire, eds. 2005. *La fracture coloniale: La société française au prisme de l'héritage colonial.* Paris: Decouverte.

Blatt, Ari J. 2008. "The Play's the Thing: Marivaux and the Banlieue in Abdellatif Kechiche's *L'Esquive.*" *French Review* 81 (3): 516–527.

Blowen, Sarah, Jeannine Picard, and Marion Demossier, eds. 2001. *Recollections of France: Memories, Identities, and Heritage in Contemporary France.* Oxford, UK: Berghan.

Bordes, Philippe. 2007. *Jacques-Louis David: Empire to Exile.* New Haven, CT: Yale University Press.

Bordwell, David, Janet Steiger, and Kristin Thompson. 1988. *The Classical Hollywood Cinema: Film Style and Mode of Production to 1960.* London: Routledge.

Bosseno, Christian. 1992. "Immigrant Cinema, National Cinema—The Case of Beur Film." In Dyer and Vincendeau, 1992, 47–57.

Bouchareb, Rachid. 2006. Interview. "Debt of Honor." *Time,* September 28. http://www.time.com/time/world/article/0,8599,1540655,00.html.

Bourdin, Alain. 1984. *Le Patrimoine réinventé.* Paris: Presses Universitaires de France.

Boutry, Philippe. 1997. "Le Clocher (The church tower)." In Nora, 1997, 3081–92.

Bowen, John R. 2006. *Why the French Don't Like Headscarves: Islam, the State, and Public Space.* Princeton, NJ: Princeton University Press.

Bretèque, François de la. 1992. "Images of 'Provence': Ethnotypes and Stereotypes." In Dyer and Vincendeau, 1992, 58–71.

Brubaker, Rogers. *Citizenship and Nationhood in France and Germany.* Boston: Harvard University Press.

Brown, Terence. 1996. *Celticism.* Amsterdam: Rodopi.

Bruno, G. 1877. *Le Tour de la France par deux enfants.* Paris: Editions Belin.

Buffière, Félix. 1985. *Ce tant rude Gévaudan.* Mende, France: SLSA Lozère.

Buffon, Comte de Georges Louis Leclerc. 1804. *De l'homme: histoire naturelle.* Paris.

Burgière, André. 1997. "La génélogie." In Nora, 1997, 3980–908.

Burke, Peter. 1990. *The French Historical Revolution: The Annales School 1929–1989.* Stanford, CA: Stanford University Press.

Callahan, Vicki. 2005. *Zones of Anxiety: Movement, Musidora, and the Crime Serials of Louis Feuillade.* Detroit, MI: Wayne State University Press.

Calmettes, Gérard. 2005. *Enrico Macias: Rien que du bleu.* Paris: Editions Christian Pirot.

Caroll, David. 1998. "The Art of the People: Aesthetic Transcendence and National Identity in Jules Michelet." *Boundary* 2:111–38.

Chafer, Tony, and Amanda Sackur, eds. 2002. *Promoting the Colonial Idea: Propoganda and Visions of Empire in France.* Basingstoke, UK: Palgrave.

Chevalier, Denis. 2003. "Le patrimoine rural, outil politique ou enjeu de société?" *Modern and Contemporary France* 11 (3): 279–92.

Chevalley, Abel. 1972. *La Bête du Gévaudan.* 1936. Paris: Editions J'ai lu.

Citron, Suzanne. 1987. *Le mythe national: L'histoire de France en question.* Paris: Editions ouvrieres.

Climo, Jacob, and Maria G. Cattell, eds. 2002. *Social Memory and History: Anthropological Perspectives*. New York: Altamira.

Conklin, Alice L. 1997. *A Mission to Civilize the Republican Idea of Empire in France and West Africa, 1895–1930*. Stanford, CA: Stanford University Press.

Conley, Tom, and Steve Ungar, eds. 1996. *Identity Papers: Contested Nationhood in Twentieth-century France*. Minneapolis: University of Minnesota Press.

Connerton, Paul. 1989. *How Societies Remember*. Cambridge: Cambridge University Press.

Coras, Jean de. 1560. *Arreste Memorable du parlement de Tolose*. Lyon, France: Antoine Vincent.

Cousins, Russell. 2006. "Jean de Florette." In Powrie, 2006, 185–96.

Crisp, Colin. 1997. *The Classic French Cinema, 1930–1960*. Bloomington: Indiana University Press.

Crossley, Ceri. 1993. *French Historians and Romanticism: Thierry, Guizot, the Saint-Simonians, Quinet, Michelet*. London: Routledge.

Dacascos, Mark. 2001. "Mark Dacascos—Interview." With Rob Blackwelder. *Contactmusic.com*. http://www.contactmusic.com/new/home.nsf/interviewee/mdacascos.

Darwin, Charles. 1859. *On the Origin of Species*. London: Murray.

Davis, Natalie Zemon. 1983. *The Return of Martin Guerre*. Cambridge, MA: Harvard University Press.

———. 1988. "On the Lame." *American Historical Review* 93 (3): 572–603.

———. 2003. "Movie or Monograph? A Historian/Filmmaker's Perspective." *Public Historian* 25 (3): 45–58.

Derderian, Richard L. 2004. *North Africans in Contemporary France Becoming Visible*. NewYork: Palgrave Macmillan.

Desvallée, André. 1998. "À l'origine du mot 'patrimoine.'" In Poulet, 1998, 89–105.

Djebar, Assia. 2006. Speech. "Discours Prononcé Dans La Séance Publique." Paris Palais De L'institut, June 22. http://www.academie-francaise.fr/immortels/discours_reception/djebar.html.

Doane, Mary Anne. 2002. *The Emergence of Cinematic Time: Modernity, Contingency, the Archive*. Cambridge MA: Harvard University Press.

Donadey, Anne. 1996. "'Une Certaine Idée de la France': The Algeria Syndrome and Struggles over 'French' Identity." In Conley and Ungar, 1996, 215–32.

———. 2001. *Recasting Postcolonialism: Women Writing between Worlds*. New York: Heinemann.

Durmelat, Sylvie. 1998. "Petite histoire du mot *beur*: ou comment prendre la parole quand on vous la prête." *French Cultural Studies* 9:191–207.

———. 2000. "Transmission and Mourning in Mémoires d'immigrés: l'héritage maghrébin: Yamina Benguigui as Memory Entrepreneuse." In Freedman and Tarr, 2000, 171–88.

Dyer, Richard, and Ginette Vincendeau, eds. 1992. *Popular European Cinema*. London: Routledge.

Echenberg, Myron. 1990. *Colonial Conscripts: The Tirailleurs Senegalais in French West Africa, 1857–1960*. London: Heinemann.

Einaudi, Jean-Luc. 1991. *La Bataille de Paris: 17 octobre 1961*. Paris: Seuil.

Eley, Geoff, and Ronald Grigor Suny. 1996. *Becoming National*. Oxford: Oxford University Press.

Elsaesser, Thomas, and Adam Barker, eds. 1989. *Early Cinema*. London: British Film Institute.

Englund, Steven. 1992. "The Ghost of Nation Past." *Journal of Modern History* 64 (2): 299–321.

Espiard de la Borde, François Ignace. 1743. *Essais sur le génie et le caractère des nations*. Brussels: Léonard.

Esposito, Maria. 2001. "Jean de Florette: Patrimoine, the Rural Idyll and the 1980s." In Mazdon, 2001, 11–26.

Fabre, François. 2001. *La Bête du Gévaudan*. 1930. Paris: Edition de Borée.

Favell, Adrian. 2001. *Philosophies of Integration Immigration and the Idea of Citizenship*. Basingstoke, UK: Palgrave.

Feldblum, Miriam. 1999. *Reconstructing Citizenship: The Politics of Nationality Reform and Immigration in Contemporary France*. New York: State University of New York Press.

Finlay, Robert. 1998. "The Refashioning of Martin Guerre." *American Historical Review* 93 (3): 552–72.

Flood, Christopher, and Hugo Frey. 2002. "Defending the Empire in Retrospect: The Discourse of the Extreme Right." In Chafer and Sackur, 2002, 195–211.

Foucault, Michel. 1977. *Language, Counter-memory, Practice: Selected Essays and Interviews*. Edited by Donald F. Bouchard and Sherry Simon. Ithaca, NY: Cornell University Press.

———. 1978. "Politics and the Study of Discourse." *Ideology and Consciousness* 3:3–26.

Freedman, Jane, and Carrie Tarr, eds. 2000. *Women, Immigration, and Identities in France*. Oxford: Berg.

Frémont, Armand. 1997. "La Terre." In Nora, 1997, 3047–80.

Friedman, Lester, ed. 1993. *Fires Were Started: British Cinema and Thatcherism*. Minneapolis: Minnesota University Press.

Fromentin, Eugène. 1858. *Une Année dans le Sahel*. Paris: Plon.

Gans, Christophe. 2001. Interview by Anwar Brett. *BBC*, October 17. http://www.bbc.co.uk/films/2001/10/17/christophe_gans_2001_interview.shtml.

———. 2002. "Interview with Director." "Interview at Los Angeles Cinemateque." *Brotherhood of the Wolf* [*Le Pacte des loups*]. Directed by Gans. Produced by Canal Plus. Distributed by Universal.

Gemünden, Gerd. 1998. *Framed Visions: Popular Culture, Americanization, and the Contemporary German and Austrian Imagination*. Ann Arbor: University of Michigan Press.

Gillette, Alain, and Abdelmalek Sayad. 1976. *L'Immigration algérienne en France*. Paris: Editions entente, 1984.

Gillis, John R., ed. 1994. *Commemorations: The Politics of National Identity*. Princeton, NJ: Princeton University Press.

Girod, Patrice. 2001. Review of *Amélie*. *Starfix*, March–April.

Godin, Emmanuel, and Tony Chafer, eds. 2005. *The French Exception*. Oxford: Berghahn.

Goff, Jacques Le. 1988. *Histoire et mémoire*. Paris: Gallimard.

Goldhammer, Arthur. 2006. "Did Historians Make History?" *French Politics, Culture & Society* 24 (2): 102–14.

Greene, Naomi. 1999. *Landscapes of Loss: The National Past in Postwar French Cinema*. Princeton, NJ: Princeton University Press.

Grewal, Kiran. 2007. "The Threat from Within: Representations of the Banlieue in French Popular Discourse." In *Europe: New Voices, New Perspectives*, edited by Matt Killingsworth, 41–67. Melbourne, Australia: Contemporary Europe Research Center.

Guiomar, Jean-Yves. 1997. "Le 'Tableau de la géographie de la France.'" In Nora, 1997, 1073–102.

Gunning, Tom. 1989. "The Cinema of Attractions: Early Film, Its Spectator, and the Avant-Garde." In Elsaesser and Barker, 1989, 56–62.

Hage, Ghassan. 2000. *White Nation: Fantasies of White Supremacy in a Multicultural Society*. London: Routledge.

Halbwachs, Maurice. 1997. *La mémoire collective*. 1950. Paris: Albin Michel.

Hall, Stuart. 1997. "The Question of Cultural Identity." In Hall, Held, and McGrew, 1997, 273–326.

———. ed. 1997. *Representation: Cultural Representation and Signifying Practices*. London: SAGE.

———. 2005. "Whose Heritage? Un-Settling 'The Heritage,' Re-Imaginging the Post-Nation." In Littler and Naidoo, 2005, 21–31.

Hall, Stuart, David Held, and Tony McGrew, eds. 1997. *Modernity and Its Futures*. Cambridge: Polity.

Hamilton, Peter. 1997. "Representing the Social: France and Frenchness in Post-War Humanist Photography." In Hall, 1997, 75–150.

Hannaford, Ivan. 1996. *Race: The History of an Idea in the West*. Baltimore, MD: Johns Hopkins University Press.

Hargreaves, Alec G. 1995. *Immigration and Identity in "Beur" Fiction*. Oxford: Berg.

———. 2001. "Resuscitating the Father: New Cinematic Representations of the Maghrebi Minority in France." *Research in African Literature* 4 (2): 343–52.

———. 2005. "An Emperor with No Clothes?" *Riots in France, Social Science Research Council*, November 28. http://riotsfrance.ssrc.org/Hargreaves/ (accessed December 12, 2005).

———. 2006. "Broader Trends in Representation of Ethnic Minorities in France." Keynote address, French and Italian Graduate Student Conference, Austin, Texas, April 21.

———. 2007. "Indigènes: A Sign of the Times." *Research in African Literatures* 38 (4): 242–46.

———. 2007. *Multi-ethnic France: Immigration, Politics, Culture, and Society*. London: Routledge.

Hargreaves, Alec G., and Jeremy Leaman. 1995. *Racism, Ethnicity, and Politics in Contemporary Europe*. London: Elgar.

Hargreaves, Alec G., and Mark McKinney, eds. 1997. *Post-Colonial Cultures in France*. London: Routledge.

Hayward, Susan. 1993. *French National Cinema*. London: Routledge.

Hayward, Susan, and Ginette Vincendeau, eds. 2000. *French Film: Texts and Contexts*. London: Routledge.

Hewitt, Nicholas. 2004. "Gabin, Grisbi and 1950s France." *Studies in French Cinema* 4 (1): 65–75.

Higbee, Will. 2001. "Hybridity, Space, and the Right to Belong: Maghrebi-French Identity at the Crossroads in *Karim Dridi's Bye Bye*." In Mazdon, 2001, 51–64.

———. 2001. "Screening the 'Other' Paris: Cinematic Representations of the French Urban Periphery in La Haine and Ma 6-T Va Crack-er." *Modern and Contemporary France* 9 (2): 197–208.

Higgins, Lynn. 1996. "Pagnol and the Paradox of Frenchness." In Conley and Ungar, 1996, 91–112.

———. 1998. *New Novel, New Wave, New Politics: Fiction and Representation of History in Postwar France*. Omaha: University of Nebraska Press.

Higson, Andrew. 1993. "Re-presenting the National Past: Nostalgia and Pastiche in the Heritage Film." In Friedman, 1993, 109–29.

―――. 2003. *English Heritage, English Cinema: Costume Drama since 1980*. Oxford: Oxford University Press.

Hobsbawm, Eric. 1992. *Nations and Nationalism since 1780: Programme, Myth, Reality*. London: Canto.

Hobsbawm, Eric, and Terence Ranger, eds. 1992. *The Invention of Tradition*. London: Canto.

Hunt, Lynn, and Jacques Revel. 2006. *Histories: French Constructions of the Past*. New York: New Press.

Hutcheon, Linda. 1989. *The Politics of Postmodernism*. London: Routledge.

Imache, Tassadit. 1989. *Une Fille sans histoire*. Paris: Calmann-Levy.

―――. 1995. *Le Dromadaire de Bonaparte*. Arles, France: Actes-Sud.

Jacono, Jean-Marie. 2002. "Musical Dimensions and Ways of Expressing Identity in French Rap: The Groups from Marseilles." In *Blanc, Black, Beur: Rap Music and Hip-Hop Culture in the Francophone World*, edited by Alain-Philippe Durand, 22–32. Lanham, MD: Scarecrow.

Jeunet, Jean-Pierre. 2002. "Interview with Director." DVD. Miramax.

Kastoryano, Riva. 2002. *Negotiating Identities: States and Immigrants in France and Germany*. Princeton, NJ: Princeton University Press.

―――. 2006. *Territories of Identities in France. Riots in France, Social Science Research Council*, June 11. http://riotsfrance.ssrc.org/Kastoryano/ (accessed July 3, 2006).

Katriel, Tamar. 1999. "Sites of Memory: Discourses of the Past in Israeli Pioneering SettlementMuseums." In Ben-Amos and Weissberg, 1999, 99–135.

Keaton, Tricia Danielle. 2006. *Muslim Girls and the Other France: Race, Identity Politics, and Social Exlcusion*. Bloomington: Indiana University Press.

Killian, Caitlin. 2006. *North African Women in France*. Stanford, CA: Stanford University Press.

Koselleck, Reinhart. 2004. *Futures Past: On the Semantics of Historical Time*. New York: Columbia University Press.

Laachir, Karima. 2005. "The Interplay between History/Memory/Space in Tassadit Imache's *Presque un Frère* and *Le Dromadaire de Bonaparte*." *Modern and Contemporary France* 13 (4): 449–64.

Lacassin, Francis. 1995. *Maître des lions et des vampires: Louis Feuillade*. Paris: Pierre Bordas.

Laderman, David. 2002. *Driving Visions: Exploring the Road Movie*. Austin: University of Texas Press.

La France en Question. 1996. Paris: Gallimard.

Landy, Marcia. 1996. *Cinematic Uses of the Past*. Minneapolis: University of Minnesota Press.

Lanzoni, Remy Fourmier. 2004. *French Cinema: From the Beginnings to the Present*. New York: Continuum.

Laqueur, Thomas W. 1994. "Memory and Naming in the Great War." In Gillis, 1994, 150–67.

Lay-Chenchabi, Kathryn. 2001. "Writing for Their Lives: Three Beur Writers Discover Themselves." *Mots Pluriels*. http://motspluriels.arts.uwa.edu.au/MP1701klc.html.

Lazarus, Neil, ed. 2004. *The Cambridge Companion to Postcolonial Literary Studies*. Cambridge: Cambridge University Press.

Lebovics, Herman. 1992. *True France: The Wars over Cultural Identity, 1900–1945*. Ithaca, NY: Cornell University Press.

―――. 2004. *Bringing the Empire Back Home: France in the Global Age*. Durham, NC: Duke University Press.

Le Goff, Jacques. 1988. *Histoire et mémoire*. Paris: Gallimard.

Le Sueur, Guillaume. 1561. *Histoire admirable d'un faux et supposé Mary*. Lyon, France: Jean de Tournes.

Littler, Jo, and Roshi Naidoo, eds. 2005. *The Politics of Heritage: The Legacies of 'Race.'* London: Routledge.

Lormier, Dominique. 2006. *"C'est Nous les Africains": l'épopée de l'armée française d'Afrique 1940–1945*. Paris: Calmann-Lévy.

Lotman, Yuri, and B. A. Uspensky. 1978. "On the Semiotic Mechanism of Culture." *New Literary History* 9 (2): 211–32.

Lowenthal, David. 1998. *The Heritage Crusade and the Spoils of History*. Cambridge: Cambridge University Press.

Marx-Scouras, Danielle. 2005. *La France de Zebda 1981–2004: Faire de la musique un actepolitique*. Paris: Autrement.

Matsuda, Matt K. 1996. *The Memory of the Modern*. Oxford: Oxford University Press.

Mazdon, Lucy, ed. 2001. *France on Film: Reflections on French Popular Culture*. London: Wallflower.

Mazierska, Ewa, and Laura Rascaroli. 2003. *From Moscow to Madrid: Postmodern Cities, European Cinema*. London: Tauris.

———. 2006. *Crossing New Europe: Postmodern Travel and the European Road Movie*. London: Wallflower.

McCullough, Mary. 2003. "No More Silencing the Past: First Generation Immigrant Women as Bricoleuses de mémoire." *International Journal of Francophone Studies* 6 (2): 119–34.

Mehrez, Samia. 1993. "Azouz Begag: Un di zafas di bidoufile or the *Beur* Writer: A Question of Territory." *Yale French Studies* 82 (1): 25–42.

Ménatory, Gérard. 1991. *La Bête du Gévaudan*. Paris: Editions Loubatieres.

Michelet, Jules. 1834. *Introduction à L'Histoire universelle*. Boston: Eilbron, 2007.

———. 1847. *Histoire de la Révolution française*. Paris: Gallimard, 1952.

———. 1869. *Histoire de France*. 1845. Paris: Hachette.

———. 1876/1974. *Le Peuple*. 1846. Paris: Flammarion.

Miller, Christopher. 2008. *The French Atlantic Slave Trade*. Durham, NC: Duke University Press.

Moine, Raphaëlle. 2007. "Generic Hybridity, National Culture, and Globalised Cinema." In Vanderschelden and Waldron, 2007, 36–50.

Molia, Francois-Xavier. 2007. "Peut-on être à la fois hollywoodien et francais? French Superproductions and the American Model." In Vanderschelden and Waldron, 2007, 51–62.

Monaco, James. 1977. *The New Wave*. Oxford: Oxford University Press.

Montesquieu, Charles de Secondat, baron de. 1721. *Lettres persanes*. Paris: Larousse, 2007.

———. 1758. *De l'Esprit des lois*. Paris: Larousse, 2006.

Morris, Alan. 1992. *Collaboration and Resistance Reviewed: Writers and 'la Mode retro' in Post-Gaullist France*. London: Berg.

Naficy, Hamid. 2001. *An Accented Cinema: Exilic and Diasporic Filmmaking*. Princeton, NJ: Princeton University Press.

Nettelbeck, Colin. 2007. "Kechiche and the French Classics." *French Cultural Studies* 18 (3): 307–20.

Neupert, Richard. 2007. *A History of the French New Wave Cinema*. Madison: University of Wisconsin Press.

Noiriel, Gérard. 1988. *Le Creuset français*. Paris: Seuil.

———. 2001. *État, nation et immigration: Vers une histoire du pouvoir*. Paris: Gallimard.

———. 2004. *Gens d'ici venus d'ailleurs: La France de l'immigration de 1900 àjours*. Paris: Chene.

Nora, Pierre. 1997. "Entre mémoire et histoire." In Nora, *Les Lieux de mémoire*, 1997, 1:23–43.

———. 1997. "Lavisse, instituteur national." In Nora, *Les Lieux de mémoire*, 1997, 1:230–94.

———, ed. 1997. *Les Lieux de mémoire*. 3 vols. Paris: Gallimard.

———. 1997. "La Nation-mémoire." In Nora, *Les Lieux de mémoire*, 1997, 2:2201–18.

———. 1997. "Présentation." In Nora, *Les Lieux de mémoire*, 1997, 1:15–22.

———. 1999. *Michelet, Historien de la France*. Paris: Gallimard.

Norindr, Panivong. 1996. "Filmic Memorial and Colonial Blues: Indochina in Contemporary French Cinema." In Sherzer, 1996, 121–46.

———. 1996. "La Plus Grande France: French Cultural Identity and Nation-Building under Mitterrand." In Conley and Ungar, 1996, 233–58.

Ozouf, Jacques, and Mona Ozouf. 1997. "La Tour de la France par deux enfants." In Nora, 1997, 277–302.

Pagnol, Marcel. 1962. *L'Eau des collines*. Paris: Flammarion, 2004.

Pearson, Roberta. 1999. "Custer Loses Again: The Contestation over Commodified Public Memory." In Ben-Amos and Weissberg, 1999, 176–201.

Peer, Shanny. 1996. "Peasants in Paris: Representations of Rural France in the 1937." In Conley and Ungar, 1996, 19–49.

Pidduck, Julianne. 2005. *La Reine Margot*. Urbana: University of Illinois Press / IB Tauris.

Poirrier, Philippe. 2004. *L'Invention du patrimoine en Bourgogne*. Dijon, France: Editions de Dijon.

Poirrier, Philippe, and Loïc Vadelorge, eds. 2003. *Pour une histoire des politiques du patrimoine*. Paris: La Documentation Francaise.

Porton, Richard. 2005. "Marivaux in the Hood: An Interview with Abdellatif Kechiche." *Cinéaste* 31 (1): 46–49.

Poulet, Dominique, ed. 1998. *Patrimoine et modernité*. Paris: Harmattan.

Powrie, Phil. 1996. *French Cinema in the 1980s: Nostalgia and the Crisis of Masculinity*. Oxford, England: Clarendon.

———, ed. 1999. *French Cinema in the 1990s: Continuity and Difference*. Oxford, England: Oxford University Press.

———. 2006. *The Cinema of France*. London: Wallflower.

Prevost, André. 1998. "L'évolution de la banlieue française: Un nouveau trajet des modes." *Contemporary French Civilization* 22 (1): 71–88.

Prost, Antoine. 1997. "Les Monuments aux morts." In Nora, 1997, 199–223.

Reader, Keith. 1995. "After the Riot." *Sight and Sound* 5 (11): 12–14.

———. 1998. "Cinéma." In *Encyclopedia of Contemporary French Culture*, edited by Alex Hughes and Reader, 103–6. London: Routledge.

Rebichon, Michel. 2001. Review of *Amélie*. *Studio*, April.

Renan, Ernest. 1882. "*Qu'est-qu'une nation?*" ("What is a nation?"). In Eley and Suny, 1996, 41–55. First given as a lecture in 1882.

Revel, Jacques, and Lynn Hunt, eds. 1996. *Histories: French Constructions of the Past*. New York: New Press.

Rignol, Loïc. 2002. "Augustin Thierry et la politique de l'histoire. Genèse et principes d'un système de pensée." *Revue d'histoire du XIXe siècle* 25:87–100.

Roberts, Warren. 1992. *Jacques-Louis David: Revolutionary Artist*. Chapel Hill: University of North Carolina Press.

Rogers, Susan Carol. 1987. "Good to Think: The 'Peasant' in Contemporary France." *Anthropological Quarterly* 60 (2): 56–63.

Rollet, Brigitte. 1999. "Identity and Alterity in Indochine." In Powrie, 1999, 37–46.

Rosello, Mireille. 1993. "The Beur Nation: Toward a Theory of Departenance." *Research in African Literatures* 24 (3): 13–25.

———. 1997. *Declining the Stereotype: Ethnicity and Representation in French Culture.* Danvers, MA: University Press of New England,.

———. 2001. "Agnès Varda's *Les Glaneurs et la glaneuse*: Portrait of the Artist as an Old Lady." *Studies in French Cinema* 1 (1): 29–36.

———. 2001. *Postcolonial Hospitality: The Immigrant as Guest.* Stanford, CA: Stanford UniversityPress.

Rosen, Philip. 2001. *Change Mummified: Cinema, Historicity, Theory.* Minneapolis: University of Minnesota Press.

Rosenstone, Robert A. 1995. *Visions of the Past: The Challenge of Film to Our Idea of History.* Cambridge, MA: Harvard University Press.

———. 2006. *History on Film, Film on History.* New York: Longman.

Ross, Kristin. 1996. *Fast Cars, Clean Bodies: Decolonization and the Reordering of French Culture.* Cambridge, MA: MIT Press.

Rousso, Henry. 1990. *Le Syndrome de Vichy de 1944 à nos jours.* Paris: Seuil.

Roy, Olivier. 2005. "The Nature of the French Riots." *Riots in France, Social Science Research Council,* November 18. http://riotsfrance.ssrc.org/Roy/ (accessed December 12, 2005).

Sala-Molins, Louis. 2002. *Le Code Noir ou le calvaire de Canaan.* Paris: Presses universitaires de France.

———. 2002. Interview with Eric Pincus. *Historia* (November–December):34–37.

Sayad, Abdelmalek. 2004. *The Suffering of the Immigrant.* Translated by David Macey. Cambridge: Polity Press.

Schneider, Cathy Lisa. 2008. "Police Power and Race Riots in Paris." *Politics and Society* 36 (1): 133–59.

Schroeder, Erin. 2001. "A Multicultural Conversation." *Camera Obscura* 16 (46): 142–80.

Scott, Joan Wallach. 2007. *The Politics of the Veil.* Princeton, NJ: Princeton University Press.

Sebbar, Leïla. 1981. *Fatima, ou les Algériennes au square.* Paris: Stock.

———. 1982. *Shérazade: 17 ans, brune, frisée, les yeux verts.* Paris: Stock.

———. 1985. *Les Carnets de Shérazade.* Paris: Stock.

———. 1991. *Le Fou de Shérazade.* Paris: Stock.

———. 1999. *La Seine était rouge.* Paris: Thierry Magnier.

Seliger, M. 1958. "Race-Thinking during the Restoration." *Journal of the History of Ideas* 19:272–82.

Shepard, Todd. 2006. *The Invention of Decolonization: The Algerian War and the Remaking of France.* Ithaca, NY: Cornell University Press.

Sherman, Daniel J. 2004. "'Peoples Ethnographic': Objects, Museums, and the Colonial Inheritance of French Ethnology." *French Historical Studies* 27 (3): 669–703.

Sherzer, Dina, ed. 1996. *Cinema, Colonialism, Postcolonialism.* Austin: University of Texas Press.

Silverman, Maxim. 1992. *Deconstructing the Nation: Immigration, Racism, and Citizenship in Modern France.* London: Routledge.

———. 1995. "Rights and Difference: Questions of Citizenship in France." In Hargreaves and Leaman, 1995, 126–52.

Silverstein, Paul A. 2004. *Algeria in France: Transpolitics, Race, and Nation*. Bloomington: Indiana University Press.

Silverstein, Paul A., and Chantal Tetreault. 2006. "Postcolonial Urban Apartheid." *Riots in France, Social Sciences Research Council*. June 11. http://riotsfrance.ssrc.org/Silverstein_Tetreault/ (accessed July 3, 2006).

Sire, Marie-Anne. 1996. *La France du Patrimoine: Les Choix de la mémoire*. Paris: Gallimard.

Souchard, Maryse, Stéphane Wahnich, Isabelle Cuminal, and Virginie Wathier, ed. 1997. *Le Pen, les mots: Analyse d'un discours d'extrême droite*. Paris: Editions le monde.

Staum, Martin S. 2003. *Labeling People: French Scholars on Society, Race, and Empire*. Toronto: McGill-Queen's Press.

Swamy, Vinay. 2007. "Marivaux in the Suburbs: Reframing Language in Kechiche's *L'Esquive*." *Studies in French Cinema* 7 (1): 57–73.

Tai, Hue-Tam Ho. 2001. "Remembered Realms: Pierre Nora and French National Memory." *American Historical Review* 106 (3): 906–22.

———. 2005. Review. *Les Lieux de mémoire*, by Pierre Nora. *European Journal of East Asian Studies* 4 (2): 315–27.

Tarr, Carrie. 1997. "French Cinema and Post-colonial Minorities." In Hargreaves and McKinney, 1997, 59–83.

———. 1999. "Ethnicity and Identity in the cinéma de banlieue." In Powrie, 1999, 172–83.

———. 2005. *Reframing Difference: Beur and Banlieue Filmmaking in France*. Manchester, UK: Manchester University Press.

———. 2007. "*L'Esquive* (Kechiche 2004): Reassessing French Popular Culture." In Vanderschelden and Waldron, 2007, 130–41.

Terdiman, Richard. 1993. *Present Past: Modernity and the Memory Crisis*. Ithaca, NY: Cornell University Press.

Thierry, Amedée. 1845. *Histoire des Gaulois*. 1828. Paris: Jules Labitte.

Thierry, Augustin. 1840. *Considerations sur l'histoire de France*. Brussells: Riga.

Todorov, Tzevtan. 2004. *Les Abus de la mémoire*. Paris: Aléa.

Turim, Maureen. 1989. *Flashbacks in Film: Memory and History*. London: Routledge.

Vadelorge, Loïc. 2003. Introduction. In Poirrier and Vadelorge, 2003, 11–24.

Vanderschelden, Isabelle. 2005. "Jame Debbouze: A New Popular French Star?" *Studies in French Cinema* 5 (2): 61–73.

———. 2007. *Amélie, French Film Guides*. Urbana: University of Illinois Press.

Vanderschelden, Isabelle, and Darren Waldron, eds. 2007. *France at the Flicks: Trends in Contemporary Popular French Cinema*. Cambridge, UK: Cambridge Scholars.

Van Dijk, Maria. 2002. "Return of the Repressed: The Resurgence of the French B Movie." *Bright Lights Film Journal* 35 (January). http://www.brightlightsfilm.com/35/french-bmovie1.php.

Véray, Laurent, and Bill Krohn. 2005. "1927: The Apotheosis of the French Historical Film?" *Film History* 17 (2/3): 334–51.

Vico, Giambattista. 2002. *Scienza Nuova*. 1725. Cambridge: Cambridge University Press.

Vincendeau, Ginette, ed. 1995. *Encyclopedia of European Cinema*. London: Cassell / British Film Institute.

———. 2000. "Designs on the Banlieue: Mathieu Kassovitz's *La Haine*." In Hayward and Vincendeau, 2000, 310–27.

———, ed. 2001. *Film/Literature/Heritage: A Sight and Sound Reader.* London: British Film Institute.

———. 2005. *La Haine.* Champaign: University of Illinois Press.

Volney, Constantin François de. 1787. *Voyage en Égypte et en Syrie.* Paris: Volland et Desenne.

Vyverberg, Henry. 1989. *Human Nature, Cultural Diversity, and the French Enlightenment.* Oxford: Oxford University Press.

Warne, Chris. 1997. "The Impact of World Music in France." In Hargreaves and McKinney, 1997, 133–49.

Weil, Patrick. 2005. *La République et sa diversité: Immigration, intégration, discriminations.* Paris: Seuil.

Wieviorka, Michel. 1996. "Culture, société, et démocratie." In *Une société fragmentée? Le multiculturalisme en débat,* edited by Wieviorka, 11–60. Paris: La Decouverte.

———. 2005. "La République, la colonisation, et après. . . . " In Blanchard, Bancel, and Lemaire, 2005, 117–23.

Wihtol de Wenden, Catherine, ed. 1987. *Citoyenneté, Nationalité, et Immigration.* Paris: Arcantère.

———. 1987. *Philosophies of Integration: Immigration and the Idea of Citizenship.* Paris: Arcantère.

Wilder, Gary. 2005. *The French Imperial Nation-State: Negritude and Colonial Humanism between the Two World Wars.* Chicago: Chicago University Press.

Winock, Michel. 1990. *Nationalisme antisémitisme et fascisme en France.* Paris: Seuil.

Zerubavel, Eviatar. 2003. *Time Maps: Collective Memory and the Social Shape of the Past.* Chicago: University of Chicago Press.

Zisserman, Katya, and Colin Nettelbeck. 1997. "Social Exclusion and Artistic Inclusiveness: The Quest for Integrity in Mathieu Kassovitz's *La Haine.*" *Nottingham French Studies* 36 (2): 83–98.

Index

Djebar, Assia, 101
documentary, 11, 90, 135, 136, 141, 151
Doisneau, Robert, 80, 87, 88
Donadey, Anne, 22, 102, 118, 159, 185n8
Dormann, Jacques, 2
Douce France (Chibane), 106
DRAC (Directions Régionales des Affaires Culturelles), 178n10
Dréville, Jean, 36, 38
Dridi, Karim, 11, 103, 122, 186n15; *Bye Bye*, 106, 113–19, 156, 185–86n14; *Pigalle*, 113
Duby, Georges, 25
Durand, Jean, 38
Dusk till Dawn (Rodriguez), 75
Duvivier, Julien, 107

Eau des collines (Pagnol), 49, 182n11
1812 (Morlhon and Zecca), 35
Einaudi, Jean-Luc, 182n15, 185n6
empire, 14, 37, 58, 115, 137, 161; in cinema, 54, 55, 57, 79; and heritage, 8, 9, 23, 24, 27, 163; loss of, 6, 22, 26, 37, 56, 167, 178n14. *See also* colonialism; mission civilisatrice
Enfant roi, L' (Kemm), 35
Enfants du paradis, Les (Carné), 36, 81
Enfants du pays, Les (Javaux), 156
Enlightenment, 74, 75, 79, 122; legacy of, 123, 124, 125, 134; and slavery, 16, 180n6
Entre les murs (Cantet), 107, 186n18
Espiard de la borde, François Ignace, 17
Esquive, L' (Kechiche), 11, 107, 121, 122–30, 148
ethnic minorities in France, 5, 7–9, 13, 100–101, 114, 147–49; discrimination against, 116, 134, 144, 167; and heritage, 12, 27, 104, 106, 109, 115, 135; and identity politics, 23, 42, 46, 52, 54, 110, 112; representation of, 11, 83, 102–3, 106–7, 110, 111, 113, 114, 121–29, 135–43, 145–63. *See also* Beur; colonialism; immigration
Europeanization, 1
European Union, 5
evolution, 15, 99, 179n4; and historiography, 18–19, 178n9
Exposition coloniale (Colonial Exposition of 1931), 27, 168, 179n16

Fabuleux destin d'Amélie Poulain, Le (Jeunet), 79–89, 90, 112, 183–84

Fabulous Troubadours, Les, 134
family values, in heritage films, 44, 46, 47, 52–55
Fanny (Pagnol), 185n14
Fantômas (Feuillade), 107
Faute à Voltaire, La (Kechiche), 107, 115, 122, 156, 186n2
February 2006 law on history, 167, 181n12, 182n14
Femmes d'Islam (Benguigui), 136
Feuillade, Louis, 87, 107, 108, 111, 185n11
film noir, 36, 70, 74
flashback, 40, 41, 81, 146, 162; embedded flashback, 40, 41, 44, 45, 62, 69–70; in heritage films, 40, 41, 45, 57, 65
Flaubert, Gustave, 148
FLN (National Liberation Front), 153
folklore, 42, 44, 67, 68, 82
Fontaine, Anne, 106
Foster, Jodie, 109
Foucault, Michel, 29
400 coups, Les (Truffaut), 81, 148, 150
fracture coloniale (colonial fracture), 9, 20, 22, 78, 113, 116, 117, 178–79n16, 179n18
fracture sociale (social breakdown), 26, 111, 112
framing, 160; in film, 80, 84–85, 116, 125–26, 139, 149, 152, 153, 157–58; in narrative, 69–70; of the past, 26, 59, 167, 168
francité (Frenchness), 11, 26, 28, 39, 42, 62, 88, 92, 94, 104, 147, 178n2, 183n8; as hereditary, 3, 7, 13, 14, 18–20, 28; and heritage, 4, 5, 14, 105, 130, 131, 146, 163; multicultural conceptions of, 11, 12, 132–35. *See also* French exceptionalism
Franc-Moisin, 122
François Villon (Zwoboda), 36
François Premier, 44
Franco-Maghrebis, 9, 100, 101, 103, 105, 114, 122, 144, 184–5n3; vs. French of European origin, 138, 141, 143, 144, 148, 150; representation of, 103, 115, 121, 123, 135, 136, 151. *See also* Arab; Beur; immigration
French Colonial/African Army, 137, 138, 154, 156, 157, 161, 186n2, 187n11
French exceptionalism, 4, 178n8. See also *francité*
Frenchness. See *francité*

history (*continued*)
64, 84, 94, 100, 103, 112–13, 119, 123, 155,
166; and immigration, 55–57, 113, 115, 130,
133–43, 182n12, 184n14, 185; and memory,
1, 25, 28, 31, 32, 60, 71, 103–5, 114, 117, 157;
and national identity, 3, 8, 9–10, 14, 19,
21, 30, 38, 101–2; recorded history, 69,
72, 73, 158; reformulation of, 37, 40, 66,
68–70, 72, 73–74, 76, 78, 102, 150–54, 159,
162, 167–68; transmission of, 3, 20, 58,
86, 148, 166
HLM (public housing), 9, 110, 111, 122, 142,
144. See also *banlieue*; *cité*
Hoberman, J., 183n8
Hollywood, 67
horror film, 75
Hôtel du nord (Carné), 80
Howard's End (Ivory), 33
Hugo, Victor, 111, 133, 134, 186n2
Hunébelle, André, 36, 38
Hussard sur le toit, Le (Rappeneau), 2, 64,
182n10
hybridity, 102, 114, 115, 120, 122, 134, 145–46,
183n6. *See also* liminality; *métissage*

IAM, 120, 134, 185n14
identity, 43, 46, 48–49, 51–55, 61–64, 101, 104,
106, 124, 133, 137, 163, 165, 177n2; collective, 12, 18, 19, 51, 58, 100, 102, 104, 123,
144, 169; crisis of, 22–23, 29, 33, 38, 41, 65,
121, 145, 149; individual, 16, 42, 45, 46,
80, 89, 120–21, 124, 127, 182n11; multicultural, 115, 120, 132, 134–35, 145, 167; national, 1–5, 7–10, 11, 14, 17, 21, 19, 26–28,
31, 34, 47, 62, 94, 103, 130, 136, 178n14;
179n1; politics of, 42, 55–56, 60, 89, 99,
100–101, 109, 141, 162, 166; regional/lo-
cal identity, 6, 41, 42, 67, 76, 103, 105, 111,
123, 132, 134–35, 143–44, 163, 180–81n11,
183–84n11, 185n14; transmission of, 20,
39, 46, 95, 144, 182n16
Imache, Tassadit, 103
immigrant labor, 102, 116, 117, 133, 139, 141,
150, 151, 152
immigration, 5, 6, 42, 107, 120, 130, 132, 137,
139, 141, 143, 145, 146, 154; and cinema,
135–43, 154–56, 163, 186n2, 187n12; and
collective memory, 102, 104, 113, 133, 134,

136, 151–52; and history, 8, 11, 12, 58, 111,
135, 139, 143, 168, 178–79, 184n14; politics
of, 6–7, 29, 45–47, 52, 55–56, 64, 133, 155,
178; "second-generation," 119, 121, 136,
142, 150, 163, 183–84n3. *See also Beur*;
Cité national de l'histoire de l'immigration; *intégration*
"inassimilability," 7, 111, 138, 147, 150, 163
Inch'Allah dimanche (Benguigui), 136
Indigènes (Bouchareb), 12, 106, 154–63, 167,
168, 187n14
Indochina, 55–60
Indochine (Wargnier), 11, 40, 43, 55–61
Inrockuptibles, 82
insiders vs. outsiders, 45–46, 47, 48, 52–53,
63, 182
intégration (integration) 60, 94, 104, 115,
122, 129, 130, 144, 151; debates about, 7,
52, 56, 61, 100–101, 106, 138, 141, 144, 155,
179n17; problems of, 61, 100, 114–16, 122,
123, 129, 130, 138, 140–41, 148, 153; process
of, 46–47, 100–102, 117, 128, 136, 154; republican model of, 60, 101, 123, 128. *See
also* Beur; immigration
interracial romance, depiction of, 43, 103
Introduction à l'Histoire universelle, 18,
180n7
Islam, 141, 155, 161–62. See also Muslim

J'accuse (Gance), 35
Jacquot, Benoît, 2, 40, 66
Javaux, Pierre, 156
Jean Chouan (Luitz-Morat), 35
Jean de Florette (Berri), 2, 11, 43, 49–55, 57,
58, 105, 143
Jeu de l'amour et du hasard, Le (Marivaux),
122, 124, 125
Jeunet, Jean-Pierre, 164, 183n10, 184; *Fa-
buleux destin d'Amélie Poulain, Le*, 11,
79–90, 99, 112, 183n2, 183n6
Jews, 84, 109, 112, 140
Joan of Arc, 21
Jordan, Neil, 75
Journal des chasseurs, 68
Jules et Jim (Truffaut), 80, 81
jus sanguinis, 52, 182n12. *See also* citizen-
ship
jus soli, 52, 182n12. *See also* citizenship

Kaganski, Serge, 82–83, 183n8
Kassovitz, Mathieu, 80, 84, 88, 110, 122 ; *Haine, La*, 110
Kastoryano, Riva, 7
Kechiche, Adbellatif (Abdel), 103, 122, 128, 129; *Faute à Voltaire, La*, 107, 115, 156; *L'Esquive*, 11, 107, 130, 148
Kemm, Jean, 35, 38

L.627 (Tavernier), 106
Lacombe Lucien (Malle), 187n15
laïcité, 66
Laissez-passer (Tavernier), 159
Lalanne, Jean-Marc, 80
Lamorisse, Albert, 81
Lang, Jack, 2
Laplanche, Jean, 96
Lavisse, Ernest, 27, 28
Lebovics, Herman, 1, 6, 7, 14, 25, 26, 105, 177n1, 178n6, 178n11, 179n1
Leconte, Patrice, 2, 40, 66, 74
Lee, Spike, 110
Le Goff, Jacques, 2, 8, 25
Le Henaff, René, 38
Le Pen, Jean-Marie, 53, 61. *See also* Front National
Lettres persanes (Montesquieu), 180n4
Libération, 80, 82, 187n13
Libertin, Le (Aghion), 2, 66
lieu de mémoire (space/site of memory), 21, 25–29, 58, 82, 90–92, 95, 98, 102–3, 143, 144, 147–50, 152, 156–58, 184n16. *See also* heritage; memory; nostalgia
Lieux de mémoire (Nora), 9, 10, 25–31, 32, 66, 79, 168, 181n14, 187n10
liminality, 102, 118, 119–20, 121, 168. *See also* hybridity; métissage
Longest Day, The (Annakin, Marton, and Wicki), 168
Louis XIV, 16, 24
Louis XV, 66, 68, 69, 71, 72
Lowenthal, David, 1, 2, 6, 8, 177n3, 178n7
Lumière, Auguste and Louis, 4, 34, 157, 181n16

Macias, Enrico, 140, 141
Madame Bovary by Chabrol, 66; by Flaubert, 148
Madame Du Barry (Christian-Jacque), 36

Maghreb, 120, 142, 144, 155. *See also* Beur; Franco-Maghrebis; North Africa
Maigret tend un piège (Delannoy), 36
Malaysia, 55
Malle, Louis, 187n15
Manau, 134
Manon des sources: by Berri, 11, 43, 49–55, 57, 58, 182n11; by Pagnol, 49, 182n11
March against Racism, 143, 187n8
marginalization, 11, 14, 92–98, 110, 111–16, 130–34, 146, 148. *See also* racism*Marie du port, La* (Carné), 36
Marius (Pagnol), 182n11, 185n14
Marivaux, 122
marriage and family, treatment of, 43, 44, 45, 51, 53, 54, 58–59, 117, 119–20, 140, 141, 145, 182n16
Marseille, 32, 114–20, 121, 134, 185n14
"Marseillaise, La" (French national anthem), 161
Marseillaise, La (Renoir), 36
Marton, Andrew, 158
Marx-Scouras, Danielle, 186n1, 186n3
Massilia Sound System, 120, 134, 185
Matisse, Henri, 82
Matrix, The (Wachowski and Wachowski), 67
M'Bowolé, Makomé, 110
Mediterranean, the, 116, 119, 120, 134, 185
melodrama, 68, 109, 136
Melville, Jean-Pierre, 108
Mémoires d'immigrés, l'héritage maghrébin (Benguigui), 11, 135–43, 157
memory, 2, 8, 20, 24, 45, 47, 51, 57, 64, 71, 74, 95, 139, 144–45, 149, 154, 156; and cinema, 3, 4, 11, 31–32, 33–34, 39–48, 64, 74, 78, 79, 92, 99, 137, 156–60; collective, 1, 4, 11, 14, 22, 29, 38, 42, 58, 62, 67, 68, 88, 100–102, 119, 132, 133, 138, 139, 144, 147, 150, 163; of colonial past, 8, 10, 11, 20, 22, 26–27, 55–58, 61, 105, 134, 137, 140–43, 152, 156–60, 163, 178–79; countermemory, 9, 12, 25, 66, 77, 98, 102–5, 131, 133, 136, 147, 151, 154, 163; crisis of, 3, 9, 15, 26; and heritage, 2, 5, 7, 8, 13, 21–30, 124, 130; national, 10, 12, 18, 21–31, 57–59, 125, 136, 154; personal, 58, 59, 87, 117, 148; and repression, 116, 117, 118, 138, 139, 152–53, 157,

memory (*continued*)
158, 159, 163, 166; screen, 3, 56, 158, 159; transmission of, 11, 15, 25, 26, 59, 113–14, 124, 144, 146, 178n9. *See also* heritage; *lieu de mémoire*; nostalgia
Mercanton, Louis, 35
métissage, 102, 120. *See also* hybridity; liminality
Métisse (Kassovitz), 106, 110
Michelet, Jules, 3, 10, 18–21, 26, 28–31, 35, 41, 180, 181n14
Millet, Jean-François, 91, 92, 94, 95
Miracle des loups (Bernard), 35
mise-en-abyme, 71, 72, 73, 74
mise-en-scène, 3, 11, 33, 43, 47, 50, 75, 77, 81, 82, 91, 110, 114, 130, 140, 141, 153, 156
Misérables, Les (Hugo), 133–34
misrecognition, 147–48, 152
mission civilisatrice (civilizing mission), 20, 21, 78, 161, 166
Mitterrand, François, 2, 23, 25, 37, 38, 43, 92, 177
mobility vs. immobility, 85, 86, 90, 92, 111–19, 122, 124–30, 144, 149, 151, 153
Mode Retro, 187n15
Molière (Tirard), 2
Môme, La (Dahan), 2
monarchy, 16, 20, 74, 75, 76
Monde, Le, 26, 57, 81, 138, 142, 161, 186n4, 187n12, 187n14
Monet, Claude, 177n1
montage, 94, 117, 139
Montand, Yves, 38, 49, 182n13
Montesquieu, Charles de Secondat baron de, 17, 179–80
Montmartre, 28, 79, 81, 85, 88, 108
Morlhon, Camille de, 35, 38
Morocco, 82, 155, 161
Mort de Marat (Hatot), 4, 34
Mort de Robespierre (Hatot), 4, 34
Mort du Duc d'Enghien, La (Capellani), 4
Mounsi (Mohand Nafaa Mounsi), 103, 142
multiculturalism, 9, 12, 116, 119, 122, 124; and heritage, 9, 98, 105, 121, 130, 132; and identity, 115, 124, 132–35; multicultural narratives, 11, 102, 103–5, 144–50, 156–57, 184n5
Muriel (Resnais), 37

Musée de la France d'outre-mer, 168, 179n16
Musée d'Orsay, 91, 92, 94
Musée national des Arts d'Afrique et d'Océanie, 168, 179n16
museum, 67, 92, 168, 179n16
Muslim, 124, 162. *See also* Islam
myth of return, 119–20, 139–40, 143, 154

Naceri, Sami, 154, 155
Naficy, Hamid, 62, 163
Name of the Rose, The (Annaud), 75
Nana (Renoir), 108
Nanterre, 151, 152
Napoléon (Gance), 24, 35
Napoléon, 24, 26.
narrative, 20- 23, 30, 32, 36, 40, 48–49, 58–60, 64, 71, 74, 77, 89, 107, 112, 114, 148, 151; film narrative, 3–4, 11, 32–35, 37, 39, 40–43, 48–51, 66, 67, 70, 72, 79–84, 86, 91–92, 109, 111, 119, 133, 160, 165–66, 181n2; historical narrative, 4, 14, 19, 21, 23, 34, 37, 39, 40, 42, 69–70, 73–76, 153–54; multicultural narrative, 11, 102, 104–5, 149, 184–85n3; and the nation, 5, 8, 9, 11, 13, 20, 22, 31, 45–46, 60, 90, 130–31, 167; structure of, 3, 19, 30, 32–35, 39, 40–45, 50, 57, 62, 69, 78, 162
Native American, 68, 78, 79
New Wave, 37, 81, 108–9, 111, 177, 181, 184n13
Noiriel, Gérard, 7, 19, 156, 178n15, 181–81n15, 184n14
Nora, Pierre, 2, 9, 10, 25–30, 50, 52, 57, 65, 66, 69, 77, 79, 103, 136, 143, 151–53, 167, 181, 184n16
Norindr, Panivong, 23, 24, 56–59
North Africa, 37, 83, 84, 88, 95, 102–6, 116, 120, 133, 135, 140, 143, 146, 147, 148, 154–59, 161, 183n11, 185n7
nostalgia, 25, 26, 33, 36, 44, 49, 50, 54, 57, 64, 65, 80, 87, 136, 139, 145, 149, 151, 156, 182n11
Nouvelle France (New France), 78, 79
Nuit de Varennes, La (Wazjde), 40, 181n9
Nuytten, Bruno, 2

October 17, 1961, 102, 138, 152, 153, 154, 182n15, 285n6
Œil de Vichy, L' (Chabrol), 159

100% Arabica (Zemmouri), 106
Oscar (Academy Award), 56, 79, 155
Outremer (Roüan), 55
Ozouf, Jacques, 27, 29
Ozouf, Mona, 27, 29

Pacte des loups, Le (Gans), 11, 66–79, 80, 87, 89, 90, 99, 123, 168, 183
Pagnol, Marcel, 49, 50, 80, 82, 103, 146, 182; *Manon des sources*, 51 ; *Trilogie marseillaise, La*, 185–86n14
Palais de la porte dorée, 168, 179n16
Panier district (of Marseille), 114
Papon, Maurice, 116
Paris, 67, 71, 82–86, 102–3, 115, 119, 134, 135, 138, 141, 154; representation of, 80, 83, 87–90, 108, 110, 114, 118, 112–23, 140, 152, 184n13; sites in, 28, 82, 111, 151
partie de campagne, Une (Renoir), 82
Passage to India, A (Merchant), 33
past, 7, 8, 61, 78, 85, 87–90, 91, 99, 107, 136, 143, 155, 165; alienation from, 54, 105–6, 111–15, 120, 122, 155, 178–79n16; decolonization of, 8-12, 23–25, 58, 78–79, 102–4, 135–38, 159, 162–63; glorification of, 2, 29, 33, 49, 55-57, 64–65, 145, 149; memory of, 1, 21, 22, 25, 27, 101; national past, 13, 14, 19–20, 26, 60, 62–63, 130, 131, 136, 142; relationship to present, 5, 6, 15, 19, 28–32, 55, 70, 84, 95, 98, 119–21, 167–68; representation of, 3, 4, 34–50, 66–70, 80, 83–87, 70–77, 104, 108, 109, 116–18, 122, 135, 152, 157–58, 164, 166; transmission of, 15, 58–59, 136, 165; as trauma, 84–86, 115–20, 178n14
pastiche, 33, 74, 80, 86, 183n6
patriarchy, treatment of, 44, 54, 58, 146
patrimoine, 1–3, 5, 15, 24, 112, 122, 127, 177–78, 181n1; post-colonial version of, 102, 123, 129, 135, 168. *See also* post-colonial
Perec, Georges, 81
Perles de la couronne, Les (Guitry), 35
Péron, Didier, 80
Peuple, Le (Michelet), 18, 20, 21, 180n7, 180n11
Pied-noir, 84, 103, 140, 141, 149, 160
Pierre et Djemila (Blain), 106
Pigalle (Dridi), 113, 114
Poetic realism, 82, 108, 109, 111

polar (detective film), 36, 70, 71, 75, 106
police, representation of, 110
Pons, Louis, 96
popular music, 133, 134, 157, 169
Porton, Richard, 130
post-colonial, 10, 12, 78, 151, 155, 167, 186n2; and ethnic minorities, 14, 21, 22, 62, 113, 121, 129, 131, 137, 138, 152, 163, 167; history, 137, 165, 266; identities, 135, 166; version of heritage, 8, 10, 11, 12, 100–105, 134–35, 154. *See also* ethnic minorities in France; *patrimoine*
postmodernism, 12, 13, 24, 74, 80
Pouctal, Henri, 35, 38
Powrie, Phil, 2, 33, 38, 41, 49, 50, 58, 181–81n9
"present absence," 21, 26, 37, 89, 102, 105, 109, 112, 138, 178–79n16, 180n10
production values, 33, 34, 37, 38, 43, 47, 55, 65, 67, 156, 177–78n5
Prost, Antoine, 25
Provence, 8, 49, 50, 57, 94, 103, 156, 161
Pyramide du Louvre (Louvre Pyramid), 24–25

racism, 8, 17, 83, 110–21, 134, 141, 143, 144, 156, 159, 160, 183n8, 183–84n11
raï, 132
Reader, Keith, 108, 110
realism, in cinema, 70–71, 74, 76, 77
Rébichon, Michel, 80
regionalism, 6–8, 12, 41, 42, 76, 105, 178n10; and heritage films, 38, 41, 42, 67, 90, 105; and multiculturalism, 94, 104, 105, 119, 123, 132–35, 146
Reign of Terror, 69
Reine Margot, La: by Chéreau, 2, 38, 64, 65, 66; by Desfontaines, 38; by Dréville, 36, 38; by Morlhon de, 38
remake, 38, 42, 49, 51, 65, 80, 82, 92, 182n11
Renan, Ernest, 13, 14, 15, 28, 178n9
Renoir, Auguste, 81, 82, 86
Renoir, Jean, 25, 82, 108
republic, 7, 16, 18, 24, 27, 56, 78, 141, 162, 180n6; Fifth Republic, 137, 138, 160, 161; Fourth Republic, 137; Third Republic, 14, 20, 27, 38. *See also* citizenship; democracy
Resnais, Alain, 37, 109, 181n6

Dayna Oscherwitz is associate professor of francophone studies at Southern Methodist University, where she teaches courses on French and African cinema and francophone culture. She is coauthor of *The A to Z of French Cinema* and has published articles in such journals as the *French Review*, *Research in African Literatures*, and *Studies in French Cinema*.